The Miniature Epic in Vandal Africa

The Miniature Epic
in Vandal Africa

BY

DAVID F. BRIGHT

UNIVERSITY OF OKLAHOMA PRESS : NORMAN AND LONDON

By David F. Bright

Haec mihi fingebam: Tibullus in His World (Leiden, 1978)
Elaborate Disarray: The Nature of Statius' Silvae (Meisenheim, 1980)
(editor, with E. S. Ramage) *Classical Texts and Their Traditions: Studies
in Honor of C. R. Trahman* (Chico, 1984)
The Miniature Epic in Vandal Africa (Norman, 1987)

Library of Congress Cataloging-in-Publication Data

Bright, David F.
    The miniature epic in Vandal Africa.

    1. Epic poetry, Latin—Africa, North—History
and criticism.   2. Dracontius, Blossius Aemilius,
5th cent.—History and criticism.   3. Christian
poetry, Latin—History and criticism.   4. Mythology,
Greek, in literature.   5. Africa, North—Intellectual
life.   6. Vandals.   I. Title.
PA6098.A4B75   1987   873'.01'0996   87–40211
ISBN 0–8061–2075–4 (alk. paper)

The paper in this book meets the guidelines for permanence and dura-
bility of the Committee on Production Guidelines for Book Longevity of
the Council on Library Resources, Inc.

Contents

Preface

THIS WORK grew out of a plan to examine all the Greek and Latin epyllia of late antiquity. That ambition arose from the realization that one of the more interesting phenomena in classical literature had never been systematically studied. The so-called miniature epic, a strange mixture of conflicting expectations created by using epic meter and subject matter but giving the story a treatment more reminiscent of the smaller genres, had a long and varied history. Specimens are found unevenly distributed over time, from the Hellenistic era which gave it its basic form down to the Renaissance and beyond. Over that range there have been studies of separate authors or poems, but there exists no comprehensive study of the epyllion over that span.

Indeed, there is no systematic study even of the separate phases of that history, except for the earliest period, for which we have M. M. Crump's *The Epyllion from Theocritus to Ovid* (1931). As will be clear from the first chapter of this book, the absence of a history of the epyllion even in antiquity springs from various causes. The relevant corpus lacks superficial cohesiveness because of the tremendous variety of subject matter, of date, of scale, and of style. The implications of this diversity will be a starting point for this study.

The most striking lacuna in the scholarship on the epyllion was a full scale study of the poems from the latter stages of antiquity—roughly from the beginning of the fourth century until the end of the fifth. This was an age which saw a vigorous revival of the epyllion tradition (it is more correct to think of a tradition than a genre), and there are numerous poems which answer the description of the epyllion; yet there is no large scale examination of the evidence, much less an effort to relate the later period to the classical phase. It was this double task which I had in mind as I began this project: to look at all the late epyllia and to set them in the context of tradition from the classical era.

It soon became obvious, however, that this was far too much to fit into a single volume because so many crucial areas had not been explored fully. I have limited myself at this point to a segment of the material which can stand on its own, but which I hope will also be of use in studying the other epyllia from the late period. This volume deals specifically with the epyllia of Dracontius and the anonymous *Aegritudo Perdicae*, all from North Africa during the Vandal rule. There was a temptation to aim at comprehensive coverage of the North African materials by including Reposianus' *De concubitu Martis et Veneris*, which is now generally accepted as being of Vandal date, and perhaps even the centos from the *Anthologia Latina;* but these both differ from the poems under review in such important ways that they would have impaired the unity of the volume.

Reposianus' work is less a narrative than a tone poem, and the atmosphere and exotic situations give the *De concubitu* the effect of an idyll. It has a theme of admittedly epic provenance, picking up on the famous and delightful song of Demodocus in *Odyssey* 8, but the story was scarcely epic in tone or effect even there: it is a mythological *divertimento* which rapidly became more at home in the slighter genres. Reposianus has created a poem more reminiscent of the idyll or the elegy than of epic or drama.

The Vergilian centos present another kind of contrast entirely. They are closer to the expected range of topic, but in most cases they are so brief that they can hardly be called narrative. The longest of them (*Hippodameia*) is 164 verses, virtually the same length as Dracontius' *Hylas*, and comparisons might be possible between these poems. But there are centos on appropriate topics running no more than 16 lines (*Hercules et Antaeus: Anth. Lat.* VI.12) and these cannot be treated side by side with Dracontius' *Orestis tragoedia*, which extends to nearly a thousand verses. Moreover, all these works are dominated by the bizarre nature of the cento tradition. Every line is taken from Vergil and reapplied to alien topics and contexts, and the contrast with original composition is distracting to say the least.

Thus the other specimens of Latin hexameter poetry from Vandal Africa on heroic themes are inappropriate to a study which is mainly concentrated on Dracontius. The *Aegritudo* offers, as will be seen, a species of the epyllion closer to the earlier tradition with regard to form and various stylistic conventions, while Dracontius is more representative of the serious hexameter tradition in his stories but more innovative in treatment. Reposianus and the centos are further from the tradition in both respects. I have therefore deferred them to a second study which will treat the rest of the later Latin epyllia and have used Dracontius and the *Aegritudo Perdicae* to present the central characteristics of the late miniature epic.

The approach taken in this study is to examine the epyllia individually, with particular emphasis on literary questions. I have tried to place the poems in their context: first with a preliminary depiction of the literary tradition of the epyllion itself and of the world in which Dracontius and the poet of the *Aegritudo* wrote (Chapter 1); and, after the individual analyses, with a reexamination of the epyllion in light of the evidence displayed in this study. I believe that the basic concept of the epyllion must be rethought in order to accommodate a far wider range of literary and subliterary influences which affected the epyllion in late antiquity, without, however, severing its clear connection to the earlier phases. The miniature epic is a flexible form, at home in widely different contexts. It is surprising to find both the continuity of form and conception and the radical changes in style, influences, and intention. Dracontius emerges as an impressively creative writer, ready to reshape myths to new purposes, displaying a wide learning in both Greek and Latin letters and showing how much his era and his culture were at the crossroads of ancient and medieval, pagan and Christian, Roman and barbarian. He is, I believe, a much underrated poet.

There has been no complete edition of the works of Dracontius since Vollmer (1905). That is a pity, as there has been considerable work done on Dracontius since then. Some of the poems have been separately edited in this interval: for the *Romulea*, J. M. Diaz de Bustamante's *Draconcio y sus carmina profana* (1978) offers a very thorough introduction, particularly on the rhetorical qualities of the poems, and many suggestive contributions to the text; for the *Orestis tragoedia*, Emmanuele Rapisarda has provided a much improved text and a stimulating commentary (1964); and F. Speranza's edition of the *Satisfactio* lays out a great deal of information clearly and usably. I have used these editions alongside Vollmer without consistently following any one editor's text. There is, alas, no complete edition of the *De laudibus Dei* more recent than Vollmer.

The early phase of the project was supported by a Research Fellowship from the American Council of Learned Societies, to whom I am glad to record my indebtedness. And the Research Board of the Graduate College in the University of Illinois at Urbana-Champaign has generously provided funding both for publication subvention and for research assistants: I am particularly grateful to George Panayiotou and Fred W. Jenkins for their work in this latter capacity, and to C. R. Shea, who offered characteristically imaginative ideas and criticisms at several stages. In addition, I have benefited greatly from the discrimination and learning of my colleagues David Sansone and Howard Jacobson. They have my best thanks. Naturally, when my stubbornness overrode their caution, they are not to blame.

DAVID F. BRIGHT

Urbana, Illinois

List of Abbreviations

THE FOLLOWING abbreviations have been used for citation of frequently used texts and scholarly materials. I have also used the standard abbreviations for ancient texts and for journals such as may be found in *L'Année philologique*. Fuller information on the books cited compendiously is given in the Bibliography.

Ancient Texts

AP	*Aegritudo Perdicae*
Ch.	Aeschylus, *Choephori*
Declam.	*Declamationes*
DLD	Dracontius, *De laudibus Dei*
El.	*Electra*
Epit.	Apollodorus, *Epitome*
Eum.	Aeschylus, *Eumenides*
Fab.	Hyginus, *Fabulae*
Hel.	Dracontius, *De raptu Helenae*
Herc. Fur.	Seneca, *Hercules furens*
Hyl.	Dracontius, *Hylas*
IA	Euripides, *Iphigenia at Aulis*
IT	Euripides, *Iphigenia in Tauris*
Med.	Euripides, Seneca, Dracontius, *Medea*
Or.	Dracontius, *Orestis tragoedia*
Ph.	Seneca, *Phaedra*
PV	[Aeschylus], *Prometheus vinctus*
Rom.	Dracontius, *Romulea*
Sat.	Dracontius, *Satisfactio ad regem Gunthamundum*
Theb.	Statius, *Thebaid*

Thy.   Seneca, *Thyestes*
Troad.   Euripides, *Troades*
Vat. Myth.   Vatican Mythographers

Modern Works

A&R   *Atene e Roma*
Aricò   G. Aricò, "Mito e tecnica narrativa nell'
                *Orestis tragoedia" Atti dell 'Accademia di
                Palermo* 37 (1977–78) 405–95
Barwinski   B. Barwinski, *Quaestiones ad Dracontium et
                Orestis tragoediam pertinentes (1887–88)*
Courtois   Christian Courtois, *Les Vandales et l'Afrique*
                (Paris 1955)
Diaz   J. M. Diaz de Bustamante, *Draconcio y sus
                carmina profana* (Santiago de Compostela
                1978)
Kuijper   D. Kuijper. *Varia Dracontiana* (The Hague
                1958)
MGH   *Monumenta Germaniae historica*
Phil.   *Philologus*
Provana   E. Provana, "Blossio Emilio Draconzio. Stu-
                dio biografico e letterario" (Torino 1912)
Quartiroli   A. M. Quartiroli, "Gli epilli di Draconzio"
                Athenaeum 24 (1946) 160–87; 25 (1947)
                17–34
Rapisarda   E. Rapisarda, *La tragedia di Oreste*, 2d ed.
                (Catania 1964)
RCCM   *Rivista di cultura classica e medievale*
RE   Pauly-Wissowa, *Realencyclopaedie der
                klassischen Altertumswissenschaft*
RFIC   *Rivista di filologia ed istruzione classica*
Romano   D. Romano, *Studi draconziani* (Palermo
                1959)
SIFC   *Studi italiani di filologia classica*
Türk   G. Türk, *De Hyla* (Breslau 1895)
ULG   E. Baehrens, *Unerdite lateinische Gedichte*
                (Leipzig 1877)

Vollmer	*Fl. Merobaudis reliquiae, Blossii Aemilii Dracontii carmina, Eugeni Toletani episcopi carmina et epistulae* (Berlin 1905)
WS	*Wiener Studien*
ZPE	*Zeitschrift fur Papyrologie und Epigraphik*

The Miniature Epic in Vandal Africa

Chapter 1

Introduction

The Epyllion

FROM THE THIRD to the first century before Christ, one of the most admired accomplishments for a poet was to compose a miniature epic poem, a general category of composition which since the midnineteenth century has been called the epyllion. From Callimachus to Theocritus to Bion, from Catullus to Vergil to Ovid, the keenest talents were attracted by this exercise. Yet it is one of the ironies in the study of classical literature that the epyllion is a nongenre. The ancients themselves never adopted a distinct term for the form, and there is no ancient discussion of what its rules or limits should be.

The study of this nongenre has always been fragmented and plagued by incomplete or contradictory definitions. This is a significant problem in view of the quality of the poems involved and the centrality of the poets who worked in the tradition. Yet there is a tendency to treat individual epyllia with reference to some others within the general group in recognition of a kinship which is sensed even if not successfully articulated. The Hellenistic epyllia have now been treated as a group,[1] and Marjorie Crump's effort at a definitive study is just over a half-century old.[2] The basic division, however, marked by her confident claims about the characteristics and subdivisions of the epyllia and by Walter Allen's acerbic rejection of the whole category,[3] has been modified but not resolved. Is there such a thing as an epyllion distinct from other kinds of poetic composition, or

3

is the *Kreuzung der Gattungen* so extensive in both the Hellenistic and Roman phases that the pursuit is pointless? The fact is that we are dealing not with a settled form at any stage, but with a tradition of experimentation which accommodated a wide range of options in both subject and treatment. The traditional terms for genera had long since been established, and the tendency to combine features from disparate literary strands meant that there was no perceived need to give names to such shifting experimental performances. In modern times, however, the fact that there was a relatively brief but intense and frequently brilliant production of poems with several features in common has led to one apparently unshakeable orthodoxy about the epyllion. The category, if it exists (so runs the accepted approach), is defined exclusively by the poems "from Theocritus to Ovid," and deliberations on the evolution and evaluation of the epyllion are bounded by these limits. Sometimes the axiom is stated the other way round: as these are the only poems meeting the criteria so vaguely expressed, the form must exist only within this time frame. At any rate, there has been no dispute with the proposition that the poems are narrative hexameter compositions on heroic or quasi-heroic topics displaying the highest form of Alexandrian polish. It is the quintessential neoteric ambition to create such a work. How could it be at home in another era?

But even within the confines of the Hellenistic-Roman era, this view is only partly accurate. The association with epic based on meter is after all an assumption, and there are elegiac poems which share with the epyllia all essential characteristics except meter. One thinks of Propertius' *Hylas* (I. 20) or Tibullus (I. 7) on the exploits of Messalla.[4] If we do not insist on weighing meter above all else, then the center of gravity shifts, and a new perspective on the experimentation emerges. We are back at the *Kreuzung der Gattungen,* a notion frequently misunderstood to require that a single genre be manipulated by the application of features from other genres, like plastic surgery. But the process of combination is more open and less predictable. The experimentation is not a disruptive factor to be worked around in getting at the real form: in the case of the epyllion there is no real form, only a common bond consisting precisely of this experiment within broad limits, allowing differing elements to dominate from one case to the next. The epyllion presented a wonderful challenge precisely because there was so much room for the individual stamp of genius. No wonder that the neoterics were so fond of it, and that it attracted most of the first-rank talents.

The fragmentation in studying the epyllion is exacerbated by the fact that there is a pause in the production of works which might reasonably be nominated for membership in the group, starting immediately after Ovid.[5] It would be difficult to give a convincing reason for this sudden decline in interest in a form which had attracted such varying talents, but it is certain that the short hexameter (or even elegiac) poem turns in other directions during the Silver Age: the *Silvae* of Statius illustrate most clearly the new preferences among formal poets. At the same time, the Vergilian revival of epic on the grand scale, coupled with the triumph of rhetoric in all branches of Roman letters, encouraged poets to treat narratives once more on a vaster canvas.

Thus there ensued a period of dormancy for the kind of poetic experiment which the "classical"[6] epyllia represented. From the death of Ovid to the early fourth century there was virtually nothing produced along the lines of Catullus 64 or even the *Culex:* one possible exception is the recently published *Alcestis* from Barcelona, but it probably belongs in the late third or the fourth century rather than the Silver Age.[7] Yet this silence did not signify the death of the epyllion. In the later stages of antiquity a form of epyllion came into favor once more in both Greek and Latin, and we have as many relevant poems from the fourth and fifth centuries of our era as from the entire Hellenistic-Roman phase.[8] It will be admitted at once that these are not by Vergils and Catulluses, but they are precious evi-

dence of the survival value of this tradition and offer valuable insights into the late antique concepts of narrative poetry and of the influences which shaped the imaginations of
the latest poets of classical antiquity.

But two results—one ancient and one modern—flow
from this separation of the two stages of the ancient epyllion. First, scholars have considered the later poems in isolation from the earlier, and just as they have treated the
classical phase without regard for subsequent development, so they have generally studied the later works only
in their own context. Usually these are scholars who have
less interest in the classical phase but are instead concerned with historical topics in late antiquity or looking
ahead to medieval literature rather than to the classical tradition from which the poems sprang.

In antiquity itself, during the long quietus from Ovid to
Claudian, the influences at work on literary tastes had
changed very significantly. In the case of genres with well-
defined traditions and expectations, there was a more
stable frame of reference for gradual modification to meet
evolving tastes. But the epyllion had never been a stable
compound, and there was no definite form to serve as a
point of reference. Thus the epyllion was all the more open
to fundamental changes of style, emphasis, and outlook. At
all times during the classical phase, the epyllion had applied the literary and aesthetic preferences of the day to
narrative poetry on a modest scale. In the earlier phase this
meant conventions and innovations linked to Hellenistic
poetry and, to a lesser extent, Roman elegy. But in late antiquity the short narrative poem soaked up the prevailing colors of its own day, and the result was a whole new
picture.

The literary climate of the later Empire was very different from either the Republic or the early Principate, although it drew on both periods. There emerged what has
been called a "new Alexandrianism":[9] after the relatively
uninteresting lull of the third century, authors began again
in the fourth century to be absorbed by *variatio* and by the

joy of elaborateness. The use of rare or obsolete words and the formation of neologisms contribute to the rich texture and frequent obscurity of late authors, and the relative lack of restraint in employing rhetorical embellishment means that the texts are more intense in their hues than even the work of such a poet as Statius. If we move further ahead in time, it is hard to read a page of Sidonius without feeling that the language is very nearly out of control. This enjoyment of extremely elaborate and dramatic effects, so closely allied to other aspects of life seen in the late imperial courts, affects choice of subject matter, structure and disposition of material, and style. There is less subtlety in even the best of the late poets (e.g., Claudian) than in the Silver poets, but there is a compensating vigor and panache for those who take the time to learn how to enjoy it.

Yet if we ask what the poets of late antiquity thought they were doing, one part of the answer will be that they were building on the tradition of poetry which they inherited from the earlier ages of Latin letters. Their most available and admired models were the poets of the Silver Age, and we shall see how much influence can be traced from Dracontius back to the Silver epic poets as well as to Senecan drama; but at least in the fourth century the figure of Vergil overtopped all other poets, and the veneration of his works was a prime consideration in any poet's activity. Thus even though the Silver Age, which was so important for the later period, had nothing to correspond to the epyllion, the link to Vergil provided a tie to the Golden Age, which saw the perfection of the epyllion in Latin.

But the poetic preferences of that earlier era had been replaced by other genres, and what is more significant, prose had risen to a place of dominance in literature, which meant that even poetic forms were very heavily influenced by the canons of taste in prose. If we look for the literary forms, apart from epic itself, which had the greatest influence on the later epyllion, the list will include the *Rezitationsdrama* on the poetic side and also the rhetorical exercises from the schools, panegyric and invective (which

were the most characteristic voices of the later Empire),
and the prose romances. The combined effects of these
new influences make the later epyllion strikingly different
in both style and tone, and it is perhaps not surprising that
the gap of both time and manner should have led scholars
to consider the early and late groups apart from each other.

Yet there is another result of this isolation of the late
from the early poems. They have not been thought of as a
group in themselves either, so they have never been studied together. Dracontius himself offers a striking instance
of this problem: there is only one essay on all four of his
epyllia.[10] The huge recent edition of the *carmina profana*
by Diaz de Bustamante does not include the *Orestis tragoedia*, the longest and most imposing of his pagan poems.[11]

Having lodged this complaint, I must at once plead
guilty to the same fault. It is manifestly impossible to treat
all the epyllia within the confines of a single volume, and so
I have decided to focus this study on Dracontius, both because of the intrinsic interest of the four epyllia we have
from his pen, and because within the unity of artistry of a
single poet's work we also find a remarkable variety of subject and of influences. Dracontius thus provides a good
measure of the possibilities of the late epyllion. Indeed, he
is a stern test of the relationship between these late poems
and the classical phase, for he belongs to the latter part of
the fifth century, after the main revival was past, and he
indulges more than any of his predecessors in effects derived from lower prose genres.

I have also included the much-maligned *Aegritudo Perdicae*, which certainly belongs to the same North African
context as Dracontius' work, and even shows some affinities
with the greater poet's art: in fact, the *Aegritudo* has frequently—but falsely—been attributed to Dracontius himself.[12] Perhaps the comparison of the two poets' works will
help to expand our base for further investigation.

The Vandals

All the poems studied in this volume come from the Vandal kingdom of North Africa during the latter part of the fifth centry. It is a curious and perhaps accidental contribution of modern times that the Vandals are a byword for wanton destruction and brutish insensitivity.[13] Barbarians they most assuredly were, and destructive of much that fell in their path, but there is no reason to think of the Vandals as more savage than many of the other Germanic and non-Germanic peoples who moved across the face of Europe in late antiquity and indeed no less civilized than some representatives of the Roman order itself. Our sources from the time of the Vandals are all unremittingly hostile, for obvious reasons: they spoke for the victims of the Vandals and were little inclined to see good in the conquerors who demolished what had formerly been the Roman world.[14] Modern scholarship has developed a more dispassionate record on the Vandals, and the folk who emerge from this more careful scrutiny are no more lovable than Procopius and Victor of Vita said they were, but they are more believably human, and more interesting.[15]

The movements of the Vandals, who separated into two streams as early as the third century B.C. (Asdingi and Silingi), took them across much of Europe in a variety of conditions. Until the opening years of the fourth century, they remained outside the limits of the Empire, although they were known in a shadowy fashion to the Romans from the time of Pliny and Tacitus and joined the Marcomanni in the wars against Marcus Aurelius. But from the time the Vandals crossed the Rhine in 406, they were alternately lured and impelled across the Empire in company with the Suebi and the Alani. At one time or another, the Vandals were simple invaders and plunderers; they were named *foederati* of the Empire in an effort to acknowledge their gains and discourage them from seeking any more; they were the victims of the concentrated power of the Visigoths in Spain, where the Asdingi and Silingi had

descended with all the ferocity that imagination attributes
to barbarians, together with the Alani and Suebi. Much of
the Iberian peninsula had fallen into their hands, and when
Wallia led his Visigoths against these cruel invaders in 416,
he did so in the name of the Empire which had purchased
his services. Visigoths were no less bloodthirsty than Vandals, and the Silingi were extirpated by 418. The Alani
were severely reduced in numbers and strength, and their
remnant attached themselves to the Asding Vandals. From
that time on, the full title of the Vandal ruler was "King of
the Vandals and the Alans."

It was soon clear that the surviving Vandal and Alan populace could not safely remain on European soil. When
Gunderic died in 428, he was succeeded by his brother
Gaiseric, one of the most remarkable of all the barbarian
rulers. Gaiseric it was who led the Vandals to an adventure
not undertaken by any other migrating people of the time:
he led his entire people by sea over to Africa. The use of a
fleet was to be a crucial feature of the Vandal success story
over the next century, and certainly the mobilizing of a
populace reported at 80,000[16] to cross at Gibraltar and
move across North Africa expeditiously and victoriously
called for extraordinary leadership. But in 429, Gaiseric
did precisely that. Spain felt itself freed of a great threat,
but the departing Vandal horde would return to harry the
continent it had abandoned.

After being invading marauders, allies, settlers, enemies,
and refugees, the Vandals found their last home in the best
part of North Africa. The march eastward from Gibraltar to
Numidia met with surprisingly little resistance, but the
success in the more developed provinces of Numidia and
Proconsularis seem to have relied in part on the treachery
of the Roman Bonifacius. Hippo fell to the Vandals in 431,
and after further victories they were able to bring the Romans to sign a treaty in 435 which ceded to the barbarians
much of Numidia, the most important part of Sitifensis,
and part of Proconsularis. In return, the Romans accepted
the Vandals as *foederati* and assigned them to nominal ser-

vice of Valentinian III. But in this disposition, as in all deal-
ings with the Empire, Gaiseric was neither satisfied nor
trustworthy. In 439 the Vandals took Carthage and therewith established themselves in the second greatest city of
the Western Empire. They were now in a position to re-
negotiate their relations with Rome, and the outcome, in
the form of a new treaty in 442, was predictably more favorable to the conquering Vandals. They were now an indis-
putably independent kingdom, and their claim was granted
for all of Proconsularis, much of Numidia, all of Byzacena,
and part of Tripolitana. The sequence of events between
429 and 442 perfectly illustrates what Bury called Gaiseric's
gift for astute and perfidious diplomacy.[17]

This was not the end of the Vandal expansion. Their role
as an aggressive sea power allowed them to conquer the
Balearic Islands, Corsica and Sardinia, parts of western Si-
cily and of southern Italy, culminating in a sack of Rome
herself in 455, thus returning the favor precisely six hundred years after the destruction of Carthage by the Romans. Ironically, the marauding Vandals were much less
thorough in their sack than the earlier Romans had been in
representing civilization.

With the conquest of Carthage, the Vandals moved their
seat of government to the great city, and there a series of
six kings ruled for nearly a century.[18] All were of the house
of Gaiseric, although none had his flair for the use of power
or his subtle cunning.

One quality, however, all the Vandal rulers had in common: their ruthless adherence to the Arianism to which the
Vandals had been converted, ruthless because they would
tolerate no opposition and no alternative creeds including
that of the Donatists who had figured so prominently in the
African church.[19] The result was an ongoing persecution of
the far more numerous Catholic populace of the kingdom.
The degree of severity in that persecution varied from one
king to the next, with Huneric and Gelimer perhaps the
most fanatical of all, but for every Vandal ruler, Arianism was the sole official creed. This in part was to be the

downfall of Dracontius, as we shall see. The distrust and dislike of orthodox Christians—including orthodox princes in other realms—was one of the driving forces of Vandal policy through the years.

Another feature must be mentioned if only for the paradox it implies. To judge from all the evidence, the Vandals were entirely illiterate. The inscriptions and coins from the kingdom are in Latin, the language which the rulers were content to leave in place as the instrument of government. And yet from this kingdom, ruled by illiterate barbarians, there emerged a modest revival of letters. The Vandal monarchs apparently tolerated the continuation of the intellectual traditions for which Carthage had long been famed; for there is no other way to account for the continuity of culture which Dracontius and Corippus display. The schools and the fostering of learning continued, undoubtedly at a lower level and tenuously but without entirely breaking the links to the past. In fact, after the loutish Gunthamund, Thrasamund actually encouraged the cultivation of letters and gathered to his court an assortment of poets, theologians, and historians. Dracontius illustrates the upper limit of letters in Vandal Carthage, and Luxorius is probably more typical of what one might hope for in the early sixth century. The *Latin Anthology*, compiled in the latter days of the Vandal regime but certainly bringing together poems from a long time-span, contains a vast rambling array of material, much of it appallingly bad. It is, one fears, a fair measure of the taste and aspirations of the Latin-speaking literate (hardly literary) community of that era.

And yet despite the repressive and frequently violent regime, especially in matters religious, the conduct of everyday life seems often to have gone on in a fairly orderly fashion. After the initial upheaval and the imposition of absolute Vandal authority, there was apparently some gradual restoration of older arrangements. The celebrated *Tablettes Albertini*[20] provide a precious glimpse into the mundane operations of an unremarkable community and show how land was in some cases restored (under Gunthamund?) to folk who had lost it under the early repressions of Gaiseric. It is likely that life was no worse for the lower strata of the African-Roman populace under the Vandal regime than before, and to the extent that the marauding of the Circumcellions was reduced, life had improved.

The point is that the daily administration of the kingdom retained much of the pre-Vandal method. The Roman law and its language were kept, and even the terminology of offices was preserved: the proconsul was now simply attached to the Carthaginian court. The content of this administration was modified to the autocracy of the Vandal kings, who cared above all else to provide security and land for the Vandal population and to favor the Arian church above the Catholic; but the long-established patterns of civil service, of the law and the bureaucrats, was not a threat to the Vandals and relieved them of a major problem of preserving (or creating) order at the lower levels.

What emerges from our evidence on Vandal Carthage, then, is a picture of a busy capital city which retained something of its texture as a cultural center of long standing, despite a total change in the structure of authority and the unpredictability of a regime which repressed or persecuted in pursuit of material goods and religious supremacy, but which also tolerated the civilized elements of the civilization now in its power.

North Africa had always been an area which accommodated a blend of cultures: not only the mix of native origins and Punic, but of Greek as well as Roman had produced a cosmopolitanism such as no other city except Rome could match. The addition of the Germanic element in the Vandals (and therewith the non-Germanic Alan component) will not have been as tremendous a jolt in *cultural* terms as in many other parts of the Empire. The Vandals seem to have kept more or less to themselves culturally, but obviously there was some intermingling, at least at the higher levels of social status. Dracontius is apparently an illustration of this process.

Dracontius

By any measure, the most talented poet in fifth-century Africa was Blossius Aemilius Dracontius, who had both the learning and the imagination to exploit the cultural heritage of Carthage. It is a considerable frustration that we know so little about this man, but in fact there are virtually no sources of information outside of the poems themselves. The paucity of good evidence has not prevented—indeed, has prompted—a large literature of speculative scholarship on Dracontius' biography.[21] I have no desire to add to that literature, but only to lay out a few of the questions connected with Dracontius' career.

We have one more or less fixed date on which to peg our poet's biography: he was imprisoned by Gunthamund between 484 and 496. From this rough marker, we must calculate the rest of his biography. For instance, his birth date is variously reckoned from this bit of evidence. We know that Dracontius was a lawyer, and apparently a prominent one:[22] it is reasonable to assume that he attained that prominence before rather than after the disgrace of his incarceration, and this would seem to move the date of his birth back to 450 or perhaps a bit earlier. Other guesses have gone as far back as 420 (in order to allow him to recite *Rom.* V before the proconsul of an unconquered Carthage),[23] and as far forward as 460.[24]

His family is another mystery. The name would appear to guarantee a Roman line, generally estimated as senatorial, and there is no reason to think that Dracontius was born anywhere other than in Carthage. But there has been a lively debate over the possibility that he may have been of mixed Roman and Vandal lineage. This hypothesis was first advanced by Kuijper, and fervently attacked by Romano.[25] Diaz has more recently rejected the idea completely,[26] and yet it would seem to fit with other considerations not raised thus far in the discussion,[27] and I am inclined to believe that Kuijper was correct in postulating a Roman father and

a Vandal mother. The link to the Vandals will become important in another context.

At any rate, the young man studied in the rhetorical
school of Felicianus in Carthage; some parts of the *Romulea*
are dedicated to his teacher, and all show clearly enough
the imprint of the training he received from Felicianus. But
Dracontius also acquired a wide and thorough familiarity
with Latin literature beginning with Lucretius, and it is
very probable that he knew Greek poetry or parts of it as
we shall see in examining the *Orestis tragoedia*. There had
been a long tradition of Hellenism in Carthage, and two
generations earlier there was nothing startling in a poet's
showing a knowledge of Greek poetry. But the coming of
the Vandals is often thought to have eradicated that strain
of culture.[28] Whether Dracontius was very unusual for his
day we cannot tell, but there is good reason to think that he
had read Homer and at least parts of the Attic tragedians
and possibly much more.

After attaining some degree of repute in the law, Dracontius committed the most serious mistake of his life. Unfortunately, we are badly informed on the offense, as the poet's
own statement is obscure:

culpa mihi fuerat dominos reticere modestos
    ignotumque mihi scribere vel dominum,
qualis et ingratos sequitur qui mente profana,
    cum dominum norunt, idola vana colunt. (*Sat.* 93–96)

Clearly, Dracontius wrote a poem in which he expressed
praise of a foreign prince, and for this *carmen et error*
there was no forgiveness. The poet was turned in to Gunthamund by informers and suffered imprisonment, loss of
property, and torture. He and his family remained pris-
oners to the end of Gunthamund's reign; it was only under
the milder Thrasamund that the poet was released.

What was the nature of this tactless praise, and to whom

was it addressed? It is not at all certain that Dracontius called any foreigner *dominus* (which would surely have been high treason, and would have brought a more decisive punishment than imprisonment): indeed, *Satisfactio* 94 has been altered to *nec dominum* so as to avoid such a situation.[29] We have no trace of the offending poem so as to assess the poet's words, but it is hardly likely that such a piece would be preserved and circulated. It is more probable that Dracontius wrote enthusiastically of a foreign leader, not inviting intervention to rescue Africa from the Vandals or the Catholics from the Arians but merely extolling the deeds of a leader (probably military) from another land.

It was long assumed that the recipient of the poem was the Emperor Zeno, but there are severe problems with such a notion as has now been recognized.[30] The Emperor was hardly in a position to intervene in the affairs of Africa during the reign of Gunthamund, and after the publication of the *Henotikon* (481) there would be little enough reason for him to wish to rescue the Western Catholics in any case. His relatively unwarlike temperament also argues against the idea.

If not Zeno, then who? Kuijper suggested Theodoric,[31] but his candidacy is not without its difficulties either, partly chronological and hinging upon the date at which Theodoric assumed the title of king.[32] Corsaro made an equally intriguing suggestion:[33] that the object of Dracontius' praise was Odovacar, who was king at the necessary moment, as he had assumed the power in Italy in 476 and was in the ascendant until 489 when he suffered losses to Theodoric. He would have been closer to the Vandals in the sense that he was at least mildly Arian but maintained good relations with the Catholic structure both East and West, so that Dracontius might well have felt him to be a more admirable model of behavior than the narrowly Arian Gunthamund.

The question is unanswerable, but the offense and its consequences loom over any study of Dracontius. Two complementary points do arise, however, no matter who

the addressee was. First, it is obvious that Dracontius enjoyed some prominence if his views on foreign princes were
of interest to the Vandal king. Indeed, the fact that Dracontius found himself in a position to express such views—that
is, that his composition would have found a hearing in high
places—shows some status in the realm. And by the same
token, the fact that such a diplomatic gaffe should have led
not to execution but only to imprisonment under a repressive and jealous monarch like Gunthamund is a further
indication that Dracontius was well connected with respect
not only to the Roman subjects but to the Vandals. In view
of the overall separation of Roman and Vandal in the political sphere, is it likely that Gunthamund would have spared
a mere Roman meddling in foreign relations? It seems to
me more likely that he might have done so if Dracontius
himself was partly of Vandal stock and thus more closely
linked to the ruling class. A Roman who enjoyed the favor
of the Vandals could easily be the sort of person to stir jealousy and motivate an informer.[34]

In any case, while in prison our poet wrote *Satisfactio ad
regem Gunthamundum*, a work of elaborate apology and
justification reminiscent of Ovid's equivalent efforts in the
Tristia. Unfortunately, it had no more effect than the poems
from Tomi, and Dracontius later wrote a more ambitious
work, *De laudibus Dei* in three books. That work is incidental proof that the poet's offense cannot have been the
profession of Catholic doctrine in the face of Arians, for
Dracontius not only details impeccably orthodox views in
De laudibus Dei, he even goes so far as to describe Arius as
insipiens (I.738)—hardly the posture designed to win pardon if that was the nub of the original offense.

It is a plausible enough conjecture that the poet regained
his freedom at the start of Thrasamund's reign, and that the
monarch may have used that event as an opportunity to display his magnanimity and at the same time to secure the
goodwill of his subjects in the face of threats from the neigh-
boring Moors.[35] The family of Victor—for whose sons the

poet wrote the epithalamium *Romulea* VI—apparently
played a role, as verses 36–40 imply:

> . . . quorum umbone tegor vel quorum munere vivo:
> post varios casus, post tot discrimina vitae
> porrexere piam placido pro tegmine dextram
> et, quod maius erat, laesi tribuere salutem
> fortunamque mihi reducem pietate novarunt.

Dracontius responded to this act of belated clemency from
the king by writing a panegyric of Thrasamund, which has
not survived even though we have hints of its existence.[36]

Of the remainder of Dracontius' life we likewise have no
record. Did he regain his standing in the community along
with his freedom? Did he return to the practice of the
law?[37] And what poems, if any, should be assigned to the
period after his incarceration? None of these questions can
be answered with any confidence, although it is likely that
at least some of the *Romulea* fall into this later period, and
perhaps three of the four epyllia which are to engage our
attention.[38]

The *Romulea* is itself a peculiar assemblage of poems.
The ten pieces are of very uneven merit, and it is nearly
certain that what we have now does not represent the original collection.[39] The components are:

I. Dedicatory preface,[40] addressed to Felicianus, lead-
    ing into
II. *Hylas* (ch. ch. 2);
III. Dedicatory preface, addressed to Felicianus, leading
    to
IV. *Verba Herculis cum videret Hydrae serpentis capita
    pullare post caedes*, a remarkably silly *ethopoeia*
    which does little to suggest the quality of which Dra-
    contius is capable and shows him still a prisoner of
    the rhetorical school mentality rather than its master;
V. *Controversia de statua viri fortis*, treating the sort of

wildly improbable situation on which students had
trained in the schools since the days of Quintilian;[41]
VI. *Epithalamium in fratribus*, addressed to Victorianus
and Rufinianus the sons of Victor and showing the
poet's mastery of a particularly artificial genre; apparently composed after the poet's release (496 or later);
VII. *Epithalamium Iohannis et Vitulae*, written from
prison and thus datable to 484–96;
VIII. *De raptu Helenae* (cf. ch. 4);
IX. *Deliberativa Achillis an corpus Hectoris vendat*, a
work nearly as silly as V.;
X. *Medea* (cf. ch. 3).

It would appear that the *Romulea* brings together materials
from the poet's early phase: the starkly rhetorical exercises
which are so redolent of his school days, at least one poem
from his prison years and one from later, and in all probability some more ambitious and serious works which should
be assigned to his full maturity. Is it fanciful to imagine that
a man who had been punished long and severely for political indiscretion might turn to less controversial activities
after finally obtaining his freedom? Perhaps Dracontius focused more on poetry and less on foreign relations in his
later years.

One of the epyllia is not preserved with the *Romulea*,
although it surely was attached to the rest of Dracontius'
poetry on traditional themes at some stage. The *Orestis
tragoedia* (cf. below, ch. 5) is the longest and most ambitious of Dracontius' poems apart from the *De laudibus;* I
am inclined to see it as one of his later works, possibly even
from a time after his imprisonment. It survived separately
from the other *carmina minora*, and enjoyed considerable
influence in the Middle Ages while the *Romulea* were apparently unknown.

There is no doubt that the narrative poems are the most
interesting and successful of the compositions on pagan or
rhetorical themes. Several reasons come immediately to

mind. The rhetorical poems are productions from the poet's youth (admittedly, *Hylas* dates from this early phase as well), while *Helen, Medea,* and *Orestes* all come from a more mature stage of the poet's art.[42] Moreover, the epyllia—including the relatively slight *Hylas*—all work from fully developed literary traditions in both Greek and Latin, which the poet has exploited in various ways to lend depth and significance to the poems. It is obvious that the themes of these poems are inherently meatier and invite a more significant treatment than Hercules agape at the Hydra's sprouting heads, or even more significant than the wedding of a friend. Perhaps it was the hard challenge of the tradition already behind these stories that prompted Dracontius to develop and invent his own treatment of major myths: in the *Orestes* at least, one cannot escape the sense of direct confrontation between Aeschylus and Dracontius. We can hardly feel surprised that the Roman poet has failed to surpass the *Oresteia,* but the effect of his model has been impressive. And finally, as will emerge from the analysis of the individual poems, Dracontius as a Christian poet could not look at the great stories of pagan mythology without some impact from his own beliefs reshaping what he saw. It is very difficult to tell how extensive and how conscious this process was. Dracontius undoubtedly loved the stories on which he had been raised—why else would he pursue them in the peculiar world in which he lived—but as the *Satisfactio* and *De laudibus Dei* show, the urge to spell out his faith was powerful.

Thus the epyllia of Dracontius are of interest as a group and separately, as they show the imagination of an author who was at the confluence of so many cultural factors: Greek and Latin letters, a new Germanic strain, the clash of pagan and Christian, and we may say from this vantage point, the transition from antiquity to the medieval world.

Chapter 2

Hylas (Rom. II)

Background and Tradition

FROM ONE END OF antiquity to the other we encounter the story of the young Hylas, beloved of Hercules and taken from him into the water.[1] The myth was especially popular in the Alexandrian period, from which we have treatments by Theocritus and Apollonius and know of treatments by Callimachus, Nicander, Philetas, and Euphorion.[2] It remained more widely treated in Greek authors than in Latin, but Propertius (I.20) and Valerius Flaccus offer well-known versions.

The features of the story which are invariable are relatively few but crucial. Hylas always has some association with Hercules. As Türk showed, the linkage results from the cult of Hylas in Bithynia, specifically near Cius, which Hercules was credited with founding.[3] Thus for most of the literary tradition, the association with Hercules and with the Propontis persists. This provides a third feature, the association with the Argonauts, since that adventure accounts for the presence of Hercules in the region. And the Hylas story in turn explains—or permits—the fact that Hercules was not one of the Argonauts who actually reached Colchis: he must be distracted from his mission. Hylas had always been associated with a spring (so Hesychius),[4] which dictates the manner of his loss. And finally, Hercules always laments the boy's disappearance.

Within this framework the poets and mythographers embellish the story in many ways, and use the myth for a variety of purposes. In some cases, the story is imbedded in a

21

larger narrative (e.g., Apollonius, Valerius Flaccus) of the
Argonaut saga;[5] in others it is an independent tale (e.g.,
Theocritus, Propertius, and Nicander). In the epic narratives Hercules is the center of attention and Hylas a sub-
sidiary figure, while the elegiac and epyllionic versions
turn more on erotic aspects and thus dwell more on Hylas than his heroic companion. Propertius, for example,
scarcely mentions Hercules, and expressly makes Hylas
a lesson in the perils of entrusting one's love to others.
Another major variable is the presence or absence of Hercules' fellow Argonaut Polyphemus, who sometimes appears instead of Hercules as Hylas' lover, and frequently
helps search for the lost boy.

In seeking to recognize subgroups within the tradition,
one may look at the treatment of particular features. Agudo
Cubas argues, for example, that the fundamental split is between those accounts with a single nymph capturing Hylas
and those with a conflux of nymphs, the latter always being
the more popular.[6] And yet as we shall see, Valerius Flaccus
is in some respects a model for Dracontius, though he
presents a single nymph; while on the contrary Propertius
and Theocritus share with Dracontius the multiple nymphs,
but almost nothing else. The central distinction is rather
the role of the boy: for some poets Hylas is the protagonist,
while for others he is a mere lay figure. Moreover, his relationship with Hercules varies considerably. He is generally
the beloved of the hero (although some versions, including
Dracontius, make relatively little of this); nearly all poets
recall that Hylas was acquired in battle by Hercules as
a servant. Some cast the relationship rather as that of a
young squire to the hero. There is even the version of So-
crates, and perhaps Euphorion, which makes Hylas the son
of Hercules.[7] The balance of prominence given the two
characters and the nature of their relationship offer a much
more appropriate basis for sorting out the tradition.

These distinctions are relevant to a consideration of
Dracontius' *Hylas* because they show what aspects of the
tradition are constant, and what features were always regarded as open to variation. In light of these facts it is clear

that Dracontius has moved in a very independent fashion, introducing novelties even in areas previously regarded as fixed.[8]

The most notable change is that Dracontius has divorced the tale from the context of the Argo, or rather has suppressed that connection. Hercules appears *post bella suis*, and no mention is made of Argo or its crew. But as reported by Apollonius (I.122), it was immediately after capturing the Erymanthian boar that Hercules heard of the Argonautic expedition and hastened to join Jason. Thus Dracontius has followed the Greek tradition, which is nowhere else recorded in the Latin authors, setting in sequence the capture of the boar, the Argonautic expedition, and Hylas. Yet he has suppressed the second of these in order to focus our attention more sharply on Hercules and Hylas themselves and to allow room for his other innovations. Indeed we find novelty even here, for the tradition—including Apollonius—specifies that Hercules' task was to capture the boar alive.[9] He was carrying it in chains and left it behind in Mycenae when he went to enlist for *Argo*. But in Dracontius, Hylas is carrying the boar's hide.

The second major innovation is made possible by eliminating the Argonautic setting. The abduction of Hylas is now prompted not by the spontaneous passion of nymphs who see Hylas, nor by Juno's anger at Hercules, but by Venus' desire for revenge against Clymene, who has been rehearsing the story of Venus' dalliance with Mars. In no other version is any such idea found. The motif of Venus' anger as the catalyst of action is popular in late African poets, and it is reasonable to assume that Dracontius himself introduced it here.

And third, our poet has concomitantly changed the place of the action. Instead of the Mysian locale reported elsewhere, we are now *Penei sub fonte* which is where Vergil places Clymene and her company in the account of Aristaeus:

Pastor Aristaeus fugiens Peneia Tempe . . .
tristis ad extremi sacrum caput astitit amnis. (G. 4.317, 319)

Clymene is also telling the same story as in the Aristaeus episode, so it is even clear when the *Hylas* takes place.[10] As Aristaeus arrives at the spring, Clymene is singing her tale, and Hylas arrives in the aftermath of that action.

A fourth relatively minor alteration is that the motivation for Hylas to be near the spring is now unclear. He comes *hauriturus aquas,* but no explanation of his being in the area is provided. Hercules and Hylas pass by in their travels: presumably from Mycenae, but whither? Basically, Hylas must be there to be available for abduction.

And last, Dracontius presents another detail which is otherwise found only in the Greek tradition. Cupid en route back to heaven appears to Hercules and tells him of Hylas' fate. This may eventually go back to a lost Greek tragedy on Hercules and Hylas. Aristophanes *Plutus* 1127 reads

$$\pi o \theta \epsilon \hat{\iota} s \ \tau \dot{o} \nu \ o \dot{v} \ \pi a \rho \acute{o} \nu \tau a \ \kappa a \grave{\iota} \ \mu \acute{a} \tau \eta \nu \ \kappa a \lambda \epsilon \hat{\iota} s$$

and it is conjectured that the comic poet culled the line from a tragic source.[11] The link with Hylas is provided in the scholia on the play, which report that $\pi o \theta \epsilon \hat{\iota} s \ \tau \dot{o} \nu$ $o \dot{v} \ \pi a \rho \acute{o} \nu \tau a$ became a proverbial expression for fruitless searching.[12] One scholion states that Ἡρακλῆς πολὺν χρόνον ἐζήτει· ὕστερον δὲ ὑπό τινος αἰθερίας φωνῆς ἤκουσε ποθεῖς κτλ. The other specifies that Hercules was searching παρὰ τῶν πηγῶν. This last detail is significant because the hero is once again near the spring when he hears Cupid's voice. In Dracontius, as in the scholiast, the hero is still searching frantically (*adhuc furibundus*), a point emphasized by the repetition in line 141 of the line describing his first arrival there (94).

It is clear that Dracontius has felt free to rework even the most traditional features of his story, and this freedom makes it difficult to decide what parts of the tradition he knew. Some aspects are clear enough. Contrary to the common view that Dracontius knew only Latin sources,[13] it is probable that he used Apollonius, and he may also have

known the Greek tradition about the voice announcing
Hylas' fate. It is less likely that he is using Theocritus, who
like Dracontius portrays the nymphs consoling Hylas after
his capture (XIII.53–54). It is far more probable that he
derived the detail from Silius Italicus (V.8ff.), whose account of the abduction of Thrasymenus by the nymph concludes with Agylle consoling the youth.[14]

I think we can simplify the question further. There is no
need to look beyond the Vergilian passage and Aristaeus
himself: after he is taken below the water, he is consoled by
Clymene and the other nymphs. At any rate, if Dracontius
did have Theocritus in mind or even knew the poem, it was
reflected only in this one detail, while he diverged from
him on many matters of importance.

We might expect our poet to use Propertius extensively,
as the elegist's treatment in I.20 offered a ready model for a
free-standing poem on the theme. But there is no recognizable echo of Propertius. Procacci believed[15] that

> quem rubor ut roseus sic candor lacteus ornat;
> illi purpureus niveo natat ignis in ore (66–67)

was an imitation of Propertius I.20, 45–46:

> cuius ut accensae Dryades candore puellae
> miratae solitos destituere choros.

The shared word *candor* (in different forms) is hardly
enough to show influence—it is an appropriate and not un-
common word for a necessary notion. And this is all that
anyone suggests. It is surely more reasonable to conclude
that Dracontius did not follow the elegist. This is explained
not by Dracontius' determination to keep his distance from
an earlier rendition of the theme, but by the absence of
Propertius from the entire Dracontian corpus. I believe
that our poet did not know Propertius' work, at least not at
first hand, as Propertius seems not to have been used by
fifth-century writers generally.[16]

Three Latin poets were certainly drawn upon. Vergil we have already noted. He provided the setting, the nymph Clymene and her song, the cause of the offense against Venus, and the nymph named Deiopea who consoles Hylas.[17] He also served as a model for Venus' address to Cupid, appealing to his superior powers and imploring his aid:[18]

> ergo his aligerum dictis adfatur Amorem:
> "nate, meae vires, mea magna potentia, solus,
> nate, patris summi qui tela Typhoea temnis,
> ad te confugio et supplex tua numina posco." (*Aen.* 1.663–66)

There is an obvious temptation to regard as likewise Vergilian the picture with which the poem opens, namely Cupid coming to see his mother. But Dracontius was looking to Lucretius' celebrated tableau of Mars and Venus in the first proemium (1.31–40). The pose of the two figures, with Cupid flinging himself into Venus' lap and the goddess gazing upon him, strongly recalls the vivid picture in Lucretius of Venus seated and looking down at the infatuated god (1.33ff.). The son has replaced the lover, but there is an imitation of the ferocity of Lucretius' Mars in Dracontius' Cupid who embraces his mother *violentis ulnis* (5). That Dracontius had the passage in mind as he wrote the poem is established by the explicit quotation of *De rerum natura* I.1 in verse 74, where Cupid is *hominum divumque voluptas*. Moreover, Dracontius has echoed the Lucretian tableau quite unmistakably in *Medea* 126ff., where once again Venus addresses Amor.

The third Latin poet used in this epyllion is, appropriately, Valerius Flaccus, and yet Dracontius' independence is shown by the fact that he draws a few details from Valerius but has a basically different story. Valerius belongs to the minority tradition which has a single nymph (in his case Dryope) as Hylas' captor; and of course the event is set in the Argonautic expedition, and a major role is assigned to Hercules. And yet the picture of Hylas struggling with gear too big for him is surely derived from Valerius:

> cui iunctus Hylas pulcherrimus haeret
> gestans fulminei pellem cum dentibus apri;
> et licet invalidus haec pondera ferre laborat,
> ipse tamen gaudet, quasi iam commune trophaeum
> gestet. . . . (95–98)

So Valerius (I.108–11):

> Protinus Inachiis ultro Tirynthius Argis
> advolat, Arcadio cuius flammata veneno
> tela puer facilesque umeris gaudentibus arcus
> gestat Hylas; velit ille quidem, sed dextera nondum
> par oneri clavaeque capax.

There are other incidental echoes of Valerius,[19] but the other detail of significance comes at the end of the poem, when Hercules frets about telling Hylas' mother of the boy's fate:

> quid matri narrabo tuae, quae te mihi parvum
> deposuit pietatis inops? (159–60)

This is a more lively version of Valerius III.733–35:

> Amphitryonides nec quae nova lustra requirat,
> nec quo temptet iter, comitis nec fata parenti
> quae referat videt. . . .

This anxiety is not expressed anywhere else in the tradition. It is characteristic of Dracontius that he should pick up two vivid details such as these and yet leave aside the essential structure of the story in which he found them. He is always eager for novelty and is most attracted, as Provana shows, to the lively sentimental touch.[20] Dracontius shows his originality precisely in taking over phrases and details and turning them into a strikingly new version of an old tale. This may be seen most readily in the structure of the poem and in the characters as he develops them.

Structure

It is readily apparent that the poem falls into four separate scenes, some of which are complex and others quite
simple.[21] The scenes are also quite unequal in length. Procacci was merely following the prevailing view when he
spoke of "gravi difetti di proporzione fra le varie parti"[22] but
he did not recognize the interrelation of the scenes. For example, he regarded lines 4–94 as a single segment, merely
because they precede the "real" theme, that is, the arrival
of Hylas; but there is no unity to 4–94, and he was therefore justified in lamenting a lack of harmony and organiza-
tion. Quartiroli a generation later still argued that Dracontius merely composed a series of scenes with no control
over the narrative flow or internal coordination of parts.[23]

But in fact, the poem displays a surprisingly careful architecture, as will be seen for each of the epyllia. Diaz' discussion shows a more positive approach, dealing mainly with
the rhetorical arrangement.[24] The relatively small scope of
the poem certainly encouraged polishing, and the influence
of the poet's school training was still very strong at this
stage of his work. The structure (apart from the prefatory
lines 1–3) is as follows:

A	Venus and Cupid	4–70	67 vv.
B	Transformation of Cupid	71–93	23
C	Capture of Hylas	94–140	47
D	Lament of Hercules	141–63	23

Note that panels B and D are equal in length, while A and
C are very uneven. For this there is good reason, as will
appear shortly. Note also that the first scene is nearly as
long as the next two combined. Clearly the interview between Venus and her son is the most important single element in the poet's design. This is not surprising, since it is
the poet's own contribution to the story.

Each scene is marked by the entrance of the principal
speaker or figure on stage. In fact, the dramatic influence is

quite striking, shown in the role of the speeches and in the stage directions accompanying entrances and exits. The first scene opens with Cupid flinging himself into his mother's lap:

> fuderat Idalius gremio se forte parentis
> penniger et collum violentis cinxerat ulnis
> oscula pura rogans. mater devota coruscos
> indulget vultus roseoque est orsa labello. (4–7)

This picture of the two figures embracing is an image of the scene's structure. Venus and Cupid speak almost equal lines (Venus, 32, Cupid, 30), but they are not presented as a conversation. Venus begins with her prayer to her son but does not get to the specifics of her petition. She is interrupted by the impatient boy and then resumes her speech in 45 with another declaration of his power, thus encircling with affirmations his own assessment of his abilities. This time she also gives details of the situation. The intertwined speeches seem to be an extension of the physical position of the speakers. Virtually the entire scene consists of speeches, 61 of 67 lines.

As we have seen, the breathless arrival of Cupid and the goddess' prayer are an echo of Lucretius' tableau, but that picture has been converted from a described scene into a dramatic moment. Morelli observed that the conversation between Venus and Cupid is a regular part of the late epithalamia, including those of Dracontius (*Rom.* VI and VII).[25] Cupid's boasts of past triumphs or promises of future conquests are likewise from this tradition, reflected both here and in *Medea* 49ff. The passage also bears some formal resemblance to Eros' words in Nonnos XXXIII.118–39, but the lines of influence cannot be untangled.

Both speeches have complex structures. Cupid's breaks into four parts: general boasting (15–18), Jupiter's loves (19–27), Cupid's power to afflict other gods—even Minerva (28–30) or Neptune (31–35)—and a gleeful prediction of what he will be able to do to mere mortals (36–44). The

emphasis throughout is on the unnatural or even perverted. After his claims, it is almost a relief to hear Venus'
request for something less flamboyantly unnatural. Her second speech also falls into segments. After reaffirming Cupid's
power (46–52), she tells the story of Clymene and laments
the nymph's impertinence (53–61) and finally makes her
request (62–70). On a small scale the structure of this
scene is itself like the traditional epyllion format, with di-
gressions and emotional speeches forming a kind of chinese-
box maze, all on bizarre erotic themes.

Thus the first scene of the poem is busy and dramatic,
with carefully placed speeches. The contrast with the second portion of the poem could scarcely be greater. Venus
has now left the stage and will not reappear. Cupid's swift
preparations and travel to earth mark the opening of the
scene, as his entry began the first. This part of the epyllion
(panel B in the scheme given above) likewise falls into three
segments: Cupid's preparations and departure for the spring
(71–79), his change in appearance (80–89), and his meeting
with the naiads (90–93). But by contrast with A, there is no
direct speech here at all. Cupid has the stage to himself but
does not indulge in soliloquy. Instead, he is presented in a
pantomime as he changes costume. Indeed, we may say
that while the stage influenced the poem as a whole, it was
more particularly the pantomime with its silent, irreverent,
and lewd conduct which prompted this picture of Cupid.[26]

There is a sharper break between the second and third
scenes, as Hylas finally comes on stage in the company of
Hercules:

> interea post bella suis Tirynthius ibat
> victor ovans, cui iunctus Hylas pulcherrimus haeret
> gestans fulminei pellem cum dentibus apri. (94–96)

After the mincing steps of Cupid and the twittering of the
nymphs, this triumphal procession is arresting. But the
scene belongs to Hylas, not Hercules. The hero is not mentioned again after his entrance, and our attention, like that
of the nymphs, turns to the delicate youth. We are given

four reactions to Hylas and his beauty, including the poet's
pulcherrimus. The nymphs express their astonishment even
before they are smitten by the god's darts, comparing Hylas
to various personages including Apollo (100–108). Then
after Cupid shoots them, the poet tells us again of their frantic reaction (echoing Vergil's description of the enamored
Dido). Third, Clymene fittingly speaks for all of them—
she had after all caused the situation by her earlier words—
and recommends capturing Hylas for their common pleasure (111–22). Like her sisters, she thinks of legendary
archetypes, for example, Paris and Oenone.[27] The capture
itself now takes place (123–30), and Deiopea after exhort-
ing her sisters (for unspecified purposes) consoles Hylas.
Her language is filled with the beauties of nature and gives
a new perspective on the quality of his charm. Thus we
have, as in the first segment, three speeches on a single
topic with the central one being the most complex. The
balance is emphasized by the fact that the central panel in
A is Cupid's boast of his powers, and the central panel in C
is on Cupid's exercise of those powers. Venus' lament focuses on Clymene's "crime" (viz., reciting Venus' *crimina*),
and Clymene by her speech exculpates herself:

> nec erit mihi crimen amanti. (118)

and as the end of the first panel contains Venus' scheme for
the nymphs to suffer,

> hoc puero viso Nympharum turba calescat;
> haec illis sit poena nocens, ut vota trahantur
> ipsarum in longum, donec pubescat amatus, (68–70)

so this third panel ends with Deiopea's contented announcement to Hylas,

> tu noster iam sponsus eris sine fine dierum. (139)

The fourth scene is intended to be parallel to the third in
at least one respect. The opening lines bring us back to
Hercules. Now it is time for his performance, and once

again the beginning of the segment is marked by the arrival
of the principal actor. The echo of 94 is sharp and clear:

> interea furibundus adhuc Tirynthius ibat
> et clamans quaerebat Hylan. (141–42)

But instead of Hercules *ovans* (95), we find Amor *ovans*
(147). Yet Amor's words to Hercules are only reported: the
hero delivers the only speech (151–63).

Thus the demarcation of scenes is achieved by the entrance of the principal figure, with an impression of stage
directions as the poet ushers in the speaker. In three cases
the emphasis is on speeches exclusively by or about the
central figure. In the fourth the effectiveness depends precisely on the absence of speech.

Moreover, there is a network of echoes and parallels
serving to bind the four scenes together in various ways, all
pointing eventually to the main purpose of the poem. The
equal length of B and D draws our attention to the essential
opposition between Hercules and Cupid, for the poem reports a test of strength between these two, each invincible
in his own way. Cupid's arrival at the spring (B) is matched
by Hercules' double entry, first in triumph (C) and then in
panic (D) as Amor assumes the role of *triumphator*. These
two entrances themselves serve to set C and D side by
side; and the same phenomenon should be noted for A and
B, which both start with the arrival of Cupid. Thus Hercules and the god each have two scenes marked by their
presence, and it is fitting that the final scene should show
their meeting.

Cupid is the fulcrum of another balance as well. The poem
opens with Venus attesting to her son's power and closes with
Hercules acknowledging and bewailing that power. Further-
more, the mother-son theme stands out in both these scenes.
Venus is the *mater devota*, doting on the son she must pray
to, and the poem closes with Hercules' planned words to
Hylas' mother to report his deification (note *genetrix* in
162, which perhaps is a final Lucretian echo).

This further suggests that Cupid and Hylas are to be

seen in counterpoint to one another. They are the two beautiful sons, and the two inner panels (B and C) focus on them in turn. The account of Cupid's disguise, for all its qualities of parody, emphasizes his beauty, which is the focus of all the speeches about Hylas.

Thus we can see that the poem is built up from a series of contrasts between Cupid and all three other characters. It would be fair to say that the poem is about Cupid rather than Hylas. For this reason alone, Procacci's stricture about the proportions is unfounded. As in the classical epyllia, the actual focus of interest is not the nominal topic. And, as often in the Hylas tradition, the beautiful youth is a mere pawn.

If we would understand the poet's purpose in this poem, we must look more closely at the four characters to see how they are depicted, and more important, how they act.

Characters

In brief, one may say that Dracontius presents an exaggerated version of tendencies found in the literary tradition from the Hellenistic era on; but he does so, I believe, for a particular purpose not represented elsewhere in the Hylas tradition, namely, to parody the story and its characters. The case can best be seen by considering these figures separately.

Cupid was long depicted as a spoiled little boy, most notably by Apollonius (especially III. 111–53). But unlike the little brat in Apollonius and others, who must be coaxed or bribed into cooperation, this Cupid is straining at the bit to go into action.

When he flings himself onto his mother's bosom, the dangerous blend of his character is seen in the juxtaposition of *oscula pura* and *violentis ulnis*. The same combination is found in Venus' reaction to him, for she speaks first of his power (8–9) and only then calls him *nate* (12).[28] The paradox of the son mightier than the mother in her own sphere of activity is played against his childlike devotion to his mother. Once we compare the scene to the Venus-Mars

tableau, we see that the relative dominance is reversed:
whereas Lucretius emphasizes the subjection of Mars to
Venus, here the son is the dominant figure. The irony lies
in the fact that it is precisely the Mars-Venus liaison which
Venus protests as the topic of Clymene's song.

Cupid breaks in on his mother's address, eager for the
challenge and boasting wildly. His tone is as playful and
childlike as in Apollonius, but the collection of examples he
uses is alarming: Jupiter transformed, Minerva diverted
from her true nature, the paradox of the water god aflame,
and in the human realm a persistent emphasis on incest.
These were popular stories, and the *Aegritudo Perdicae*
shows what kind of treatment they might receive in Dracontius' day. Perhaps Ovid (*Met.* 6.103–20) was a partial
model, at least for the transformation of Jupiter,[29] but the
rest of the list does not appear anywhere else. It is interesting to note the similarity between this catalog and the list
in Firmicus Maternus, *De errore profanarum religionum*
(12.2). He gives many of the same stories, and includes
Herculem . . . Hylan impatienti amore quaerentem.[30] That
impassioned document had urged the damaging and pre-
posterous untruth of the pagan myths. Is Dracontius making the same point? Poets always pointed to the mixed character of Amor, the bright lure and the threat of tears, the
compulsion to abandon one's true nature for love. But the
unrelieved emphasis on perversion and incest offers no balance here.

After Venus tells her story, Cupid cuts her off and takes
command of the action. As if to underscore Cupid as taking
over from Venus, the poet uses Lucretius' most famous
phrase for the goddess:

> arcu cinctus erat, dantur post terga pharetrae,
> accipit et flammas hominum divumque voluptas. (73–74)

In his swift descent from heaven with his weapons on his
back, he recalls a tradition going back to the angry Apollo
in Homer.

So far, the picture of Cupid in this scene has been vigorous and impressive. But we are being set up for the farcical episode which ensues. Cupid will apparently undergo metamorphosis into the likeness of a naiad. The plan is not inherently ludicrous, but hear how the poet tells it:

> volucer fugiens nemus intrat opacum
> moxque dei vultus Naidis vestivit imago;
> tendit membra puer, longos ut crescat in artus,
> ut possit complere dolos ac iussa parentis;
> ‹usque› pedes fluitans vestis laxatur ad imos,
> candida diffusi ludunt per colla capilli
> et vento crispante gradu coma fluctuat acta,
> frons nudata decet diviso fulgida crine;
> et velut invitos gressus pudibunda movebat
> incedens fluxoque latent sub tegmine pennae. (80–89)

The scene has been generally misunderstood—certainly by Agudo Cubas, who finds it the finest and most delicate scene in the poem, with no suggestion that it is anything other than a straightforward transformation.[31] In fact, the grand language only serves to point up the absurdity of the visual scene. Cupid's actions are a pantomime, and Dracontius has carefully evoked the elements of that immensely popular art form.[32]

First, Cupid conveys his intentions and meaning without speaking. He strains and stretches his limbs—like the dancer—in order to pass for a naiad (82), and he walks about mincingly to mimic the dainty steps of the nymphs (88). Moreover, he wears the costume of the pantomime: ancient sources both literary and visual frequently depict the long flowing robe essential for the artist,[33] which Cupid likewise wears (84). The other feature of the pantomime's costume was the mask,[34] and verse 81 is certainly suggestive: *vultus vestivit imago* is not how one would normally describe a transformation, but it is an apt description of donning a mask. And finally, note that Cupid's "transformation" has not removed or concealed his wings: he must tuck them under his robe lest they stick out and betray

him. The line merely emphasizes that Cupid is in costume,
playing a role. The final incongruity is the regal *incedens*
(89) to describe this little boy in ladies' clothing who struts
self-contentedly around the pool. It is impossible to take
him—or, as a result, his powers—seriously.

The pantomime was used for all types of subjects, both
tragic and burlesque, but the great majority treated mythological themes. There was an emphasis on erotic topics, including incest and other unnatural propensities: Myrrha
and Cinyras, Stratonice and Antiochus. This also fits well
with what we have already heard Cupid tell of his intentions and accomplishments. Moreover, we know of pan-
tomimes on Mars and Venus, the judgment of Paris, the
rape of Helen[35]—all of which are themes in epyllia by
Dracontius and his contemporaries.[36]

The pantomime was accompanied by an orchestra and
chorus. In *Hylas* we find the nymphs performing the function of the chorus. They have already been singing in the
pool and now rise to accompany Cupid.

This emergence from the water points to a special form of
the pantomime which became very popular in the later Empire: the aquatic mime. Traversari has studied the growth
of this curious entertainment, found all round the Mediterranean in theaters converted into swimming pools.[37] There
the "dancers" could treat virtually any theme, and elude
the prohibition on female nudity, which traditional pantomime had prompted, by appealing to the obvious necessity for swimmers to be free of clothing. Myths with an
inherent link to the water were no doubt tried first, but
as this would provide a limited repertoire, other stories
were modified to include aquatic scenes. Choruses of water
nymphs were naturally suited to this environment, and one
can readily see how Dracontius could be influenced by the
popular entertainment in dealing with Hylas. G. d'Ippolito
conjectured the influence of the *idromimi* in the arrival of
Hylas (*Hyl.* 94ff.) and in Cupid rising from the sea (*Med.*
96ff.).[38] But the most completely developed specimen of
pantomime is this scene of Cupid playing the naiad, with
the chorus twittering around him. It combines the formal

features of pantomime—mask, robe, dance, and silent performance—with a setting, theme, and chorus suited to the
aquatic mime. This may explain in part the poet's alteration
of the myth to include Clymene and her sisters: they are
not merely water nymphs, but a *chorus*, uniting the musi-
cal with the aquatic. This also explains the poet's description of Hylas' singing as he approaches the spring, *cantabat
Hylas fontemque petebat* (123).[39]

Hercules and Hylas enter, and our thoughts leave Cupid
for a time, until the mischievous god retires into the woods
to collect his bow (how careful of Dracontius to remember
that he would not be carrying it!) and shoots the nymphs.
But they had already shown all the signs of falling in love
with Hylas, so that Cupid's efforts are superfluous at this
point. More important, they are ineffectual, since the goal
of his mission is never accomplished. The nymphs do indeed fall in love with Hylas, but they suffer not at all from
the experience. Where then is Venus' revenge?

Cupid is shown in the last scene as returning in triumph
to his mother:

> cum iam remearet ad ‹astra›
> post factum pennatus Amor matrique triumphum
> adportaret ovans. . . . (145–47)

Whether Venus will feel she has gained anything, one cannot say, but Cupid keeps the appearance of a victor, with
the echo of Hercules' entrance in 94. He has changed from
the naughty little boy of the opening scene into an apparently mighty god with his epiphany to Hercules. But we
know that it is a sham.

Standing in contrast to Cupid is the other boy, Hylas. They
are utterly different, and yet the poet compels us to run
them together in our imagination, not least by his use of
puer referring now to the god, now to Hylas. The appearance of both is emphasized, and in both cases it is beauty
which dominates. Both are sons of doting mothers, and
both make conspicuous entrances at the spring.

Yet while Cupid has a well-developed character, Hylas is
a mere pawn in this game of revenge. He says not a word,
in contrast to the long self-presentation of Cupid. Indeed,
although he is referred to several times in the first half of
the poem, his name does not occur until he arrives at the
spring (95). Earlier he is merely *Alcidis comes* (3, 65; also
149). Even when he is finally named, it is in the description
of Hercules, *cui iunctus Hylas.*

We may go further. In other versions of the story, there
is an element of deliberate choice in the capture of this particular boy, either because of his unparalleled beauty or (in
Valerius Flaccus) because Juno can punish Hercules by the
abduction of his favorite. In this version Venus wishes to
punish not Hercules but the nymphs, and it is sheer accident that Hylas is available to cast in their path. Hercules is
the one who is wounded by the event, although he has
done nothing to deserve it. Even Hylas' beauty is described in the most conventional terms, mostly conveyed
by the excited cries from the nymphs.

When Hylas arrives accompanying Hercules, he reminds
us of the young Iulus in the company of Aeneas.[40] The reaction of the nymphs, *horrent Alciden nymphae, mirantur
Hylanque* (100), echoes the reaction of the Carthaginians to
the arrival of "Iulus" and his father (*Aen.* 1.709), *mirantur
dona Aeneae, mirantur Iulum.* But of course the Iulus they
see is really Cupid disguised as the boy, and Dracontius
plays an elaborate game in imitating that line to present
Hylas while a transformed Cupid watches from the side.
The parallel between Cupid and Hylas is enhanced by
Hylas' eagerness to associate himself with the victories of
Hercules (96–99). His boyish enthusiasm and eagerness for
challenges suggests the zest of Cupid in the first scene, and
like Cupid in the second scene, his actions constitute a
pantomime.

The nymphs compare Hylas to five heroes and gods:
Hippolytus, Paris, Jason, Bacchus, and Apollo. Paris and
Jason continued to appeal to Dracontius as he wrote epyllia
on both, and Hippolytus reminds us that Cupid has already
alluded to Phaedra's passion. Diaz observes that Dracon-

tius does not cite either of the figures who come most naturally to mind, Ganymede and Adonis,[41] but this may simply be due to the poet's preference for novelty.

When Cupid disguised himself, his assumed appearance was naturally called *imago* (81). The nymphs use the same word in praising Hylas:

> felix sorte sua, cui talis semper imago
> serviet et roseis recubans dabit oscula labris. (107–108)

Thus we are drawn back to the unreality of Cupid's beauty, and thereby perhaps a doubt is cast on the reality of Hylas' charms—or at least on their permanence (cf. *semper*). In short, the praise has gone too far:

> cum nimium laudatur Hylas. . . . (109)

This is particularly noticeable since Cupid has not even shot the nymphs as yet. The sequence is wrong. The naiads see Hylas and exclaim over him (100), then Cupid shoots them (111), leading to renewed swooning (112–15), and finally in 125 Hylas heads for the spring. Apparently Cupid's intervention was quite unnecessary.

Hylas is understandably alarmed at being seized, and Deiopea comforts him. Her words to Hylas recall Venus' address to Cupid, including *alme puer* in 133 (cf. 50 and 53). Thus in every point, Hylas is drawn as a parallel or contrast to Cupid. The final touch is the report which Hercules will take to Hylas' mother: he has become a god. The similarity between the victor and the victim is completed. The claim with which Dracontius began,

> Fata canam pueri Nympharum versa calore
> *in melius,* (1–2)

is justified at the end.

The two other significant figures, Venus and Hercules, are practically confined to opposite ends of the poem. Venus we

have already seen as the doting mother. She is also garru-
lous, vain, petulant, and vindictive. Venus very frequently
shows these qualities, but the picture is normally balanced
by her charm, her beauty, or some saving grace. Here the
poet stresses the beauty of Hylas and of Cupid but says not
a word on the goddess of beauty.

Her prayer to her son runs on until he interrupts her
each time, and the tone of the prayer is first obsequious
and then indignant. In her second speech (45–70) Venus is
principally concerned with what others will think of her—
first because she must ask her son for help, and then because Clymene is telling stories about her. She refers to
mea crimina and admits that the story is true. She might
have added that it was also well known, making discretion
irrelevant because it is impossible.

> sed si de nobis certe cantare placebat,
> iudicium Paridis vel nostros, nate, triumphos
> cantarent fluidae carpentes pensa puellae. (59–61)

The blame has spread from Clymene to all the nymphs, and
all will suffer. Venus is still warming to her improbable
scheme of punishment by frustration when Cupid cuts her
off again.

We hear nothing more from Venus. She is mentioned
twice in connection with Cupid's efforts to carry out her
orders, but these are mechanical references. As in the
Aegritudo Perdicae, she sets the story in motion and that
is all.

Hercules scarely fares better. His single scene at the end
balances Venus at the start. He is not named until that final
scene (*Hercules* only in 147; *Herculeus* 143 and 150). Earlier the poet uses only *Alcides* (3, 65, 99, 100) and *Tiryn-
thius* (94). Hercules is opposite and parallel to Venus. As
she sets Cupid in motion, so he brings Hylas into the picture; as Venus laments in the first scene, so Hercules ends
the poem with his lamentations; and as Venus confesses her

submission to Cupid's power, so Hercules ends by admitting his helplessness in the face of the god's power.

Traditionally, since Hylas is beloved of Hercules, the hero's love for his young squire is prominently developed as motivation for his search and is the theme of his lament. Provana regarded the poet's characterization of Hercules as deft and sentimentally effective, the lament as sincere and moving.[42] But a closer look at the hero may suggest otherwise. Compared with earlier poets, Dracontius presents a less passionate picture of Hercules, and a less appealing one. There is no hint that Hercules loves, or even notices, the boy who trails so devotedly behind him: *ibat victor ovans*. In the last scene, to be sure, Hercules is distraught:

> interea furibundus adhuc Tirynthius ibat
> et clamans quaerebat Hylan, cui litus et unda
> Herculea cum voce sonant, et nomen amati
> montes silva vocant. (141–44)

The hero's love is indeed mentioned, although these are almost formulaic lines (cf. for example Vergil's summary, *Ecl.* 6.43–44). If these lines were all Dracontius gave us, our sympathy would be greater. But when Hercules gives voice to his sorrow, he turns out to be very self-centered. He says nothing to suggest affection, or interest in Hylas' fate. Rather, the hero has lost a squire and a looking glass in which to admire himself:

> O frustra nutrite puer, spectator ubique
> virtutis per cuncta meae (te teste pericla
> saepe tuli, cum victus aper, cum fracta leonis
> colla Cleonaei telo parcente necantur,
> cum simul Antaeum rapui telluris alumnum):
> quis mihi sudorem lasso post proelia terget?
> quis comes alter erit cum dat fera bella noverca?
> quid matri narrabo tuae . . . ? (152–59)

A less tender lament would be hard to construct. Of course, Hylas is not dead, and Hercules knows this now, so that

Dracontius need not have him bewail the death of his friend. But the hero's words are devoted to his accomplishments, as admired by Hylas, and the inconvenience his abduction has caused. This is a rather unsympathetic treatment. To be sure, Hercules was frequently accorded antiheroic, and especially comic, depiction. Galinsky surveys the "Comic Hero" noting that for the stage, at least, "the number of serious dramas in which he has a part is a small trickle compared to the torrent of satyr plays, farces, and comedies in which Hercules kept entertaining his audiences."[43] Certainly poets and artists never tired of depicting the mighty Hercules in a humorous fashion which helped measure the awe-inspiring distance between him and mere mortals. In the Hellenistic period we find Apollonius going in one direction by presenting Hercules as an impossible dinosaur looming over the rest of the Argonauts who are drawn on a human scale; and Theocritus in another by humanizing Hercules through humor and incongruity in three idylls (XIII *Hylas;* XXIV *Heracliscus;* XXV *Hercules the Lion-Slayer).*[44] In all these representations there was a strong element of affection and admiration.

It was rather the other side of the picture—the awesome deified Hercules, especially as found in Seneca—which drew the fire of the Christians. The attack is persistent and focuses on those qualities which could make Hercules an apparent rival of Christ. The time has not yet come when he can be admired for his virtues by Christians or even employed as a symbol of Christ:[45] instead, he is to be brought down and shown to be a sham or worse. This is the emphasis in Dracontius' Hercules.

With this point, we have already moved toward the next question. Why has Dracontius presented all four of his main characters in such an unflattering light? What is the purpose of this epyllion?

Purpose

If we consider the cumulative effect of the poet's characterizations, it becomes clear that he has reduced all the figures to objects of parody. Venus achieves nothing in pursuit of a pointless vengeance—indeed quite the opposite, for the nymphs end up perfectly happy. Cupid, who is the focus of the poem, is ridiculed in the "transformation" scene and has little effect, yet he reports his triumph at the end; Hercules is unattractively unheroic. In each instance, Dracontius has begun with the basic character from the tradition and then has turned it into a caricature.

At one level his purpose was certainly to produce an exercise in rhetorical composition: the dedication to his teacher Felicianus is sufficient indication of this. At another level, I suspect Dracontius was operating as a Christian apologist and writing a *reductio ad absurdum* of a famous myth. His concern with Christian themes and his defense of his faith were to occupy most of his literary career and would perhaps even account for his incarceration.

A young, intense student in the rhetorical school might well feel the urge to exercise his talents in order to advance the faith he felt so keenly. If the story of Hylas was a familiar theme for composition in the schools, it would recommend itself to such a student for attack from within. Under the guise of presenting a sympathetic treatment of a familiar subject, Dracontius has actually turned the story inside out.

Quartiroli recognized occasional Christian influences in the *Romulea*, except in the *Hylas*, but she saw them as incidental or even accidental.[46] As will become apparent in the course of examining the other epyllia, the Christian content is far from incidental, and the *Hylas* is not an exception.

In the case of the *Hylas*, we may think not only of the attraction inherent in attacking an anti-Christ like Hercules, but also the pagan personification of Love so sharply different from the Christian conception. I believe we can also detect the instinctive attitudes of the Christian even where Dracontius is not trying to emphasize a point against paganism or for Christianity. Despite the parodic tendency in his treatment of Cupid and Venus, for example, he has infused the scene of Venus praying to her divine son with a tone suited to Mary praying to Christ:

O mundi domitor, caeli quoque, flamma Tonantis (8)

. . . .

. . . cui subiacet omne natura
quod natura creat, caelum mare sidera tellus (46–47)

Her words are in tone and even in form an actual prayer, not merely a request for aid. The mother-god relationship dominates mother-son and goddess-god.

Most particularly, the poet has tinged the closing lines with the hues of an Annunciation scene. Listen to Hercules relay the message sent down from heaven, telling Hylas' mother that her son will be a god:

Exulta, genetrix, nimium laetare, beata
ante parens hominis, pulchri modo numinis auctor! (162–63)

These lines are not the *freddo e vuoto aforismo* Provana thought them. Nor are they parodic of the Christian message. Quite the reverse, for Dracontius would not thus mock his faith: they show the instinctive casting of a divine message into the form most natural to the poet's imagination. It may be significant that Dracontius has admitted a Christian Latin word, *zelat* (119) into his vocabulary, showing that his Christian outlook was near the surface as he wrote.

Thus Dracontius shows, even in his earliest work, interests and qualities which will persist in the later epyllia. He has made a famous myth his own by introducing novel elements of plot, including an unprecedented motivation for the action. The poet's interest in his faith has emerged in the essentially mocking treatment of the pagan gods. And the method, carefully inculcated in the schools, of echoing or recalling the old masters whenever possible, demonstrates Dracontius' wide learning and his sensitive ear for poetry. Moreover, these echoes are turned to effective and subtle use, demanding learning in the reader as well as the poet. All these elements help to explain how Dracontius stands out so conspicuously from most of his contemporaries. If *Hylas* was his first serious effort, it was a strong beginning.

Chapter 3

Medea (Rom. X)

IF NOVELTY OF treatment were a sufficient basis for esteem, Dracontius' *Medea* would be regarded as a masterpiece.[1] It is filled with features, from major points of plot down to details, which are unexampled in the rest of the Medea tradition or found scattered in minor sources. As is usual in such cases, opinion is divided between those who assume Dracontius invented whatever we cannot find elsewhere and those who assume he followed unidentified lost sources.[2]

Prologue (1–31)

Dracontius gives some hint of his method, but leaves much unanswered. In the prologue, he states his sources:

> nos illa canemus
> quae solet in lepido Polyhymnia docta theatro
> muta loqui, cum nauta venit, cum captus amatur
> inter vincla iacens mox regnaturus Iason;
> vel quod grande boans longis sublata cothurnis
> pallida Melpomene, tragicis cum surgit iambis,
> quando cruentatam fecit de matre novercam. (16–22)

That is, for the first half of the poem (Colchis), the poet has followed unspecified sources related to the pantomime. We have already seen how Dracontius used pantomime traditions in *Hylas*, although the matter may be somewhat different here. Part of the difficulty is that we have no extant material which provides a version similar to that which

Dracontius gives. The pantomime libretti were ephemeral, and we should not hope to possess a script verifying his debt, but the scope of the change is remarkable in view of the prominence of the legend in its traditional form. Quartiroli suggests that Dracontius meant nothing more specific than the general similarity of the events in the first half to events likely to be found in pantomime—but she proceeds on the assumption that the poet's claim is more precise and accurate.[3] I shall return to this problem later.

The second half (Greece), according to this poet's statement, follows the tragic tradition. The statement would be more valuable if it were less obviously false. The differences between Dracontius' treatment of the story and what we find in Euripides, Seneca, or Hosidius make it hard to accept his claim. There were other tragedies on Medea, now lost—and in all probability already lost in Dracontius' day: of Ennius' *Medea Exsul* some scraps have survived, but the treatments by Lucan and Curiatius Maternus (cf. Tac. *Dial.* 3)[4] are untraceable. Of greatest potential interest, in view of Dracontius' admiration for Ovid's other works, is his celebrated play. But we have no indications that any of these dramas departed from the mainstream of the tradition as Dracontius does. Moreover it has been plausibly conjectured that influences of Ovid's tragedy may be found in Hosidius' work;[5] and in any case, Ovid treats Medea elsewhere, always within the bounds of the received tradition.[6]

Dracontius has departed from tradition in another way. Normally, the story was treated as divisible into two portions. The epic tradition dealt with the Argonauts, building on Jason and his heroic companions and treating events through the theft of the fleece and the return voyage; the tragic poets tended to focus on subsequent events in Corinth and centered their attention on Medea. There were exceptions, of course, such as Sophocles' *Colchides*, but in Dracontius' day the extant material followed this split. Dracontius has combined both parts, at least to the extent of covering both Colchis and Greece, using the epic Muse as the medium of unifying the various sources. The scope of the poem is not matched elsewhere.

The prologue sets the tone for the whole poem. Dracontius presents himself as the bard prompted to tell a ghastly tale:

> Fert animus vulgare nefas et virginis atrae
> captivos monstrare deos, elementa clientes. (1–2)

Indeed, a story so appalling that even the poet cannot know or tell all of it (13–16).[7]

Medea is clearly to be a figure of unrelenting wickedness. But that is not how she is presented in the first half of the poem. On the other hand, the wicked witch is the "true" Medea, as events will prove, and in any case that is the more popular and familiar character. Part of Dracontius' difficulty rests in the incommensurability of the two phases, the wide-eyed maiden who falls helplessly in love with the handsome prince, and the ruthless murderer-witch who commits atrocious crimes scarcely palliated by the excuse of her barbarian origins.[8]

Colchis (32–365)

The opening sentences of this section show clearly Dracontius' attitude toward his material:

> dives apud Colchos, Phrixei velleris aurum,
> pellis erat, servata diu custode dracone.
> hanc propter pelagi temerator primus Iason
> venerat ut rutilas subduceret arbore lanas. (32–35)

The background to the events in Colchis is sketched with utmost haste: we are not told the name of the ship, and no mention is made of the heroes who comprised her crew. Moreover, Dracontius does not even hint that Jason made this extraordinary voyage under any compulsion greater than his own sense of adventure: he says nothing of Pelias or the situation in Greece. These are not accidental omissions. Dracontius cannot have the Argonauts on hand because the situation demands that Jason be alone. The Argonauts would present a competing body of accomplishment, distracting our attention from the protagonist, and they would prevent Jason from staying in Colchis, as he does in this version.

The reason is simple enough. If Dracontius is following a dramatic source, as he claims, that source obviously was set in Colchis, and had a cast of characters limited to the relevant figures. Everything in the presentation argues in favor of such a dramatic model behind the epyllion: the limited dramatis personae, the use of messengers, the *deus ex machina* which Bacchus represents, the set speeches by the characters in turn, reminiscent of Senecan drama. Dracontius has not used an epic source, despite the general association between the voyage of Argo and the epic tradition. The epic impression comes from the format and style, not from the content. Among the epic features are the reaction of the Scythians to the sight of the first ship[9] (36–39) and the messenger who hastens to report the news to the king (cf. *Aen.* 7.166ff.).

But instead of the usual landing party of heroes, Jason leaps into the water and swims boldly for shore. This is the first step in the separation of the hero from his crew, which is completed when the Argo flees at the sight of Jason being pursued by the Colchians (51). Thus he is left quite alone, and the drama can begin. The arrival of the hero alone in a far country, in pursuit of a sacred object, will remind us of Orestes' arrival among the Taurians, and this parallel will be developed in several ways as the scene progresses.

Note how rapidly Jason sinks from the heroic first impression. *Temerator pelagi* (34) and *callidus heros* (41) vanish, and when the messenger returns, he sees Jason fleeing back to the water, now no more than *pavens iuvenis*. For the rest of the poem Jason will remain a weak inconstant creature, speaking only to cry for help or weep for what he has lost. The only exception is the parallel to this scene, when he first arrives in Thebes and makes a comparably favorable impression (366ff.).

Thus Jason is captured and the danger, though unspecified, is grave. Before the scene can move too swiftly to a fatal conclusion, the poet shifts to the gods, who will now play their traditional role of making Medea fall in love with Jason. But beyond this required role, the gods also provide suspense by leaving the hero in dire peril while they discuss what to do next. The scene is long and ornate, filled with familiar details (49–176).

As tradition required, Juno must ask Venus to help Jason by sending Cupid to make Medea fall in love. But as elsewhere in Dracontius, the motivation is novel. Since we have heard nothing of the Argo and nothing of Jason's background, Juno must explain her fondness for Jason when she asks for Venus' aid:

> est nimis acceptus iuvenis mihi pulcher Iason,
> qui gelidum quondam mecum transnaverat Istrum. (56–57)

This odd tale finds its match—and perhaps its source—in Hyginus (*Fab*. 13), where Jason encounters Juno, who has disguised herself as an old woman, and helps her cross the Euhenus river.[10] This was probably, as Rose notes, a folk motif. Hyginus uses it to lead into the loss of Jason's sandal and the encounter with Pelias; in the absence of that story here, it merely accounts for Juno's partiality for the hero. We should note, however, that the location has been changed. Instead of carrying Juno across the Euhenus he took her (assuming *mecum transnaverat* does not merely mean what it seems to say) across the Danube. I wonder whether this shift to the great river of the north may be ultimately connected with the Vandal-ruled society in which the poet was working, either as a gesture of accommodation or as part of the impact of Dracontius' own background. I shall return to this question shortly.

Juno's speech to Venus (52–80) is a delightful piece of rhetoric, designed in some respects like a small *suasoria*.[11]

It shows marked resemblances to Venus' appeal to Cupid in *Hylas*, as indeed does the entire celestial scene. Juno's tone combines supplication with reproach, flattery with scorn: she gives a long list of Venus' epithets, but does not fail to specify her own status: *te divum regina precor, matrona Tonantis* (55). The lure which she holds out to Venus is the chance to diminish her rival Diana by drawing her priestess away from her duties. Venus does not respond to this opportunity, although Cupid takes note of it in his choice of weapon (cf. below). But the rivalry between Diana the virgin priestess and Venus is a recurring theme in these poems, as appears also in *Aegritudo Perdicae* and *Hylas*. To underscore the disadvantage to Diana, Juno addresses Venus in hymnic style:

> te solam putet esse deam, te numen adoret,
> te metuat metuenda deis, te iudicet unam,
> quam mare quam tellus quam numina cuncta fatentur
> imperio subiecta tuo per templa per aras
> esse voluptatum dominam. (67–71)

If this were a different poet, we would be tempted to see irony in the queen of the gods (as she has just reminded us) addressing a hymn of praise and supplication to another divinity, but not here. Dracontius is merely following the dictates of generic convention.

Juno has ample evidence of Venus' abilities in the unrelenting infidelities of her own spouse, and with pointed *praeteritio* she lists what she will not complain of (72–76). The combination is quite comical as Juno attempts to find humility and keep in check her tendencies to scorn.

Venus' reply is brief, almost terse. She acknowledges the tribute of the hymnic style by her own version:

> me Venerem me, Juno, decet me, blanda noverca,
> imperio parere tuo. (82–83)

There is some similarity to Aeolus' response to Juno in *Aen.* 1.76ff., but Venus has managed to avoid any impres-

sion of submission or inferiority. Her *quid plura loque-*
mur? is virtually a dismissal.

The focus now shifts to Cupid, who will do the actual
work. Again, there are striking similarities to the *Hylas.*
He is away "inflaming the divinities of the sea" (86), which
sounds almost as if we are to think of his mission to smite
Clymene and the nymphs (but admittedly they are not *sea*
goddesses). Cupid is given a long entrance scene as he is
fetched by Hymenaeus,[12] and upon his arrival he flings
himself on his mother's bosom as in *Hylas.* His mother's appeal to him is likewise reminiscent of—and probably modeled directly on—her speech in *Hylas* 46ff.

The powerful divinity suggested by Juno's remarks and
by the epiphany from the waves, however, is undercut by
Hymenaeus' summons:

> huc ades, o lascive puer; te mater ubique
> quaerit et e cunctis vestrum me misit alumnum
> ut venias parcente mora. (94–96)

This tone preserves the atmosphere of the equivalent scene
in Apollonius where Aphrodite calls him away from his
childish games (III.110ff.).

Meanwhile, his appearance from under the waves is described in awesome terms. This was the passage to which
d'Ippolito pointed quite plausibly as evidence for the influence of the aquatic mimes.[13] The poet has invested the entire scene with powerful visual effects. The model he had
in mind was probably memorable for its sights rather than
for its literary qualities. Cupid is now strongly associated
with fire: Venus calls him *Pyrois*, and the poet refers to him
as *ignipotens* (an epithet reserved for Vulcan in the epic
tradition). As the young god rises from the water, he shakes
his wings to shed the water, and the sparks fly. Dracontius
compares Cupid's rising amid sparks with the Phoenix striking the fire for its funeral pyre by beating its wings.[14] The
comparison works only at the visual level because the Phoenix was a symbol for rebirth, and most especially at this

time, for the Christian belief in resurrection (both that of
Christ from the tomb and the eschatological resurrection of
man).[15] Dracontius presumably does not want to suggest
such associations at this moment, although it is interesting
that he specifies that the Phoenix strikes its fire at the moment of daybreak: this too is a Christian association. I suppose that the poet considered this symbol, as much else, in
the light of his own Christian training.[16] But the simile is
very effective in suggesting both the shimmering beauty of
the god as he rises and the deadly effect of his touch.

After all this fanfare Cupid arrives at his mother's dwelling:

> dum loquitur lasciva Venus, venit ecce Cupido
> fessulus et gremio matris libratur anhelans. (122–23)

The charming diminutive takes us back at once to the affectionate, intimate setting of mother and son. *Ecce* has something of the effect of a stage exclamation to draw attention
to a character making his entrance: a similar effect is to be
observed in 179 and 270 (and cf. also 134). These may in
some fashion be remnants of a dramatic model for the entire scene; Venus' remarks to her son show the combination
of high and low elements observed in the scene generally.
She is fulsome in acknowledging Cupid's power (she is, after
all, the suppliant now) and gloats at the role Juno has had to
play (*venit ecce noverca / in manibus iam Iuno meis*). It is a
congenial assignment, and Cupid shares her enthusiasm.
He selects as his weapon for the occasion[17] the shaft with
which he once inflamed the moon with love of Endymion:
it will serve well now for her priestess.

His preparations complete, Cupid sets out on his mission in Colchis. The influence of epithalamic models is
very strong now, and Cupid is accompanied by a crowd of
personifications, such as Voluptas, Amplexus, and Gaudia.
The motif is familiar from Statius and Claudian, and indeed
from the late epithalamia in general.[18] Cupid indulges in
childish acrobatics in his flying car, sitting now on one yoked
dove and now on another. It is a charming scene, which like

his earlier arrival depends heavily on visual effects. We seem to fly with him, seeing the passing landscape from a height until Colchis comes into view, and gradually we see the scene we left in verse 49.

Jason is now being dragged like a bull to the altar,[19] and Medea, accompanied by her ministers, follows with dagger drawn. How has it happened that Medea is a *xeinoktonos?* Whence comes the idea? Human sacrifice was practiced, or at least reported, in the region around Colchis and eastward;[20] the practice of the Taurians comes to mind also.[21] The Taurians are most relevant, since Medea has been modeled after Iphigenia even as Jason was similar to Orestes: she is a priestess of Diana who sacrifices strangers—for unspecified reasons— to the goddess, and who is diverted in this instance by the intervention of Venus. Eventually she leaves the country with the hero, taking with her a sacred object belonging to the kingdom. The parallels are indubitable and clear, and even prompted Friedrich to speculate whether Medea was the model and Iphigenia the copy both for the slaying of strangers and for the theft of the sacred object.[22] But Dracontius is not the poet to prove that any such borrowing occurred early in the Greek literary tradition, and in any case, Medea can hardly have begun as a *xeinoktonos* of those who landed on her shores, or at least she must have had few victims before Jason himself arrived in the first ship ever made! Actually, Medea and Iphigenia offer mirror-image stories: with the daughter of Agamemnon it is the tale of a woman who is apparently to be married but instead is sacrificed (or so it seems) by a man, and escapes to a far land. Here it is the man, apparently to be sacrificed by a woman but who instead is married and is detained in the land. Both are familiar morphologies for tales, and it is the surface incident that has been borrowed (in whichever direction) rather than the underlying structure.

I shall return to this question of Dracontius' models and sources after we have seen the rest of the picture. Meanwhile, we should not forget that Carthage itself had a long and bloody tradition of human sacrifice,[23] of which Dracon-

tius' readers were presumably aware, just as they would be
alert to the long popularity of magicians and sorcerers in
Carthage when they read about the supreme witch Medea.

Into such a dramatic moment Cupid steps as he arrives
with his festive entourage. Medea hears his armor clank
and thinks the sound means the arrival of Diana to whom
she prays. Jason, however, is supine and can see Cupid
overhead waving to him.[24] He prays even more earnestly—
and to greater effect.

Medea's prayer is little more than a salutation and invocation of her patroness in all her roles and an offering of the
victim come to her shores. We are not told why Medea is to
sacrifice the stranger, and the few hints to be found in the
poem conflict with one another. The old nurse speaks of
purposes related to haruspicy, although that would be an
odd purpose in this context. Medea herself later on (443)
speaks of offering sacrifice not to Hecate but to Dis, with
no hint of divination. Some help may perhaps be derived
from a tradition preserved in Diodorus Siculus IV.46ff.[25]
According to this account, Aeetes learned that if ever the
fleece were taken away, he would die, and to prevent this
he instituted the custom of sacrificing all strangers who
came to the land. Not only would this policy eliminate each
potential threat as it arose, but as the report of his practice
spread, it would discourage others from visiting Colchis
(47.2). The king's actions were prompted both by his natural cruelty and by his wife Hecate (46.1). In this setting
Medea, by using her skills and secret knowledge for good,
habitually tried to rescue the hapless strangers who fell into
this misfortune. Diodorus goes on to tell how Medea met
the Argonauts and aided them in their mission.

This version presents serious problems for Dracontius'
account. In the first place, Medea should be the one to op-
pose the sacrifices, not the one responsible for them. Aeetes
and Hecate (who does not appear at all in this poem) should
be cruel and prominent. A remnant of this may be seen in
Juno's comment (59) that Jason is about to be sacrificed
Aeetis inmitis . . . ad aras. And second, Medea's role should

be closely linked to the Argonauts. As matters stand, we
see a kind of compromise. The tradition behind Diodorus'
account explains the practice of sacrificing strangers while
Medea's role as savior of the victims reappears in her sparing of Jason. But there is little to encourage us to think that
Dracontius was influenced by Diodorus; at most he may
have had access to a related tradition—particularly if, as
some believe, this story represents the genuine early view
of Medea.[26]

The poet calls Medea *furens, nocens,* and *cruenta,* but it
is the nurse who most deserves these epithets. It is far from
clear why Medea's old nurse should be serving as her aco-
lyte at the altar. It is she, nonetheless, who gets Jason properly placed on the altar (195–97), and when Medea first
hesitates upon being shot by Cupid, the nurse urges her
on:

> sed nutrix mirata moras "dic, virgo, quid haeres?"
> increpat, "ecce feri . . .
> cur homicida vacas et stas rea? sed rea non es,
> si fueris homicida magis." (225–26, 231–32)

She even goes so far as to pick up the dagger which Medea
has dropped and place it again in her hand. This insistence
by the *impia turpis anus* (238) brings a fresh appeal from
Jason to Cupid, who shoots again and settles the matter.

The odd point is not that Medea has a zealous assistant,
but that it is her nurse. I suspect that this is a vestige of the
main tradition, where Medea's nurse plays a significant role
as the princess' confidante and supporter. When Medea is
in love with Jason and can intervene to save him from
Aeetes' cruel demands, then the nurse can function well in
the role; but when it is Medea who is to slay Jason, the
nurse's role becomes confused. By supporting Medea as
priestess, she is thwarting her as lover. If Dracontius had
not insisted that this was the nurse, the problem would not
have arisen. On the other hand, the nurse still observes
and comments on Medea's symptoms as she falls in love,

allowing us to witness the change as if it were being depicted on stage.

Jason contributes little to the scene. His prayer to Cupid (201–208) balances, both in content and in length, Medea's prayer to Diana (188–94), but it does nothing to enhance his position as a hero. He is panic-stricken throughout the scene, begging for his life with every breath. By contrast, Cupid is quite lighthearted and reassures Jason that he has a bright future in marriage. Jason, it seems, cannot be comforted. His physical immobility is a perfect symbol of his character.

Now that Medea is incurably in love, she must find a way to spare her victim. Her problem is exactly that of Iphigenia, and she resorts to the same solution:

> effatur: "non est haec victima digna:
> nam torta cervice iacet, male palpitat, artus
> erigit impatiens et saucius ante dolorem:
> sanguine membra carent: iam non erit hostia grata
> quae sicco mucrone cadet." (243–47)

This was the ploy used already in Euripides (*IT* 1035ff.), and almost exactly the same words occur in Dracontius' *Orestes* (881):

> sanguine corda carent, non est haec victim grata.

But in the case of Iphigenia, it was prudent not to give a true explanation for her actions. She and Orestes were about to leave and take with them the cult-figure from the temple. Medea is not similarly encumbered, since no mention has been made of the fleece. She is simply to spare the intended victim because she has fallen in love with him; and since she is going to stay in Colchis and marry Jason, there is little to be gained by indulging in palpably false explanations. Medea is clearly being modeled after Iphigenia, even though the rationale does not quite work. The logical explanation for the near identity of *Orestes* 881 and *Medea* 246 is that the *Orestes* was earlier, and Dracontius

borrowed from it for his *Medea*.[27] Indeed, the several details we have noticed suggest that the Iphigenia model is
being applied more rigorously than the material can en-
dure, which surely argues for the priority of *Orestes* where
these details fit naturally.

Nor is this the last alteration in the accepted version of
the tale. Medea proceeds, while Jason lies under her knife,
to propose to him. This is an offer he cannot refuse. The
exchange tells us much about the two characters and their
interaction:

> conversa sacerdos
> ad iuvenem: "dic, nauta fugax, pirata nefande:[28]
> est consors matrona decens an caelibe vita
> degis adhuc nullumque domi ‹tibi› pignus habetur?"
> "solus" ait captivus "ego: mihi pignora nulla
> coniugis aut sobolis." dictis gavisa virago
> blanda refert: "vis ergo meus nunc esse maritus?"
> "servus" Iason ait, "tantum ne vita negetur
> te precor et dominam fateor." (247–55)

Medea takes the initiative, as Helen also does in proposing
to Paris, although Medea at least cares whether Jason is already married. Medea is also—ironically—interested in
whether Jason has any children. But he cares only for survival and will accept any offer she makes. He will make the
same mistake in Greece.

That the marriage of Jason and Medea should take place
in Colchis is not unique to Dracontius, but it is very rare.
The only other clear testimony to this is the report in the
scholia to Apollonius Rhodius, that according to Timonax
the wedding took place in Colchis, with Aeetes' blessing.[29]
But that was apparently connected with identifying numerous places around the Euxine with Jason's travels and the
Argonautic saga. It is unlikely to be linked, unless very remotely, with the story we find in Dracontius.

For the remainder of this segment of the poem (i.e., to
339), the epithalamium takes firm control. One manifestation of this is the prominent role which the gods again as-

sume. There are three vignettes, each dominated by a divinity. First, Cupid moves in triumph among the temples, attended by *mollis Lascivia, blanda Libido,* and others.[30] These are the regular trappings of the epithalamic procession, but along with the celebrating deities come two personifications who strike a somber note. At the wedding of Peleus and Thetis, likewise doomed to bring calamity in its wake, the discordant appearance of Eris undercuts the joy; so here an equivalent appearance:

> ecce triumphantes Ingratia dura iugales
> consequitur, gressus consors Oblivio iungit. (270–71)

These figures serve to remind us of the second half of the story, remote though it seems at this moment of festivity. They represent precisely the qualities which Jason will display in deserting Medea.

The festive tone is restored and reinforced by the arrival of Bacchus from India, likewise attended by his entourage and driving his car drawn by tigers. The picture, always popular, and especially after Nonnos' vast tribute to the god, lends an air of exotic intensity. Bacchus will play a further role in winning over Aeetes and making possible the happy ending to this part of the story, but at the same time the excitement which attends his coming helps to stir us in preparation for the arrival of Diana.

She is the third divinity whose response to the wedding is presented in this scene. Like Ingratia and Oblivio, she comes as a disruptive force amidst the celebration. Upon returning from the hunt, she finds her temple deserted and hears the festivities. Her priestess has abandoned her duties. Once more we see the neglected deity who demands an awful revenge. Her imprecation is a table of contents for the second half of the poem:

> ". . . non omine fausto
> coniungatur" ait "nec prospera flammea sumat:
> displiceat quandoque viro, cui turpiter audax
> sacrilegus processit amor; sed iustius opto:

> perfidus egregiam contemnat nauta iugalem,
> dulcior affectus vel amara repudia mittat;
> funera tot videat, fuerint quot pignora, mater;
> orba parens natos plangat, viduata marito
> lugeat et sterilem ducat per saecula noctem.
> advena semper eat, se tanti causa doloris
> auctorem confessa gemat." (290–300)

Even in this outburst against her apostate priestess, Diana preserves Medea's perspective. Jason is *perfidus nauta*, which is how Medea herself describes him (553); and Medea is *egregia*. But the curse is dreadful enough, including the death of the children and—a distinctive feature of Dracontius' story—the death of Jason himself. It even points to the self-recrimination which will afflict Medea in Greece (417ff.).

Dracontius is alone in using this motivation for the tragic events in Greece. In view of his fondness for this theme in other poems, we may be justified in conjecturing that he is the source of the innovation here. It provides him with a mechanism by which he can link the two halves of his story, despite their different sources and quite different tones. The first half must move to a happy resolution amid festivities and divine blessings, but the second half is unrelieved tragedy. What better way to prepare us for the shift than to insert into the beneficent actions of the gods a specific *radix malorum* in the favored form of a neglected deity? It can be seen that Diana's presence does intrude upon the otherwise consistent atmosphere of the epithalamium. It follows logically upon the fact that Medea abandons her duties as a priestess, but the poem has already moved on to the wedding celebration. If we remove the passage, the actions of Bacchus are presented continuously (270–83/311–27). I am not suggesting that the Diana passage does not belong here, but that it may be viewed as a detachable item, implanted in the scene by the poet for a recognizable purpose.

The main sequence resumes in 311 as a messenger carries to Aeetes the news of his daughter's betrothal.[31] The distraught king is compared to Agenor:

expavit genitor: sic quondam tristis Agenor
concidit Europae senior fraudatus amore,
cum nesciret adhuc generum meruisse Tonantem. (314–16)

An interesting analogy. Europa suggests abduction across the sea, and thus the more traditional story in which Jason takes Medea away at once rather than the prolonged sojourn in Colchis. It also suggests that the initiative rests with Jason (Aeetes must not have known his daughter very well!), and even more surprisingly it seems to involve comparing Jason with Jupiter himself. Rather than taking this as a fresh assertion of Jason's heroic nature, we should probably view it as part of the extravagant praise customarily bestowed on bridegrooms, who are often compared to the gods, including Jupiter.

Bacchus comes to placate the king and assure him of the blessings which are in store for Medea: if the first half of the poem were independent, there would be no incongruity in this assurance, and we would proceed to the happy finale. In view of the imprecations of Diana and the tragedy which lies immediately ahead, there is a curious irony in Bacchus' words. It is almost as if, contrary to the soothing impression of his words, he were actually luring Aeetes on to the madness and disaster so often associated with this god's appearance.

He appeals to Aeetes not only in terms of the father's love for Medea but also his desire for grandchildren. This theme of children runs disturbingly through the entire first half of the poem, and we are never allowed to forget the awful killing toward which the poet is leading us. Dracontius, even more daringly, compares Aeetes, after his acceptance of Jason, with Lycomedes:

sic meruit veniam generum confessus Achilles,
sic pater ignovit Lycomedes, pectore natae

> et Pyrrhum suscepit avus gremioque nepotem
> fovit et ad Troiam post crimina misit Achillis. (330–33)

The heroic comparison of Jason and Achilles twists uncomfortably with the reference to *crimina Achillis*, and of course Pyrrhus was a symbol of the violent wanton destruction associated with the fall of Troy. Finally, we should note that the comparison is not altogether flattering to Medea.

Once Aeetes is mollified, he praises the match his daughter has arranged and calls the happy couple to the palace for the wedding proper. The scene concludes with verses apparently joyful but rippling with irony:

> mox thalamos subiere pares: laetatur Iason
> sponsus et in castris Veneris Medea triumphat. (338–39)

Note the contrast between Jason, who rejoices, and Medea, who triumphs. The notion of victory haunts our appreciation of *pares* and points ahead to the unequal battle in Thebes. The juxtaposition of *Veneris Medea* shows how completely the affiliation with Diana has vanished, and where the blame should rest for what follows.

The portion of the poem dealing with Colchis concludes with a scene which prepares us for the shift from Medea the lover and priestess to Medea the murderous witch, although we should never forget that her essential character as a witch has been enunciated in the prologue and hangs over the entire poem. The final scene in Colchis (340–65) contains events nowhere else associated with the Medea story. Medea and Jason remain in Colchis for four years, where she bears him two sons. In most versions a hasty departure is essential since Jason has stolen the fleece. But with the quest of the fleece forgotten, and Aeetes having given his blessing to the marriage, the motivation for leaving—much less fleeing—has vanished. Yet Jason and Medea must return to Greece, for the climactic tragic events await them. Dracontius then attempts to achieve several objec-

tives in this scene: the necessary alteration in Medea's behavior, the motivation for the return to Greece, and the
theft of the fleece for which Jason originally came to Colchis. It must be admitted that he has not accomplished
these goals with great elegance.

The model for the scene is Statius *Thebaid* 2.306ff.,[32]
where Argia upbraids Polynices soon after their wedding as
he sighs in his sleep and longs to be on his way to Thebes:

> sed fida vias arcanaque coniunx
> senserat; utque toris primo complexa iacebat
> aurorae pallore virum, "quos, callide, motus
> quamve fugam moliris?" ait. "nil transit amantes."
> (*Theb.* 2.332–35)

So Jason, four years after the wedding, frequently sighs
and mutters in his sleep and Medea assumes the worst:

> cum nocte iacens suspirat Iason
> nec gemitus latuere magam: "quam, callide, fraudem
> quodve nefas moliris?" ait. "non fallis amantem." (342–44)

For the first time since the prologue, Medea is called *maga*:
she claims (as did Argia) that she knows his thoughts because she is his lover, but the ensuing lines together with
maga[33] stress the fact that it is because she is a witch from
whom nothing can remain secret. Her tone is strident, assuming Jason's intent to deceive: note how such words as
callide, fraudem (contrast *motus* in the model), *nefas* (contrast *fugam*), and *furta* pile up before Jason can even respond to her attack. In fact, Jason's sudden homesickness
may seem rather odd four years after his arrival and certainly less natural than the longings of Polynices. As we
shall see there may have been other forces at work in shaping the story at this point, forces which explain even if they
do not palliate the improbability.[34]

Jason now tells his wife why he came to her land. His
thoughts have turned to his comrades and his family, who

must think him dead by now. But his request is not what
we would expect:

> optarem revidere meos iterumque reverti
> ad thalamos, regina, tuos,[35] monstrare Pelasgis
> quid coniux, quid fata valent. (355–57)

He does not ask, even now, for the fleece, nor to return
permanently to his home. He wants only to visit and boast
of his good fortune. But in another surprising twist, it is
Medea who reintroduces the notion of stealing the fleece
and going with him to Greece. From here on, the poet
covers all the traditional elements of the story in a blind-
ing rush:

> astra vocans et signa ciens iubet illa Soporem
> in nemus ad pellem vel templum Martis abire.
> dormierat serpens: pellis subtracta marito
> traditur, et pariter fugerunt fratre necato.
> accipiunt natos et singula pignora portant. (361–65)

Note that it is Medea herself who actually steals the fleece
after subduing the serpent: usually her role is limited to
clearing the way for the hero to collect the prize.[36] Moreover, since the traditional role of Aeetes has been omitted,
we have heard nothing of the protection of the fleece or of
the king's cruelty. Abruptly, the dragon is brought to our
attention again (he has been fleetingly mentioned in verse
33) and promptly lulled. But why does Medea slay her
brother? This event is included simply because it was a traditional part of the story. We are at the juncture between
the two parts of the tale, as distinguished by the poet in the
prologue. The pantomime covered only events through the
wedding with its happy ending, and the tragic tradition will
shape the story once we are in Greece. But for this intermediate stage, Dracontius has simply strung together the
main traditional events almost without regard for their fitness or necessity.

The abruptness of this segment cannot be fully explained

as an intended disproportion in the narrative, such as frequently appears in the epyllion tradition;[37] for that would not take into account the apparent irrelevance of some details. Rather, the poet has found it necessary to hasten through this intervening moment between the two acts of his drama and has relied on the familiar shape of events. But the alterations in the first half of the story have made that traditional shape appear distorted.

So ends this unprecedented telling of the events at Colchis. Before reaching any conclusions on the role of the pantomime, we must consider the number of elements in the story which are characteristic of the fairy tale. Consider the following list of plot features, all of which are at variance with the traditional version:

1. The hero arrives alone in a strange land, having lost his companions and having traversed water (not merely in a ship, but by swimming).
2. He is captured and bound by a witch.
3. As she is about to slay him with a knife, she is prevented by the intervention of magic more powerful than her own.
4. As a direct result, and as a condition of his survival, he marries the witch and stays with her in her country.
5. He forgets about his own land and his purpose in traveling.
6. After a period of happy marriage, the hero in his sleep recalls his homeland, and wishes to return—but only to tell his family and friends he is alive and prospering.
7. He promises to return to the witch after this visit.

Each of these story elements is at home in fairy tales[38] and is not at home in the story of Medea. Taken together, they have transformed the Medea story into an almost pure representative of the fairy tale. More specifically, the motif of the lapsed time in the land of the fairy (or witch) would also explain more satisfactorily why Jason does not pursue his quest of the fleece for four years.[39]

The coherence of the story as a fairy tale may perhaps

best be seen at the point where the poet breaks away from
the morphology of the fairy tale. When Jason offers to return to Medea after visiting his family, Medea would, in the
fairy tale structure, have unwillingly agreed to the visit and
insisted on his speedy return. But Dracontius must after all
lead on to the second half of the story, and as a result Medea
grants more than Jason even asks: she offers to obtain the
fleece for him and go with him to Greece permanently.
This awkward transition is unavoidable if the poet is to accommodate the second stage of his tale, and as I noted
above, Dracontius has perhaps tried to reduce the awkwardness by the skeletal recounting of the necessary, transitional events.

With these speculations on the Colchis narrative, we return to the question of Dracontius' source, including the
more interesting question of his purpose in developing the
story along these lines. There is nothing to disprove his
claim to be working from pantomime, and as Friedrich
notes, the generally dramatic cast of the episode, the abrupt
turn of events at the altar, Bacchus as *deus ex machina*, and
the happy ending (up to the wedding, at least) all point to a
dramatic model, but one distinct from tragedy.[40] This only
moves the question back one step. Even recognizing the
affinities between isolated changes in Dracontius' account
and other myths found in classical literature, it remains
true that the story of Medea had a long and prominent history by his time (as Freidrich notes so arrestingly, Dracontius is midway in time between Homer and Goethe),[41] and
its shape had long since been fixed. How likely is it, then,
that a version so different from the canonical myth would
have survived intact through a medium such as pantomime
for any period of time?
  I wonder whether the version which Dracontius reports
as coming from pantomime may have its roots outside the
Graeco-Roman tradition. Is it possible that we see in this
epyllion a reworking of a folk tale as it was in the Germanic
traditions of the Vandals? Such folk tales certainly existed in

the popular, illiterate culture of the Vandals in Africa. But despite the lack of literary elaboration, they would be suitable material for the popular entertainment of the pantomime. There were elements available in the classical tradition which permitted recasting of the tale, and thus Dracontius could accommodate the imported tale to the outline of characters familiar to his reading audience. If this conjecture (it can be nothing more) is true, it means that pantomime presented a version of the folk tale, and Dracontius adapted what he saw there to the story of Medea, using literary models to make his new product seem more natural. But he felt obliged to identify in the prologue his source for so novel and unexpected a twist.

Why should he have wanted to take such a step? I return to Kuijper's idea that Dracontius was himself part Vandal.[42] The notion hinges in part on Dracontius' statement to Felicianus in *Romulea* I.13–14:

> qui fugatas Africanae reddis urbi litteras,
> barbaris qui Romulidas iungis auditorio.

A reference to the Vandals as *barbari* in such a context would be intolerably insulting if he were a Roman subject referring to his Vandal overlords, but acceptable if it is self-deprecatory in a collective sense. He also seems to imply (although it is not the only possible reading of the lines) in III.16–17 that he has learned Latin as a second language:

> antistesque tuus de vestro fonte, magister,
> Romuleam laetus sumo pro flumine linguam.

Kuijper notes:[43]

> Tum demum, non rationis egenus erit, qui latina lingua
> loquens adnuntiat latina lingua se carmen esse pacturum,
> cum sua natura aliam linguam anteponit. tum demum, cum
> inter suos maiores poetam barbaros Vandalosque cruentos
> habuisse statuemus, grati discipuli, non adolescentuli
> inepti haec erit comparatio.

There is no doubt that Dracontius was an apt pupil and widely read in classical literature. He could hardly have learned the first rudiments of Latin from the school, but it could certainly have been a second tongue (consider Ammianus and Claudian, whose mastery of this second language was far more precise). The young boy could then have learned at home both the Roman traditions to which he was heir through his Aemilian background, and the outlandish traditions represented by his mother's Vandal heritage. Among such traditions surely were folk tales of the sort I have postulated for the background of the first half of this poem.

Thus Dracontius could feel appreciation for this imported material, and yet have the cultural training to transform it into a classical narrative. The two halves of the poem then stand not only as the fusion of two very different literary forms—pantomime and tragedy—but also the fusion of the two cultural heritages which the poet shared, the Roman and the Vandal. This could be the point of the prologue with its stress on the difference between the two sources.

It is true at the same time that the influence of the romances is clear in our poet's work, and we may be tempted to take the simple solution of assuming that all these features, which may in many instances be paralleled in plots of the Greek and Roman novels, represent assimilation of that genre into the epic narrative. In this particular case that is the more complicated solution rather than the simpler because no one of the romances is so completely adapted to the morphology of the folk tale, and we still have to imagine Dracontius taking over romance plots and—either deliberately or unconsciously—reshaping the incidents into the form of a far different genre. Moreover, there is no comparable instance of a standard story already shaped by the mythological tradition being recast so as to conform to folk tale morphologies (the Odyssean narrative is hardly a cogent objection to this principle).

Thebes (366–569)

Ventum erat ad Thebas. Thus Dracontius begins the second half of his story by abruptly altering a point of universal
agreement, namely, that Jason and Medea went to Corinth.
Nowhere else is it stated that the scene was laid in Thebes.
On the contrary, all sources actually specify Corinth with
the silent exception of Hosidius.[44] It is impossible to believe that Dracontius did not know where the tragic tradition had placed the action: Quartiroli's suggestion of confusion on that score is quite unconvincing.[45] Yet since he
himself claims to be following the tragedians, we should assume that he means the tradition represented by Euripides, Ennius, Ovid, and Seneca, all of whom specify Corinth. One could conceivably conjecture that in a careless
moment Dracontius combined the two kings named Creon,
as Hyginus may have done;[46] and other explanations are
possible.[47] Eventually one must believe that Dracontius
never noticed so fundamental a fact as the city in which one
of the most famous of all tragedies was set.

W. Schetter has ingeniously solved the puzzle, at least to
the extent of identifying the formal basis for Dracontius' action.[48] There can be no doubt that Dracontius intentionally
set the scene in Thebes, once we notice that *Ventum erat
ad Thebas* is a quotation from Statius (*Theb.* 2.65), and that
the poet underscores the locale with *rector Thebanus* (374).
The educated Roman reader would pick up the Statian
echo and think of Thebes as it is depicted in the epic, "eine
Stadt des Unheils und der Verbrechen." Throughout the
second half of the poem Dracontius uses reminiscences of
the Statian conception of Thebes to make the reader think
of (1) the cruel and impious nature of Statius' Theban ruler
(cf. *tyrannus nocens* in 380–81) as similar to the Creon presented here, thereby underscoring the culpability of the
Theban house; (2) the other afflictions which have struck
the House of Thebes, thereby linking the tragedy of Jason
and Medea to a larger chain of calamities;[49] and (3) the associations of the Furies with events in Thebes, as depicted by

Statius and as explained by Dracontius. We shall see how
each of these ideas is worked out in the epyllion.

Nor does this exhaust the surprises contained in this first
line, for the poet goes on to report *pellis datur aurea regi.*
Why should Jason deliver the fleece to Creon? When our
story began, Jason was presented simply as an adventurer
come to capture the fleece. There was no mention of Pelias
or of any mission imposed upon our hero. Yet now, when
Jason finally returns to Greece after pleading the need to
visit his family and friends, he goes to Thebes, with which
he has no connection, and delivers his most prized possession to the king of that city without prompting or cause.
Moreover, there is no hint of visiting family or returning
home. For that very reason, Jason must have a goal when
he reaches Greece. He has stolen the fleece and must be
headed somewhere. Creon fills a gap by receiving the prize,
even though Dracontius does not suggest that it was he
who had sent Jason to get it. Dracontius has simplified the
story by omitting both the return voyage and the encounter
with the daughters of Pelias, but there is a great awkwardness at this seam in the tale as the hero is left without goal
or connections.

No sooner does Jason arrive in the city than the princess
Glauce is introduced. In more traditional versions Jason
and Medea enjoy ten years of happiness in Greece before
Jason decides to improve his standing and marry the princess, and during this time the children are born; but as that
has already happened in Colchis, Dracontius wishes to
move immediately into the climactic events. By moving the
encounter of Jason and Glauce to the time of his arrival, he
has turned this scene into a miniature doublet of the meeting of Jason and Medea. Jason is once again presented in a
favorable light for a moment at least, and is praised for his
bravery (cf. *callidus heros* in 41). The princess falls in love
with him at once, and takes the initiative in demanding him
as her husband despite the obvious objection of a previous
commitment:

regis nata decens fuerat pulcherrima Glauce,
iam cui virginitas annis matura tumebat;
haec ubi conspexit iuvenem, flammata nitore
aestuat et laudans alieni membra mariti
optat habere virum. sonuit genitoris ad aures. (369–73)

The motivation is passion, as in Colchis, rather than political gain, and it is the woman who takes the lead. As Medea had neglected her duty to Diana, so Glauce ignores the obligation of Jason's marriage, and covets her neighbor's spouse. (Is it fanciful to see the Christian poet pointing to the violation of the Commandment in these lines?) And so the curse of Diana is fulfilled as Jason gladly accedes to Glauce's request. As in Colchis, he is a passive figure throughout the action: *grates electus agit* (380).

Creon is in all essential respects parallel to Aeetes. Not only does his daughter marry Jason, but he is now the possessor of the fleece, which passes to Jason because of his marriage to the princess (378). As Aeetes was called *rector* by Bacchus (322), so Creon is called *rector Thebanus* (374). But most important, his motive for acceding to the marriage is not greatly different from Aeetes'. He believes that the fates have intended it, and that grandchildren will follow to bless him:

si Iuppiter auctor,
si Lachesis, si fata iubent, nil ipse morabor.
progenies mea turpe cupit: Fortuna favorem
praestet et innumeri laudent per saecla nepotes. (374–77)

Unlike Aeetes, he is not swayed by any direct intervention of the gods but by his own rationalization. In a sense, he is correct in assigning the union to fate, for it is the working out of Diana's curse.

Thus Dracontius underscores how the two halves of the poem may after all be united. Glauce will cause disruption of Jason's plans, and a pliant father will agree to the irregu-

lar arrangement. The thoughtless haste with which Jason
complies suggests that Medea was not altogether unreasonable in her suspicions at his nocturnal mutterings. He is
after all the unreliable creature she accused him of being,
and the rest of the poem will display Medea's revenge for
his willingness to give in to the intemperate passions of
Glauce—exactly like those by which she herself originally
won him.

Once again we are in the midst of hasty wedding preparations as Creon summons the guests. This is the point of
the action on which Dracontius has chosen to concentrate.
His purpose is related to the over-all structure of the poem,
but his model is Seneca's tragedy and to a lesser extent
Hosidius. Because of this severe concentration on what
normally comes later in the play, he has omitted crucial
items. Medea is not seen as a threat to the realm, since
Jason's marriage is unrelated to political ambition, and so
there is no negotiation between Creon and Medea: she is
not to be sent into exile, and thus does not need to ask for
one day's relief. She is simply ignored amid the preparations and can only vent her rage after she learns what has
already been planned. In short, she plays the same role in
the economy of this scene as Diana played in Colchis. And
because of the reduced and feeble character of Jason, he
contributes nothing to the action. This is a noticeable loss.
He does not explain or defend his actions, and there is
no climactic confrontation with Medea. Conversely, Medea
makes no effort to confront or challenge Jason. She learns of
the wedding and sets about exacting her revenge.

The poet's rhetorical propensities now take firm hold,
and we are treated to an exercise in *grand guignol*. Medea
is presented unrelentingly as a furious witch in touch with
the darkest powers. Her prayers to Luna (396–430), Dis
and the Furies (436–60), and Sol (497–508) occupy fully a
third of the Theban scene, and the description of her activities fills much of the rest. This poem is a fine test of the
reader's tolerance for rhetorical excess.

In her long appeal to Luna, Medea stresses the goddess'

function of punishing the wicked. There is an obvious irony
in that Medea's present situation stems directly from her
disobedience of the goddess and is in fact her punishment
for that dereliction. Yet the goddess hears her prayer readily. Though Medea has not quite realized it, her vengeance
on Jason is the enactment of her own punishment. She
grapples with this notion, admitting her own guilt but add-
ing a special concern:

> da veniam, Medea precor: cum clade suorum
> non decet ira deos. mereor pro crimine poenam,
> te feriente tamen, non ut mendicus Iason
> sit vindex, regina, tuus, qui criminis auctor
> ipse fuit. (416–20)

Dracontius has created a kind of logical puzzle by detaching
Jason's activities from the commands of Pelias. He had already neglected to collect the fleece, and when he recalled
his intention, he asked only to visit home, not to take the
fleece with him. It was Medea who revived that plan,
Medea who took the fleece and slew Apsyrtus. For all this
there was no justification in terms of saving Jason's life.
Medea is to this extent inexact in calling Jason *criminis auctor*. Yet in the traditional version Jason's urgent needs are
precisely the cause of Medea's actions, and she can with
justice claim that he drove her to them. In Dracontius,
Medea still performs the usual deeds, but recognizes—in a
way the traditional Medea cannot—that the central guilt
rests with her.

Moreover, it is precisely her sense of *guilt* which impels
her to her most desperate act. The lives she takes will be a
sacrifice of atonement:

> quinque dabo inferias (sat erunt pro crimine nostro
> inlustres animae). (425–26)

The five are Creon, Glauce, the children, and Jason himself. Thus the slaying of the children is not done, as else-

where, to cause Jason further anguish[50]—indeed he will
perish before them—but she takes the dreadful step *ne
prosit peccasse mihi* (430).[51] In this way a motivation is provided for the dénouement which the tradition demands.
Expiation is intertwined with revenge.

There was no clear basis in the previous versions for
this approach. Medea presumably had ample motive for
revenge in the fact that her husband abandoned her for
Glauce. But as I noted, the poet has cut out all those scenes
which would develop this clash of wills, and since she is ignored by all, her motivation must arise within herself. That
this urge should be mixed with remorse and with a need to
be punished for her sins is a further illustration of the poet's
Christianity asserting itself whenever he considers questions of wrongdoing.

Assured by signs in the heavens that her prayer has been
answered, Medea turns confidently to the lord of the Underworld and to the Furies, invoking their wrath upon the
House of Thebes:

> gens ‹haec› est vestra: dicavit
> mortibus impietas, affectus funera praestant. (451–52)

The crimes are not peculiar to Creon (here identified as
Iocastae frater et heres in 450) and Glauce, but are en-
demic to the house. Now we find a justification for her actions separate from her sense of guilt and in that sense
closer to the traditional view. As Schetter shows, Dracontius' depiction of the Furies, and their intended role in the
action, is derived not so much from Seneca as from Statius,
precisely because of their connection with events in Thebes
through the generations.[52] This general link is the main justification for invoking them, since Medea will prepare and
deliver the poisoned crown herself.[53]

After the subfusc atmosphere of this long scene, Dracontius switches abruptly to the dazzling light of day and the
wedding preparations in the palace:

exilit interea tecturus Lucifer astra
puniceo praevectus equo rutilusque micansque
concusso de crine iubar diffundit in orbem
flammigeri roseas praecedens solis habenas. (470–73)

As we return to the scene of the wedding, it is to see the
guests arrive. Dracontius has apparently derived from Catullus 64 the sequence for this part of the poem. The theme
of the wedding day is interrupted for an account of an abandoned and frantic heroine—we should note that Ariadne's
actions on behalf of Theseus are parallel to Medea's for
Jason—and then returns to the main narrative with the arrival of the guests.[54]

The wedding is not only ill omened but wrong, and as a
sign of the disaster to come, the witnesses who sign the
contract are the Tartarean sisters Tisiphone, Megaera, and
Allecto.[55] The motif of the Furies attending a wedding
doomed to disaster is an old and common one,[56] but Dracontius seems to be alone in having them participate as sig-
natory witnesses. No doubt it was his lawyer's instincts
which led him to take this extra step. Dracontius is also unusual, perhaps unique, in having the wedding actually take
place: generally, it is forestalled by the slaughter. But Dracontius wants to have a genuine parallel to the wedding in
Colchis and so makes a point of the ceremony. With the appearance of the ghastly divinities, the glitter implied in the
first lines of the scene is gone, and we return to the gloom
of the nether world.

The balance of this segment deals with the familiar culminating events of the tragedy: the presentation of the le-
thal gift, the deaths of those involved, and Medea's escape.
In each case there is some apparent novelty of treatment,
and some have assumed at least an indirect link with Hyginus (*Fab.* 25); but it is certainly inaccurate to say, as Provana does, that Dracontius tells the whole story as it is in
Hyginus.[57]

First, the gift. Medea makes a deadly crown which will
burst into flames when Glauce puts it on her head. More

frequently the tradition speaks of a crown and a robe, the latter eating away the flesh of its wearer. Hyginus, however, mentions only *coronam ex venenis auream* which sets the princess afire. He has perhaps combined the deadly poisoned robe with the crown which blazes. Hosidius also speaks only of a crown (*Med.* 421ff.). Dracontius has similarly combined the two motifs in the crown by dwelling at length on the deadly poisons from snakes, which Medea works into the gift, and the gilded appearance of the finished crown. In order to make the crown burn, Medea invokes her grandfather the Sun, whose fire controls all life. The passage combines two principal symbols of the poem, the snake and the flame.[58] It also recalls by contrast the Phoenix, with whom Cupid was compared: it also was kindled in its deadly pyre by the rays of the Sun. This dreadful finale can trace its origins directly to the actions of the god to whom the Phoenix was compared.

Once the crown is prepared, Medea herself delivers it to the princess. In this instance, Dracontius is not following Hyginus, who preserves the usual tradition: *eam [sc. coronam] muneri filios suos iussit novercae dare.* The only other source which may accommodate Medea delivering the crown in person is Hosidius. He does not specify, and one is left with the impression that Medea has done everything alone. In our poem Medea can indulge a grisly dramatic irony as she presents the gift to Glauce:[59]

"accipe, virgo, libens auratam in fronte coronam,
quam captiva dabo, qualem mea pignora sumant." (513–14)

Dracontius agrees with Hyginus in another important divergence from the mainstream. Jason is among the victims of Medea's crown, as the entire palace is turned into a vast pyre. Even here the poet reflects something of Medea's attitude:

uritur *ingratus* usta cum virgine nauta. (519)

This story is not found elsewhere, although Page thought it pointed to a tradition older than Euripides, which was preserved through the mythographer.[60]

There is a further curious detail which may suggest dependence on Hyginus. The names of Medea's children by Jason are variously reported, as are their numbers. The most common version is that there were two sons named Mermerus and Pheres.[61] Dracontius follows this tradition but commits an elementary blunder by calling the second boy *Pheretes* (532). Obviously he found the name in an oblique case—note Hyginus' *Pheretem*[62]—and from that deduced a false nominative.

The murder of the children shows the poet in full cry. Medea contemplates the death of her Theban rivals and her husband with ghoulish pleasure, but then *necdum satiata . . . nec secura* she turns on her children. The young ones have instinctively come to their mother for protection from the horror around them, unaware that she is its source:[63]

> ut flammas vitare queat, infantia simplex
> affectu petit ipsa necem vel sponte pericla
> quaerit inops, passura necem mucrone parentis,
> ignari quae mater erat quid saeva pararet. (533–36)

It is characteristic of Dracontius to play on this perversion of the tender relationship of mother and child. We have been prepared for this scene by the frequent references to the joys of motherhood and the expectation of grandchildren, including Medea's own comment to Jason (250). This instinctive reaching out for safety on the part of the children replaces the grotesque rhetoric of Seneca and Hosidius, where the boys plead for their lives. But Medea is beyond maternal or even human feeling. Immediately before and after the description of the children, she is called *furibunda* (531, 537). As the boys approach, she raises her sword and prays to the gods to accept the sacrifice. We are back at the moment when Medea had Jason under her sac-

rificial knife and uttered a similar prayer (188–94). This
time, however, there is no reprieve—for the children or for
us—the poet reaches for a new way to depict the crime and
settles on a grisly picture:

> haec ait et geminos uno simul ense noverca
> transegit pueros. quos sic portabat ad arcem. (547–48)

On the citadel she commits their bodies along with the
other victims to the pyre which was the palace. This particular sequence is not found elsewhere, although Dracontius is apparently reflecting the ancient association of Medea
with Hera Akraia in Corinth (the goddess had promised, in
a version obviously not followed here, to make the children
immortal), to whom Medea dedicated the children.[64] Euripides specifies that the bodies will be delivered to the citadel, but neither Seneca nor Hosidius follows him.

There is a curious coincidence—I believe it is nothing
more by Dracontius' day—in this reemergence of a tradition which associated Medea with Juno; for it had reinforced the role of Medea as the protector of Jason, even as
Juno was. Here they work at deadly cross-purposes, but
originally there was an identity of function.

And finally, her revenge complete, Medea flees in the
traditional chariot drawn by a yoke of serpents. But there
has been no Aegeus to offer her refuge in Athens. We are
not told where she will flee, but as that falls outside the
scope of the action, it does not matter to the poet. With all
her enemies dead, it is not even clear from whom she is
now escaping. The only possible ending to the scene is
Medea's mad flight, both because tradition dictates it, and
because the poet must depict the criminal fleeing from the
scene of the crime in order to emphasize once more both
her guilt and her power.

Epilogue (570–601)

Dracontius concludes the epyllion with an invective against
the assorted malevolent forces which have abused Thebes,
culminating in the disaster just presented. After the emphasis he has placed on Thebes and the role of the Furies,
it is not surprising that he should revert to the topic. Once
again there is some similarity to Catullus 64: that poem also
ends with a gloomy rumination on the loss of innocence
and of the contact between gods and men. As befits the
awful deeds reported here, the tone is harsher and the initial premise less positive.

The catalogue of disasters includes Cadmus, Athamas,
Palaemon, Jocasta, and Oedipus, and the fraternal struggle
of Eteocles and Polynices. Only the first of these is developed in any detail, but it is a logical choice for such special
treatment, for it provides one link between Colchis and
Thebes. It was Cadmus who slew the dragon, and sowed
half its teeth in the field in Thebes, whence sprang the
earth-born army. The other half of the teeth came into the
possession of none other than Aeetes of Colchis and figured
prominently among the trials set for Jason in traditional
versions of the Argonautica.[65] In this respect Jason is a
doublet of Cadmus. Dracontius has naturally eliminated
the trials from his version of events in Colchis, but this is a
way, at least indirectly, to bring in one of the most familiar
episodes in the Argonautic tradition. It also suggests a parallel between Medea's background and the city to which
she ultimately comes.[66]

The poet turns to the divinities who have played important roles in this poem—*blanda Venus, lascive puer, Se-
meleie Bacche* (587)—to ask for mercy, although he realizes
the appeal is futile. Thebes was the birthplace of Semele
and the place of the wedding of Cadmus and Harmonia:[67]
why should it suffer so extravagantly at the hands of the
gods it has welcomed? It would be better to have nothing to
do with the gods. Here the poet comes to what may well be
his main point:

sitque nefas coluisse deos, quia crimen habetur
relligionis honos, cum dat pro laude pericla. (600–601)

Schetter notes acutely that this rallying cry against the worship of the gods comes strategically at the end of the poet's
peroration.[68] The entire poem has moved to this point, and
the poet has just shown us in the epilogue how the actions
of Medea are the culmination of the destructive interaction
of the gods with men. The bond of obedience and worship
has proved itself to be fruitless at best and usually worse.
Having finally struck bottom, as it were, the relationship
should be abandoned. This is probably the poet's Christian
polemic against the pagan gods, as Schetter conjectures.[69]
The complete failure of the ancient beliefs gives room for a
fresh start, which can hardly be other than the poet's own
belief. At the same time Dracontius has created a counterbalance to the prologue. The poem opens with a description of the gods cowering at the whim of the evil Medea,
unwilling to have contact with her but unable to avoid it.
The natural relations of gods and men were perverted by
her witchcraft and tyranny over nature. In the epilogue the
poet views the question from the other end. The gods have
inflicted calamity on men, especially in Thebes, with such
unnatural deeds as incest and fratricide, until mankind
begs to withdraw from contact with the immortals.

Structure

Our analysis of the poem points to a much more coherent
structure than has generally been admitted. Obviously the
basic parts are A. Prologue (1–31); B. Colchis (32–365);
C. Thebes (366–569); and D. Epilogue (570–601). But
within this gross delineation may be discerned a genuine
architecture with symmetrical parts in each major segment.
  Both B and C begin with the arrival of Jason, setting the
stage for ensuing events: 32–49 contain his landing on the
Colchian coast and his immediate arrest, while 366–82 tell
of his arrival at Thebes with Medea and his immediate

selection as a husband for Glauce. All that follows in each segment flows from these initial situations.

The first scene now breaks off for the deliberation in heaven (49–176), which is attached to the scene in Colchis when Cupid flies down. When we rejoin the human drama, Medea is the central figure in her capacity as priestess of Diana. The sacrifice scene fills a panel of 81 verses (177–257) and is followed by a second panel of virtually equal length on the wedding of Jason and Medea: 257–339 (82 verses).[70] The final portion of this segment deals with those events subsequent to the wedding, ending with Medea slaying her kinsman and fleeing from the country: 340–65 (26 verses).

When we turn to the Theban scene, it is clear that the basic structure is precisely the same. After the hero's arrival there are two panels of equal length. The first (382–469) concentrates on Medea in her capacity as witch devoted to the triform goddess, here specifically Hecate. Length: 87 verses. The second panel deals with the wedding of Jason and the princess (47–556). In this case, of course, the princess is Glauce rather than Medea, but we have seen how Dracontius has worked on the similarities of their roles and even of their characters. Length: 87 verses. And finally, we hear of the events which follow the wedding, culminating in Medea slaying her kin and fleeing from the country: 557–69 (13 verses). Then follows the epilogue.

Considered from this perspective, the scene in heaven becomes a digression from the main action, which occurs in the human realm. The participation of the gods in the wedding scene and in the climactic revenge is different in that the gods come *into* the human arena. The action in heaven (however human in its pettiness) involves only divinities. It is segregated from the action of the real protagonist, Medea, and we are made to feel that this external stimulus is a spring mechanism to set the human plot in motion rather than the focus of attention. This contrasts with the *Hylas*: there the action is dominated by supernatural figures, both in heaven and at the pool, and it is Hylas who is drawn into the realm of the gods and sets *their* plot in motion. But the sense of separation in *Medea* accords well with the poet's lamentations in the epilogue about the futility of contact with the gods, and the cruelty of the immortals when contact occurs.

Thus the structure of the poem may be represented schematically as follows:

A. PROLOGUE	1–31	31	
B. COLCHIS	32–365		207
a. set stage: arrival of Jason	32–49	18	
digression: scene in heaven	49–176		[127]
b. Medea as priestess	177–257	81	
c. Wedding day (Jason-Medea)	257–339	82	
d. subsequent events (slay brother, leave country)	340–65	26	
C. THEBES	366–569		204
a. set stage: arrival of Jason	366–82	17	
b. Medea as witch	382–469	87	
c. Wedding day (Jason-Glauce)	470–556	87	
d. Subsequent events (slay sons, leave country)	556–69	13	
D. EPILOGUE	570–601	32	

Obviously it would be foolish to demand a mechanical exactness in the number of lines,[71] but the essential design is unmistakable: prologue and epilogue are of virtually the same size, and each half of the main body consists of comparably brief outer segments plus two larger inner panels of very equal length, the whole tied together by the parallel sequence of contents.

As to the scene in heaven, it might have been easier for Dracontius to preserve the symmetry which he was clearly at pains to achieve and introduce the plans of Venus in some other way. But the influence of generic conventions was still powerful. Dracontius is building on the tradition of the epithalamium, which since Statius had normally included a scene in heaven with Venus dispatching Cupid to inflame the bride. He could not omit this scene, despite its awkwardness structurally, and it did offer some opportunities. He could develop his view of the god's motives for dealing with mortals before plunging back into the action dominated by Medea: the digression provides suspense. Moreover, the use of a digression fits well with the traditional conventions of the epyllion.

I believe that this architecture provides a key to what Dracontius has done with the myth of Medea. His was a schematic mind, always more content to deal with paradox (especially its subspecies oxymoron) or parallel. This is due naturally to his rhetorical training, which taught him the power of persuasion and the scope for ornamentation in both these devices. And like his similarly trained Christian contemporaries, he was taught to understand his faith in the same terms. At any rate, he has presented us with a tale of Medea in which the apparently bizarre and incompatible elements are subordinated to a general scheme.

It is not a subtle scheme, but it is so pronounced as to be inescapable. By starting from the depiction of Medea as an Iphigenia figure, Dracontius (whatever his source) is able to focus on a single set of characteristics for his heroine. He can thus bind together an account of this woman as the source of passion and the source of evil. This idea, though hardly unique to Christian thought, was strongly developed in Christian writings, naturally focused on the biblical account of the Fall. The events in Eden were an immensely popular theme in poetry of the fifth and sixth centuries,[72] and Dracontius himself treated the Fall at length in *De laudibus Dei* I.459ff. Note that in both Colchis and Thebes a dominant woman lures the weaker man from his proper line of action and into ruin. Most arrestingly, Medea goes into the garden and she herself takes from the tree (where the serpent lives) what will please the man and gives it to him. This shape of events, added to the explicit censure of Glauce for coveting her neighbor's spouse and the condemnation of all that the pagan gods do, shows how Dracontius had sifted the myth in his own mind from a Christian perspective.

Chapter 4

De Raptu Helenae (Rom. VIII)

WHEREAS THE *Medea* fell neatly into two segments of nearly equal length and evoked the folk tale, the *Abduction of Helen* suggests dramatic models and in five scenes of very unequal length tells various parts of Paris' story. It will repay our attention to observe how these pieces of the story have been chosen and shaped by the poet as they display the characteristic love of repetition and echo.

In one respect at least, this epyllion is like *Medea:* we are once again treated to a variety of incidents which are normally treated in separate parts of the tradition. The events range from Paris' exposure as an infant and his return to Troy (both of which are usually associated with the dramatic tradition), his adventures in Greece (some nearly unexampled in the other literature), and his joyful return to Troy with his "bride." Thus a question must arise as to the unity of the poem: how does Dracontius combine these disparate episodes into a coherent work? And in the process we must inquire how his handling of the stories compares with our other sources on the myth.

Prologue (1–60)

The poet lays out his subject and points immediately to the moral implicit in his tale:

> Troiani praedonis iter raptumque Lacaenae
> et pastorale scelerati pectoris ausum
> aggrediar meliore via (1–3)

85

Should we interpret this as a specifically Christian distress at the actions of Paris? Is *meliore via* a claim to clearer vision or merely a poet's standard boast of his prowess as a teller of tales? Provana went so far as to claim that moral indignation was the poet's principal theme and his purpose in writing.[1] In *Medea* and again in *Orestes*, Dracontius dwells on the guilt of the woman as the initiator of mischief, and in fact he will make somewhat the same suggestion about Helen later in this poem (cf. 530ff.). This may be part of a pattern of Christian interpretation.[2] But in the prologue he blames only Paris.

This is consistent with the mainstream tradition, which always laid the principal blame on Paris the disrupter of marriage. The poets frequently spoke more in sorrow than in censure since both Paris and Helen were acting under the compulsion of Venus and of fate; and Dracontius gives the fates a particularly prominent role in the course of events.[3] They are responsible for Paris' decisions and also for Helen's aggressive cooperation. We may choose to see this as merely the poet's acceptance of the traditional concept of fate,[4] but there may be more to it than that. The peculiarly strong emphasis on characters as acting under the orders of fate provides them with an explanation, or even an excuse, for their deeds. As the author of the *Aegritudo Perdicae* uses the device of the false dream to introduce the indelicate topic of incest, so here perhaps Dracontius is using the compulsion of fate more heavily than most poets in order to have this story proceed without the suggestion of approval or indifference.[5] Yet even with this decisive role played by fate, the poet can stand outside the story he is telling and assign blame. In the prologue he has simply adopted the traditional formulation and placed the blame on Paris. Later on he will refine his accusations.

The statement of the crime shows the poet's distress in both legal and sentimental terms:

> nam prodimus hostem
> hospitis et thalami populantem iura mariti,

foedera coniugii, consortia blanda pudoris,
MATERIEM generis, sobolis spem, pignora prolis:
nam totum de MATRE venit, de MATRE creatur
quod membratur homo: *pater* est fons auctor origo,
sed nihil est sine MATRE *pater:* quota portio *patris*
omnis constat homo? MATER fit tota propago. (3–10)

We shall find a vein of legalism running through this whole
poem, as each situation is played out as though it were in a
courtroom. Here the rather peculiar distinction between
the mother's contribution to offspring and the father's
sounds legalistic, although it seems to have no genuine relation to legal texts. It is another manifestation of Dracontius' strong feelings on the subject of motherhood. The
point is underscored by the interlocking word pattern of
mater/pater, and by the almost Lucretian play on *mater/
materiem*. Dracontius may actually have regarded this as
etymologically significant, as such notions were at the heart
of the mythological ruminations by Fulgentius and his contemporaries, and Dracontius made considerable use of
such sources.

In place of an invocation of the Muse, Dracontius calls
upon Homer and Vergil:

nec dico Camenae
te praesente "veni": sat erit mihi sensus Homeri. (15–16)

Both epic poets are characterized by isolated incidents: Homer by the vengeful Menelaus leading the troops to Troy,
and Vergil by the great second book (mentioning specifically
the Trojan Horse and the impious slaying of Priam—both
instances of Greek trickery). The allusions frame the war
which will result from the action of this poem, even as
the two poets define the epic tradition. Moreover, Paris'
own arrivals at Troy prefigure the arrival of the destructive
Greeks as well as causing it. He is, like the host of the
Achaeans, an intruding and alien force who comes to claim
what is his and ends by destroying everything.

After this prefatory material, Dracontius again calls upon Vergil and Homer as his Muses—*Vulgate, precor, quae causa* (29)—and launches into his story. Yet he does so in an indirect manner. Of the wedding of Peleus and Thetis, the arrival of Eris, or the apple of discord, there is no mention. The judgment itself is already a thing of the past:

> caelicolum pastor iam sederat arbiter Idae:
> iam gremium caespes, iam surgens herbida tellus
> stabat et aetherium fuerant herbosa tribunal. (31–33)

We can see the lawyer's taste for the details of the event as a trial: the judge's bench, the courtroom, and the défendants at the bar. Inasmuch as the divinities were not on trial for any misdeed but were simply competing for recognition and a prize, this is a misleading image. Paris was settling a dispute among claimants, and so the figure of the arbiter is fitting. Yet the real value of this scene of judgment is in what follows it. Notions of guilt will pervade the poem, and the poet will quickly turn the idea of criminal behavior around. Because Paris acted as judge, he himself is judged and becomes the defendant and is found guilty.

> iudicis Idaei pretio sententia fertur
> damnaturque Paris: nec solus pastor habetur
> ex hac lite reus. . . . (39–41)

The circle of guilt and of punishment moves steadily out, with a sixfold repetition of *damnatur* (40–47), to engulf Paris, his family, the two races at war, and the great heroes.

The poet gives almost no details of the judgment itself, and this makes it difficult to determine what tradition he had in mind. The very sketchiness of the report sets Dracontius apart from Colluthus, who devotes some seventy lines to the contest itself (121–89). A few details do emerge, and they suggest that the two poets are following distinguishable traditions.[6] Most significantly, Colluthus has Aphrodite tell Paris the identity of the woman who is to be his reward (164–65).[7] It is clear that Dracontius' Paris does not know of Helen specifically, as Venus has merely promised him *talem . . . qualis nuda fuit* (64–65),[8] and it is this vague sense of anticipation and mystery which stirs Paris from his pastoral inertia; but it is Priam's request that sends Paris to Greece, not Venus' orders as in the other traditions.

Dracontius and Colluthus both preserve another element but in different ways. *Qualis nuda fuit* derives from a tradition which begins in the erotic interests of the Hellenistic period.[9] Venus won the contest because, while the other goddesses were modestly draped, she appeared nude and overawed Paris. Colluthus offers a more dramatic version of the incident:

'Η δ' ἑανὸν βαθύκολπον, ἐς ἠέρα γυμνώσασα
κόλπον, ἀνηώρησι καὶ οὐκ ἠδέσσατο Κύπρις.
χειρὶ δ' ἐλαφρίζουσα μελίφρονα δεσμὸν Ἐρώτων
στῆθος ἅπαν γύμνωσε καὶ οὐκ ἐμνήσατο μαζῶν. (154–57)

The sudden ecdysiast gesture that carries the day is novel in Colluthus but is clearly more allied to the Alexandrian tradition, which had all the goddesses totally nude, than to the older version which had them merely unveil their heads.

Dracontius points specifically to the anger of the losing contestants. As in other poems the spurned divinity is apparently to be the pivotal figure:

heu, nescia mens est
quae mala circumstent ausum dare iura Minervae! (37–38)

Then follows the summary (39–47) of the destruction which ensued. Minerva plays no further part in the action. Venus will be involved at the actual meeting of Paris and Helen, but even then there is nothing specific to mark the encounter as the goddess' reward to Paris. The judgment and the reactions of the contestants have no bearing on the poem after the prologue. Instead, the driving force, as Dracontius reminds us, is fate:

compellunt audere virum fata, impia fata,
quae flecti quandoque negant, quibus obvia numquam
res quaecumque venit, quis semita nulla tenetur
obvia dum veniunt, quibus omnia clausa patescunt. (57–60)

This does not exculpate either Paris or Helen. Paris is still, as the prologue has made plain, the moral cause of all the trouble.

Troy (61–212)

The shepherd who has presided over so tremendous an event as the adjudication of divine beauty may surely be forgiven some ennui at his humdrum pastoral life. Small wonder that Paris now looks with jaundiced eye on his flocks and countryside: *sordent arva viro post iurgia tanta dearum* (66). And so he decides to go to Troy. The story of his arrival and reception in the city forms the first of five scenes which comprise the main action of the poem; the passage is fraught with peculiarities and obscurities.

The tradition of Paris' exposure as an infant and his return to Troy as an adult was very old and thoroughly established in the literature, but within the general framework there was ample invention. Paris was perceived as a threat to his father—a common enough motif—and was to be disposed of before the prophecy of doom could be fulfilled. But of course (as fate would have it) the child was not actually destroyed but instead came into the hands of a guardian. Dracontius stands alone in having a nurse tell the prince the circumstances of his exposure and his lineage, *blandita nutrice* (69),[10] and we may ask why Paris then spent all those years living the pastoral life instead of returning to Troy far sooner; or assuming he had good reason not to try his luck by returning to the city which had tried to kill him, why he now blithely strolls into Troy simply because he is bored with the rustic life after tasting the pleasures of self-importance. The poet's answer is *mens et fata iubent*, the combination of internal purpose and external compulsion, which encodes the ambiguity of responsibility in all Paris does.

Paris has proofs of his identity, *crepundia* which were apparently given to him as a child in anticipation of just such a need to reestablish himself. The source of this tradition is unclear but would seem to go back at least as far as Ovid, who speaks of *signa* (*Her.* 16.90). Servius (*ad Aen.* 5.370) uses the term *crepundia* and gives as his source the *Troica* of Nero.[11] None of these passages gives any clue as to the nature of the *crepundia*. Thus the possession of tokens of identity was long established, but only by Dracontius is it attributed to a nurse who had long since explained everything to the exiled prince. Dracontius is then peculiarly vulnerable on the rationale for Paris' prolonged exile and this abrupt change.

In other versions, Paris returned *incognito* to enter a contest for a special bull and thereby found himself in competition with his brothers. This was the explanation given as early as the *Cypria*.[12] The quarrel which breaks out over accepting Paris back is an echo of this ancient tradition of strife, but the actual contest has been replaced by the speeches opposing his claim to a place of dignity. We shall look at these speeches in more detail shortly.

The scene is set with chilling vividness, and filled with ill-omened touches. As Paris approaches the city, the towers crumble, the earth lets out a moan and other parts of the city fall down. It emerges that the occasion was supposed to be a festive one, celebrating the rebuilding of Troy after its sack by Hercules,[13] but the whole day is suddenly turned into a prefiguration of the second and decisive sack to result from Paris' deeds. It is as if he has arrived not at the rebirth of Troy but at its funeral. The poet has borrowed from Vergil's account of the Trojan exiles' arrival at Buthrotum (*Aen.* 3.296ff.) with its haunted and hollow imitation of the ruined Troy which had been left behind. The other omens are regularly associated with the return of the dead: the sweating statue, the stream running blood red, and the statue tumbling of its own accord to the ground. The irony is presented directly:

> forte dies sollemnis erat, quo Pergama rector
> infelix Priamus post Herculis arma novarat:
> annua persolvens ingratis munera divis
> Laomedontiades capitolia celsa petebat
> reddere vota Iovi, laturus sacra Minervae. (78–82)

Priam is *infelix* not only because he is performing this ritual obligation on behalf of an ancient loss, but because he is about to welcome to his city the cause of future calamity; the gods are hostile not just for the past but for the days to come, and in particular Minerva's name reminds us of the goddess' anger at Paris himself.

Paris' arrival during a festival or ceremony will be a theme of the poem. He will do the same on Cyprus and again at his second arrival in Troy. On each occasion the ritual will assume a meaning directly opposite that intended by its participants. Here the shepherd-prince bursts in on the carefully arranged procession of his kinfolk and disrupts their actions with his shouts. We may think of Laocoon rushing in to interrupt another procession which will take place in the years ahead, as the Trojans move the fateful horse into the city in an act they think marks the end of the war.

As Paris announces himself to his astonished family, he touches on some of the crucial themes of the poem. He stresses above all his kinship and his right to be in Troy: the poet had begun with comments on the sanctity of the family, and although we assumed then that he was speaking only of the violence which Paris did to the conjugal bonds, now the larger concept of family ties comes into play. Paris is a brother—(*frater ego, fratrem cognoscite vestrum. / germanus sum vester ego* (94–95)—and a son—*Priami propago, / Hecuba mi genetrix* (95–96), and he greets all his kin by name as if to prove his relationship by displaying this knowledge he gained from the nurse along with the *crepundia* he now flings at their feet.

Paris also alludes to a second recurring theme, his role as
a shepherd. The poet, in his own voice, and various characters in the poem will imply the incongruity of a prince serving as a shepherd; here Paris links the fact of his past with
an assurance that his life has not been stained by crime—
on the contrary, it has now been distinguished by his recent
role as arbiter:

> abdicor crimine nullo:
> parvus Alexander pastor nutritus in Ida.
> nec pastor sit vile, Phryges: ego iurgia divum
> compressi, nam lite caret me iudice caelum. (96–99)

Thus Paris combines in his self-description the theme of
guilt, the contrast between shepherd and prince, and his
role as peacemaker. All of these will reappear at crucial moments. In particular, Paris thinks of himself as a source of
stability and the friend of heaven, but in fact he spends his
time on missions of diplomacy which turn into conflict and
calamity. He is not a very skillful judge of his own character. Similarly he rejects his past as a shepherd, only to look
back on it with longing when he finds himself at sea in a
storm (402ff.). The poet and the other characters persist in
calling Paris *pastor,* especially at those moments when he is
unconvincing as a prince.

The theme of the testing is continued as Paris flings down
his proofs of identity. Now it is Priam and Hecuba who are
on trial for having abandoned Paris, and his *crepundia* are
the proof of their guilt as much as of Paris' identity. The
court scene has been turned inside out. Hecuba at once
confesses her fault, and Priam follows suit:

> admissumque nefas generosa mente fatetur
> fusus in ore rubor. Paridis mox colla lacertis
> adligat et natum fletu gaudentis inundat
> convictusque pater veniam de prole rogabat. (105–108)

The floodgates of sentiment having thus been opened, Dracontius indulges his taste for emotional scenes. It must be

admitted that the display of joy and affection is somewhat
unconvincing in view of the abandonment of Paris and his
apparent disappearance from the minds of all for many
years. Moreover, at the end of the poem, the family will
again lament his presumed death not in terms of a personal
loss but simply because he is a prince and deserves a decent mourning (599ff.). But the joy of Priam and Hecuba
stands in contrast to the reactions of Cassandra and Helenus, whose speeches of resistance and prophecy will occupy most of the remainder of this scene.[14]

The entire scene displays dramatic qualities, as it consists largely of speeches by the characters (Paris, Helenus,
Cassandra, and Apollo). This feature alone would perhaps
be sufficient to raise the question of a dramatic model, but
there is more. Euripides' *Alexandros* is known only through
a tantalizing collection of fragments, and by way of Ennius'
adaptation of it in his own *Alexander*.[15] Did Dracontius
know either of these plays, and did he model this scene on
them? Buecheler argued that there was an unmistakable
resemblance between various lines of Dracontius and the
extant fragments of Ennius,[16] and Morelli was lured by this
argument into conjecturing that the late poet had Ennius'
play at his disposal as he wrote.[17] I find the proposition incredible, not because of Dracontius' supposed ignorance of
Greek, nor even because (as I think altogether probable)
the tragedies of Ennius had vanished before Dracontius'
day, but simply because the tragedy in either form and the
epyllion tell very different stories.

The dramatic tradition focused on Paris' secret return to
Troy to compete for the bull. The dominant topic is the hos-
tility toward Paris on the part of various characters, including Hecuba. There is no mention of the judgment as antecedent to his return to Troy, much less as its cause. The
only features which the stories of Euripides/Ennius and
Dracontius have in common are the fact of Paris' arrival at
Troy and the recognition scene accompanied by the prophecies of Helenus and Cassandra.

Moreover, the two strands of Paris' story—the herdsman

who adjudicates the goddesses and the prince of Troy who abducts Helen—were not always or consistently linked. In what order did the events occur?[18] Did Paris return to Troy and reestablish his place as prince before the beauty contest? If so, why does the contest occur on Ida? Or if he was still an unknown herdsman, why is he judge for the contest? The tradition that he returned to Troy for the competition over the bull is quite separate from the tradition that he was promised a bride (whether or not Helen was specified) and came to Troy for help in securing that prize. Dracontius' combination of elements is peculiar to him. Paris simply feels that his lot as a herdsman is beneath his new dignity and longs for the city. Having made that decision, he comes home and announces himself. There is no plot against Paris now and no secrecy or anonymity in his advent. In short, the crucial elements of the dramatic tradition are absent from Dracontius' treatment of the scene.

As to similarities which Buecheler and Morelli perceived between Ennius' *Alexander* and Dracontius' poem, they are illusory at best, springing from the inherent features of the scene. It is inevitable and sensible that Helenus and Cassandra prophesy at the time of Paris' arrival, given the momentous events which are to spring from his return. The dream of Hecuba giving birth to a torch was long established in the tradition, before and after Ennius. In light of these facts, then, how should we be swayed by the purported similarity of such divergent passages as these:

ENNIUS: adest, adest fax obvoluta sanguine atque incendio.
            multos annos latuit: cives, ferte opem et restinguite.

            iamque mari magno classis cita
            texitur. exitium examen rapit.
            adveniet. fera velivolantibus
            navibus complevit manus litora. (fr. XVII Joc.)

DRAC.: haec est illa tuo fax, mater, prodita somno,
            quae simul incendet Troiam regnumque parentum
            in sortem dabit illa nurus. coniurat in arma

Graecia tota dolens raptum punire Lacaenae,
litora nostra petent Danai cum mille carinis. (122–26)

The torch, which is a central fact of the story, and the prospect of that torch being applied now to Troy are the common features; there is no single verbal echo to suggest that
Dracontius was working from Ennius. The difference of the
context in which the two speeches occur and the fact that it
is Cassandra in Ennius but Helenus in the later work argue
against direct connections, and the high probability that
the tragedies were no longer available seems to turn the
odds against any such link. That the two seers of Troy should
speak out on so momentous an occasion is nearly inevitable and is common in one form or another to the entire
tradition.[19]

As Dracontius was apparently the only poet to have Paris
know of his royal lineage from childhood, on the information of his nurse and by virtue of *crepundia,* so he is apparently the only one to have Paris return home out of simple
boredom with the country life after the judgment. The two
elements do not fit well together, but other poets have had
similar inconcinnities in dealing with this story.

The twin seers, Helenus and Cassandra, deliver prophetic speeches against the acceptance of their long-
missing brother. Helenus' cry from afar is again reminiscent of Laocoon:

> tunc Helenus vates templum dimisit et aram
> et procul exclamat: "pater impie, pessima mater,
> quid pietas crudelis agit, quid perditis urbem?" (119–21)

Indeed, his whole speech is marked by even more Vergilian
features than the poem in general: the notorious *Dorica
castra* (cf. *Aen.* 2.27, just before the Laocoon scene) and
mille carinis (*Aen.* 2.198, in the heart of the Laocoon scene)
are the most noticeable examples.

Helenus makes two points in his speech: he observes the
fulfillment of the omen conveyed by Hecuba's dream of the

torch, and he looks ahead to the destruction of Troy in
terms of the heroes who will perish (128ff.).[20] Helenus sees
in his imagination the events of the war, including the identity of the woman involved (Paris himself does not know
this detail), and he laments the death of Hector, Troilus,
and many others. But like Paris, Helenus is under the spell
of fate and does not try to fight it. He seems almost to welcome this fulfillment of the prophecies.

Even as Helenus speaks, Cassandra bursts in on the
scene. Her speech is longer (135–82) and more focused in
argument, but it shares many of her brother's themes. She
emphasizes the kinship theme (not only by her words but
by embracing her mother, even in the flight of her frenzy),
yet recognition of kinship is what will destroy the city: as
Helenus had asked *quid pietas crudelis agit, quid perditis
urbem* (121), so Cassandra cries

> quid funera nostra paratis?
> immemor heu pietas: uni pia mater haberis
> pastoremque foves, sed multis impia constas
> regibus. . . . (136–39)

Note that Cassandra refuses to refer to Paris as her brother.
He is simply *pastor.* When she does call him brother (161)
it is to incite her fellow citizens to cast him down from the
walls like Astyanax. The collocation *infausto iuveni, muris
depellite, fratrem. / hic hostis . . .* shows clearly enough
what price she puts on consanguinity.

Helenus looked back to the dream of the torch and explained it by the present. Cassandra looks only ahead to the
suffering awaiting her family and herself. Like Helenus,
she sees the death and ransoming of Hector (note the pathetic triple invocation of her brother's name in 139, 140,
142) and the burning of the city. The repeated *iam . . . iam
. . . iam* (cf. 127–29) brings the events of the sack and its
aftermath vividly before us. And like her brother she accepts what fate has in store for her (143–44).[21] In both cases
it *is* fate which is to blame, and she too realizes that her

lament is futile: *quid vana cano?* (152) and *provida non credor* (159) are apt summaries of her lot and echo Helenus' *sed quid fata veto?* (131).

Helenus had identified Paris as the torch to burn Troy; Cassandra's description is parallel but less figurative: *haec est illa . . . fax* (122: Helenus); *hic hostis quem fata canunt* (162: Cassandra). The two prophecies are parallel in essential structure and content, underscoring the inescapable truth of what is said. The vision of the war to come is a blend of incidents from the *Iliad* and surrounding cyclic poems, and Vergilian phrases recalling (or, in chronology of event, foreshadowing) the *Aeneid*.

But Cassandra adds a figurative flourish drawing on medicine and the law. Many cities secure their safety by the sacrifice of innocent scapegoats, but Troy need only sacrifice one who is guilty. This return to the guilty-innocent theme fits with what we have already seen on the poet-lawyer's perspective. Here it is also related to medical practice:

> augere dolores
> ut resecet medicina solet membrisque salutem
> membrorum de parte dabit: nam corporis aegri
> fit iactura salus, at vires passio praestat
> quas auferre solet. (171–75)

Thus by sacrificing Paris—by bleeding the community through his slaying—the body politic will be made well. Implicit is the recognition which Cassandra had earlier avoided, that Paris is indeed her brother. There are only two references to Paris as her brother: in both, she calls on the citizens to slay him: *muris depellite fratrem* (161); *fraterno mucrone cadat* (178). The suggestion brings to mind Medea, who likewise hoped to secure domestic tranquillity by slaying her brother (*Med.* 364).

Thus Cassandra draws together various elements of the situation: family relationships which can only be admitted at dreadful cost but cannot be denied; the guilt which Paris carries with him even though he has committed no crime as

yet; the relations with the gods, already spoiled by deception yet inescapable. Cassandra's vision of the situation is
both clear and accurate, but of course she cannot be believed. To ensure that she and Helenus do not gain credence, Apollo appears like a *deus ex machina* to turn the
people against their plea.

The god's speech is the third and last of the scene. One is
struck by all the features of this segment reminiscent of
tragic drama: the three characters who deliver speeches, the
recognition scene, the fatal error in decision leading to the
tragic events to be presented hereafter, and perhaps most
notably this use of the *deus ex machina* to bring about an
outcome for which no other plausible impetus is available.[22]

But unlike most appearances of divinities to secure the
necessary dénouement, Apollo's pronouncement is fundamentally mendacious. He brushes aside the prophecies of
his own seers[23] and replaces them with the demands of fate:

> quid virgo canit? cur invidus alter
> exclamat? Helenus deferret Pergama verbis?
> pellere pastorem patriis de sedibus umquam
> fata vetant, quae magna parant. stant iussa deorum. (188–91)

His announcement contains two truthful elements—that
fate decrees Paris is to be received, and that the returning
prince is the one to slay Achilles (192). We almost do not
notice that this latter will be necessary only because there
will be a war with the Greeks, i.e., that Cassandra and
Helenus were telling the truth after all. The rest of Apollo's
words are cast as good news, which the Trojans will surely
be glad to accept instead of the dire visions of the seers: the
future holds great things for Troy and all will be well.

This false picture is modeled to some extent on Jupiter's
prediction (*Aen.* 1.274ff.) of what lies ahead for the Trojans
in their new identity as Romans. Apollo even quotes Jupiter as promising *imperium sine fine* (199; *Aen.* 1.279), and
again invokes fate to prove the prediction. The Trojan he-
gemony is to stretch from the rising of the sun to its setting

and last forever: but this is the Roman future. The lines also
recall Apollo's prophecy to the Trojans in *Aen.* 3.90–98.[24]
Dracontius' readers would recognize the models and recall
that in their Vergilian setting they were both true predictions. Moreover, if the Trojans are one day to produce the
Roman race, then by extension Apollo is really speaking
the truth here as well. But that is sophistry: in order to
have the events of the *Aeneid,* the war which Cassandra
predicted and Apollo brushed aside must first ruin Troy and
send her remnant across the sea.[25]

The contrast between Cassandra, who speaks the truth
but is not believed, and the god of prophecy who misleads
but is believed, is quite possibly due to more than the demands of plot. We have seen in *Medea* how the poet appears to discredit the worship of the gods, and in *Hylas*
how they may even be·objects of ridicule. This deception
by the god of truth may be another example of the Christian poet's view of the old gods. The whole scene shows
how little credence should be placed in prophecy, even
from the most authoritative source.

Apollo has a third point to make, once more backed by
fate:

> mortali divum periet quo iudice iudex?
> nec hoc fata sinunt. (200–201)

This takes us back full circle to Paris' own perception of his
worth when he decided to return to Troy at the start of this
segment. The judge of the gods should have special treatment: he should appear as the prince he is, not as the shepherd he has been.

> scindete pellitas niveo de pectore vestes,
> murice Serrano rutilans hunc purpura velet. (204–205)

Appearance and perception are central to the poem. Paris
gets himself into trouble by judging beauty; he is now to
change his outward appearance in order to conform to—and

even bring about—a change in his condition; Helenus
and Cassandra have visions of the future, as does Hecuba;
and above all it is Helen's beauty, once seen by Paris, which
brings on the fateful action. So if Paris *dresses* like a prince,
he will in some significant way *become* a prince.

And yet, Apollo hastens to add, the Trojans should not
hold Paris' experience as a shepherd against him. For the
god himself endured the same lot in the service of Admetus. Indeed, Apollo's recollection of the episode makes it
sound quite appealing.

> ego pastor Apollo
> ipse fui domibusque canens pecus omne coegi,
> cum procul a villa fumantia tecta viderem;
> Alcestam sub nocte pavens deus ubera pressi,
> Admetus intrantes haedos numerabat et agnos. (206–10)

This is a fond recollection of the pastoral life, not a scornful
or apologetic statement. The echo of the first *Ecologue*[26]
adds further warmth to the account. For Apollo, the shepherd is an admirable figure (whatever the god's thoughts
and complaints may have been at the time): has he not
called Paris *pastorem* (190) at the beginning of his speech?
Indeed Paris himself will echo this praise of the shepherd's
lot as he is tossed by the storm at sea (402ff.). In the context
of the scene at Troy there is a striking contradiction between the scorn with which Paris viewed his lot at the
opening of the segment (61ff.) and the praise which Apollo
bestows on it in the process of commending Paris to the
Trojans as a prince. This tension between Paris the shepherd (when he was inconspicuous but successful) and Paris
the public figure (who seems to cause nothing but trouble)
runs through the entire poem. But it is ironic that Apollo's
final words on behalf of Paris are a commendation of the life
he has now abandoned.

In the face of Apollo's insistence the Trojans accept the
prince. Priam's reaction, *et grates securus agit* (212), recalls
Jason's disastrous willingness to accept the hand of Glauce,

et grates electus agit (*Med.* 380). Hector simply remains silent, neutralized (*tacet optimus Hector*): this detail points
to the last scene of the poem, when Hector shows a similar
lack of enthusiasm at the second safe return of his troublesome brother: *non gaudet fortior Hector* (624). It is a somber ending to the homecoming of a prince blessed by Apollo.

Salamis (213–384)

No sooner is Paris accepted back into the bosom of his family than he once again conceives a passion to be elsewhere.
The opening of this section is clearly parallel to the beginning of the segment which brought Paris to Troy.

> iam regno non impar erat, sed sceptra tiaram
> imperium trabeas iam post caeleste tribunal
> totum vile putat, solam cupit addere famam
> maiorum titulis, vivaces quaerere laudes,
> ut celet quod pastor erat. (213–17)

As in the earlier passage (61ff.), Paris is anxious to leave behind his pastoral associations and is unimpressed with his
lot in life after the role he has played in adjudicating the
gods. We can hardly be expected to forget that this is why
he came to Troy, which he now disdains. His princely status
has been affirmed, but it is as if Apollo's kindly words for the
life of a shepherd have cast a shadow over Paris' position,
and he must seek fresh distinction—*vivaces laudes*—for
himself. The poet's fondness for parallelism has taken its toll
here, and yet the one point which *ought* to have been repeated is missing: that Paris should now move on to find the
woman promised by Venus. This had driven him from Ida
to Troy but does not prompt his dissatisfaction now that he
is in a position to pursue her. Dracontius is preoccupied
with the shepherd-prince polarity and leaves out the one
natural explanation.

Of course Paris must go to Greece, but it seems perverse
to omit the obvious reason for his doing so. As matters
stand, Paris is driven by simple pride and unfocused ambi-

tion for glory, so that the encounter with Helen will now seem accidental.

Clearly Dracontius has inherited or fallen into confusion as to whether Paris was specifically told whom he was to win. In 65 he was promised a woman *qualis nuda fuit* (sc. Venus); here he seems to have no notion of seeking a woman, but only glory. With this lack of a specific purpose goes a lack of destination: Paris is merely eager to sail the Aegean (229).

It is Priam who gives him a destination: as long as he is in the Aegean, would he mind stopping off at Salamis and asking Telamon to return Hesione? Priam's sister had been carried off as a prize of war after Hercules took Troy,[27] and it was a source of humiliation to the Trojan monarch that the captive princess could not be regained.

Note the respect with which Priam now addresses his newly recovered son:

sic pater adloquitur iuvenem sermone verendo:
"nate, redux pietatis amor, bonus arbiter Idae . . ." (220–21)

and the importance of the mission he entrusts to this diplomat of the gods. What irony that Priam should count on the diplomacy of one who is about to progress from angering the gods to starting a war which will engulf his city. As we shall see, Paris is the only diplomat on the mission who does not even speak.

Moreover, says Priam,

dum Dorica regna peragras,
det Venus uxorem, faciat te Iuno maritum. (228–29)[28]

Does this mean that Priam is aware of the promise to Paris? I think the king is merely expressing a friendly wish, which makes the entire speech the more ironic. If Priam were actually reflecting the promise of Venus, why should he mention Juno, who certainly wants nothing good for Paris? But Juno Pronuba is the appropriate goddess to invoke for marriage; Priam's wish is quite formulaic.

Paris is to be accompanied by three other Trojan *proceres,* namely Antenor, Polydamas, and Aeneas. This scheme is related somehow to a tradition preserved in Dares Phrygius, although the relationship is far from clear. According to Dares (*De excidio Troiae* 4–5), after Hercules took Troy, because Telamon had been the first to enter the city and had displayed singular heroism, he was awarded Hesione the daughter of the treacherous Laomedon to be his wife. Her brother Priam, upon assuming the throne, prepared at once for another war and sent Antenor to Greece to request the return of Hesione. Dares reports that Antenor went round to all the heroes who had supported Hercules: first to Peleus, then Telamon, then Castor and Pollux, and finally Nestor. All spurned him and he returned to Troy to report the insult and recommend war. Then Paris offers to lead a fleet against the Greeks and gives a most peculiar basis for his confidence: he dreamed that the goddesses came to him for adjudication, and Venus had promised him the fairest woman in Greece for his vote. Thus Venus would support him in this military expedition. Priam accordingly sends Paris with Polydamas, Aeneas, and Deiphobus to Sparta. They are to seek satisfaction from Castor and Pollux (but not from Telamon, who has Hesione!), and failing in this they should send word to Priam to launch the fleet.

It is clear enough that Dares and Dracontius differ in important ways in their presentation of these events, and the same will be true when we consider the later stage of the story, the abduction itself. Even here, the actions themselves and the agents are both different. It is Antenor who goes on the peaceful embassy, not Paris, and he goes to several places, not merely to Telamon. On the second embassy Antenor takes no part. For Dracontius, however, there is but one embassy, and Paris leads it with Antenor playing a major role (he speaks first). Dares, in an effort to link the pursuit of Hesione with the start of the war, sends the embassy to Sparta rather than to Salamis where the captive is living: only thus can Paris encounter Helen without another grand tour of Greece. Dracontius avoids this problem another way, by separating the two events almost entirely and relocating Helen to Cyprus. Perhaps more significant is the fact that for Dares, Paris takes the initiative, whereas Dracontius has Priam suggest the mission quite casually, as something to occupy Paris. The link to Hesione is incidental and almost intrusive in Dracontius. Paris could far more easily have gone seeking adventure and encountered Helen exactly as he does without the slightest reference to Hesione or the other Trojan legates.

Why then has he combined the stories in this awkward manner? I suspect the answer may be that the elements had already been combined in the tradition, and Dracontius could not pass up the opportunity to tell a story relying so extensively on rhetorical presentations. That would seem to imply that he had already encountered Dares' version. I shall consider this whole question again, but I am inclined to think that Dares may have preceded Dracontius, and to explain certain peculiar details as due to Dracontius' misunderstanding of Dares.[29]

In contrast to the lengthy debate reported by Dares, there is no discussion here whatever. Priam summons the *tres proceres;* they learn their destination and set out. The Carthaginian poet's geography of the Aegean leaves us agape:

> Dardana iam Tenedon classis transibat, Abydon
> et Seston dimisit aquis curvasque Maleas;
> iam Salamina vident Telamonia regna petentes. (246–48)

The fact that the poet can send his fleet both southwest and northeast at the same time is evidence of his ignorance in these matters and may shed some light on his later confusion about where the abduction itself occurs.[30]

The Greek king receives the embassy hospitably, and the Trojans are briefly placed in an unfavorable light:

> ramos frondentis olivae
> portantes ad tecta ducis sub imagine pacis
> non pacem, sed bella gerunt: nam dicta tenebant,
> quae possent armare virum, nisi iura vetarent
> hospitii, quae nemo parat violare modestus. (254–58)

Why set up the scene in this way? The Trojans have come in orderly manner, ready to discuss the return of Hesione and bearing the symbols of peace. We have had no suggestion that they are treacherous in their intent, and their speeches will be honorable and diplomatic. It is Telamon who is intemperate, and Dracontius himself points this out. Two explanations come to mind for this accusation of bellicose intent. First, the Trojans must ultimately be seen in an unfavorable light, since the major outcome of this whole voyage will be the war over Helen. The blame must therefore rest with the Trojan side; they do indeed bring war. The objection to this argument is that the war does not arise from the Hesione question at all, and in this setting they are not at fault. It could be further argued that the Trojans are necessarily doomed to failure, as the rest of the story must be worked out, including the abduction and the war. Hesione is not to be rescued, therefore the Trojans must bungle the mission. But this flies in the face of the poet's characterization of Telamon: it is he who scuttles the negotiations and decrees that the Trojans will leave empty-handed.

The other possible explanation for this accusation of warlike intent is that in Dracontius' sources the Trojans were bent on war at this stage of the action. This is in fact what we find in Dares: Paris' embassy is the prelude to a declaration of war. It is another reason for thinking that Dracontius had Dares available to him and restructured the story along original lines without altogether eliminating contradictory elements from his source.

The greatest novelty in Dracontius' treatment is the full-scale debate of Telamon and the Trojan legates. This is much the lengthiest presentation of the embassy.[31] The poet gives us three major speeches: Antenor (261–84), Telamon (292–326), Polydamas (328–48), and a briefer final statement by Aeneas (373–78). The most surprising aspect of this scene is that Paris, who was the legate originally selected by Priam, says not a word throughout the visit to Salamis. His inactivity may be explained by the fact that in the tradition as represented in Dares it is Antenor who goes to Salamis and who speaks to Telamon. When Paris goes, it is to Sparta and as prelude to war, and the party in fact never reaches its destination. This makes it more likely, in my opinion, that Dracontius was looking at the tradition found in Dares, quite possibly at the *De excidio Troiae* itself. Paris has no role to play here, and accordingly says nothing. He is along in order to be available for the real adventure which awaits him in Cyprus.

The poet has expended much effort on the three major speeches. Each of the speakers has a clearly developed character, and his speech is an effective illustration of its type. Quartiroli lamented that the rhetorician-lawyer could not make the switch to epic poet and that these speeches are the proof;[32] but in fact these are notably superior to the declamatory pieces in the *Romulea* (IV, V, and IX). They work well together as a minidrama, even as the three speeches in the first segment created the impression of a short tragic drama with its *deus ex machina* to conclude (Aeneas fulfills somewhat the same role here).

Antenor leads off *placida voce*. His words are a careful blend of diplomacy and veiled threat. He emphasizes the importance of the Trojan mission, and the high dignity of those who have come to the court of Telamon. Yet he cannot undervalue the status of Telamon, who is both king and victor. His ploy is to make constant and elaborate reference to rank—of both the Trojans and Telamon—so as to leave no doubt in the listener's mind that all parties speak as equals by nature (even if not by current circumstance).

> Troiugenas proceres et regis pignus ad aulam,
> rex Telamon venisse tuam quae causa coegit,
> insinuare decet. (261–63)

Proceres picks up for our benefit on a word which the poet has used four times in the last thirty lines (235, 244, 252, 261). These are the pick of the Trojan nobility; and in addition the son of the king himself is present.[33] This juxtaposition of *regis pignus* and *rex* already suggests the equality of the two parties, and when we add the grandiloquence of *Troiugenas proceres,* the weight is on the side of the Trojans. But Antenor picks up on the sound of *rex,* and plays it like a continuo throughout his remarks. In the space of 24 lines, we find some form of *rex* (including *regia*) nine times;[34] *regnum* three times;[35] and the syllable *re* no fewer than 24 times. The effect of the sound shifts subtly from grandness to irony and comes close to mockery by the end of the speech.

The balance is enhanced by Antenor's piling up of the Trojans' credentials—note also *regia proles* (264) and *Dardanides Priamus* (265)—intertwined with his recognition of what Telamon is: *rex* (262), *tua regna, potens* (268), *heroes* (268), and what he has achieved (266). Yet Priam is *gentis reparator et urbis* (265). It is a stalemate in the areas of lineage and valor. This allows the legate to advance his plea for favor in a far different tone from that of a simple suppliant.

Bellorum quam iure tenes in pace refundas (269). A prize of war need not be kept in time of peace. The next sentence shows the poet's skill as a pleader:

> iacet ingens Troia favillis
> excidii compressa sui, nec Pergama ductor
> surrexisse putat, nisi iam, rex magne, sororem
> reddideris regi, quae nunc captiva tenetur. (270–73)

Ingens Troia is both a recognition of the scale of Telamon's victory and—now that Troy has recovered—an implied threat.[36] Note however that Antenor simply assumes that the restoration of Troy is a goal which Telamon will applaud, and thus that the return of Hesione is a logical request. As befits a city now back on equal footing, king is to make restitution to king; and Antenor's tone finally hardens perceptibly as he bluntly states that Hesione *captiva tenetur.*

The center of gravity of the conversation has shifted: Antenor has succeeded in making Priam the dominant figure

in the negotiations. The Trojan king will regard it as an offense on Telamon's part if the matter is not resolved: *pro
rege rogaris* (276). This is a bold stance indeed for the envoy to adopt, but he presses even further. Imagine, he says,
that the situation were reversed and Priam held your sister: would you not be aggrieved? *Non dolor armaret, si non
daret ille rogatus?* (278) introduces for the first time the notion of retaliation rather than mere supplication. Antenor
develops the picture of Priam suffering the derision of his
allies and his people, and this might seem a feeble way to
end his oration. But he has already planted the idea of
Priam and Telamon exchanging circumstances, so the uncomfortable image can apply to the Greek as well as the
Trojan. Small wonder that Telamon is not amused.

Antenor has played his cards skillfully. He has placed the
victor and the vanquished on equal footing, and implied
that not only moral justice but the prospect of retribution
requires the return of the king's sister.

Telamon's reaction is intense and angry. This is no mere
possessiveness over a prize of war, but a husband and father
repelling an assault on his family.[37]

> conubium regni, thalami consortia casti
> scindere poscebant, et, quod mens nulla tulisset,
> Aiacis haec mater erat! (288–90)

With a single stroke the poet has turned the picture around.
We had obscurely seen Telamon like Paris, coming and taking away a woman to whom he had no genuine claim and
thereby causing trouble. But now the Greek king appears
as one with legitimate ties to Hesione. He is another Menelaus, and here are Paris and company trying to carry his
wife off to Troy. In light of this, Telamon is stirred to righteous anger (*iusta successus in ira* (291)—as he begins his
reply to the Trojan envoy. This makes all the more startling
his abrasive and uncompromising words. It is the reverse of
the poet's censure of the Trojans preceding Antenor's diplomatic speech.

Telemon wastes no time with tact or polite preliminaries. The embassy itself he regards as a fresh provocation:

> si *p*udor Iliacis aut mentibus esset honestas,
> excidium Troiae si *p*ectora victa dolerent,
> Herculeos comites, *P*riami gens, *p*raeda *P*elasgum,
> non magis auderent in bella lacessere Graios
> semideum *p*ost bella ducum, quibus Ilios ingens
> victa iacet. *p*lacuitne *P*hrygis *p*eriuria gentis
> solvere vos iterum? (292–98)

Telamon's rhetoric is a counterbalance to Antenor's. Whereas the first speaker had worked at implying the equality of the two sides, Telamon never even refers to Priam as a king. And while Antenor has given texture to his whole speech by the echoing alliteration of *re*, Telamon punctuates his words with a persistent, indignant *p* working from the name of the conquered Priam. Line 294 sets up the contrast between the two sides perfectly, with *Herculeos comites* at one end and *praeda Pelasgum* at the other. The Trojan's reference to *ingens Troia* (with its Vergilian echo) is now turned back on him (296); if there was any threat implied in Antenor's words, that is scornfully cast aside now with Telamon's sarcastic rejoinder.[38]

We should not ignore the dramatic irony of Telamon's question in 297–98. He assumes that the demands now being made will constitute the second instance of *periuria;* but of course it is the silent Paris, in a quite different way, who by his *periuria* will bring the house of Priam down again.

Telamon's position is elaborated in a series of indignant rhetorical questions (300–10) which amount to the simple claim that to the victor belong the spoils. He includes further reference to his legitimate marriage to Hesione, which again reminds us of what Paris is about to do.[39]

His finest rhetorical points come in 311ff. Antenor had made much of the fact that Troy has been restored to prosperity, and that the Trojan king sought his beloved sister as a matter of right.

SALAMIS (LINES 213–384)   111

si Priami recidiva domus manet illa tyranni
post ignes reparata meos, si pendit amorem
germanae rex ipse suae, pro dote sorori
vel regni pars iusta detur, ne vindicet Aiax
quod matri donasset avus, si Troia maneret. (311–15)

Telamon accepts the Trojan claim and promptly turns it into
a basis for Greek claims: my wife never brought with her
the dowry I should have gained, and I am delighted to
learn you can now pay that debt. So far from discussing the
return of Hesione, Telamon has converted her status into a
premise for further demands. Moreover, the claim is to be
enforced by her son (Priam's nephew), who will come to
Troy to collect what is his by right; it is hard not to think of
Paris who has so recently returned to Troy for the same purpose, and who will in fact be the cause for Ajax' impending
attack on that city. Telamon does not know that, and his
words work well on their own terms as an imperious rejoinder to Antenor; but the poet has also managed to link
what is happening in Salamis with the action of the rest of
the poem by the dramatic irony which runs through the
entire scene.

The idea of forces ready to attack Troy is developed in
Telamon's final lines. Ajax is not only capable of defeating
the Trojans, he is even now restless and seeking whom he
may devour. There follows a short catalogue of heroes (321–
326) who will distinguish themselves in the Trojan War:
Achilles and Patroclus, plus other looming figures from the
Iliad:

Tydides Sthenelusque fremunt Aiaxque secundus;
Nestoris Antilochus Palamedes Teucer Ulixes
exultant quod Troia redit, quod Pergama surgunt.

And on this note of mocking, Telamon ends. He has effectively answered the Trojan claim with rhetorical fencing
and with bullying rudeness. He has no more doubts about
the outcome of a Trojan war than his readers do. His words

are a reinforcement of the prediction given by Helenus and Cassandra in the first segment of the poem.

The third speaker, Polydamas, takes Telamon's warning to heart, and speaks *submissa voce*. Like Telamon he picks up on what he has just heard and turns it to his own rhetorical advantage.

> belliger armipotens, animarum iudicis heres,
> rex cui de nostris est gloria summa ruinis,
> temperet invidia, frangat dolor, ira quiescat. (328–30)

He not only acknowledges Telamon's prowess in war and implicitly accepts the Greek's assertion of superiority, but also notes that Telamon's father Aeacus was judge of the souls of the dead. In a symbolic sense this function has now been passed on to the son, for Telamon is passing judgment on the city of Troy, already crushed once and now trying to rise from its grave. It will plunge again to its death in the war.

As Telamon had emphasized that the bonds of marriage and family made it unthinkable for him to return Hesione, so now Polydamas picks up that line of thought: a brother seeks to regain his sister, made all the more precious by her new status as a queen. *Reginam frater honorat, / nos et adoramus.* With this twist Polydamas introduces a very neat ploy. Hesione has fared better than she could ever have done in Troy.

> regnum captiva meretur,
> fit felix de sorte mala, fit praeda potestas,
> imperium de clade tenet, diadema tiaram
> qui tulit ipse dedit. (333–36)

Far from humiliating the Trojans, Telamon has flattered them by elevating the sister of Priam to reign over the Greeks (*haec imperat Argis*). Why should any army wish to defeat the Greeks when by losing they can gain so much more? Indeed, the Greeks by their policy of generosity increase the number and status of kings. As Polydamas warms

to his topic, we hear once more the *re* which had marked
Antenor's speech. Note especially 340ff.:

> miranda per orbem
> mens generosa ducis, quae non vult *regna* grava*re*,
> cum ruerint virtute tua: *releva*re iacentes
> et *reges regnare* iubes *reges*que c*reare*.
> dum possint servi*re* tibi.

He thus returns to the essential point made by Antenor at
the outset, namely, that this is a conversation between
regal interlocutors, and that Telamon should not conclude
too readily that he holds all the cards. Polydamas' final
words are ambiguous (or ironic) enough to disturb even the
slowest wits:

> qui vicerit hostis
> serviet, et victi melius te praesule regnant. (347–48)

Polydamas has thus conceded that Telamon is in control,
but in view of Hesione's exalted position there is reason to
regard her as having won rather than lost. We might think
that this was Polydamas' purpose: to make Telamon regret
what he has done and impel him to send the Trojan princess
back to her own people rather than continue to compliment
her homeland by having her as his queen. If so, the ruse is
entirely unsuccessful, for Telamon is mollified by Polydamas' words—a puzzling result, since the irony seems so
heavy. Telamon should either be taken in by the ploy (if
such it is) and release Hesione or be much offended if he
sees through it. It is no compliment to the Greek hero to
have the matter end as it does.

The poet indulges in a lengthy simile to convey the relax-
ing of the king's anger. Dracontius perhaps intended it to be
Homeric in manner, since it compares the hero to a raging
lion and the Trojans to a hunter; it is certainly epic in scale
(350–64). It is also remarkably silly: as a lion when pursued
by a hunter will fly into a rage and threaten the hunter with

roars and lashings of his tail, but if the hunter throws away
his weapon and plays dead on the ground, the lion will
scorn to eat what it has not killed for itself and will leave
him alone—so Telamon was instantly mollified by Polydamas' admission of defeat. The silliness is all the more
striking after the skillful rhetoric of the three speeches just
concluded.

Interestingly, Dracontius uses the same comparison in
Satisfactio (137–48) in asking Gunthamund to pardon him.
The basic idea of the lion suddenly sparing a hunter who
plays possum is no less bizarre in the *Satisfactio* than in
Helen, but at least there it has a clear application, and the
poet works out the elements of the comparison. The two
passages are obviously related (*Sat.* 143 is identical with
Hel. 360). I believe that the more natural placement of the
comparison in *Satisfactio*, and its more appropriate usage,
indicates that the poet first wrote it for the *Satisfactio*, and
subsequently adapted it to this passage, which similarly involves a plea to a king for clemency and release. If this is
true, then the *Helen* is a relatively late work of Dracontius,
falling at least into the period of incarceration and possibly
even after it. At any rate, the epyllion will not be a work of
the poet's relative youth as we may presume *Hylas* to be;
and this in turn indicates that the poet pursued his interest
in the miniature epic and pagan themes into a later time of
his poetic career than is frequently imagined.

Telamon invites the delegation to enjoy his hospitality for
a week, and the Trojans have a chance to converse ami-
ably with their kinsmen. Hesione is glad to meet with her
nephew Paris, in whose countenance she sees the image of
her dear brother Priam (368), and we see an encounter of
two heroes who are also related.

> Cythereus et Aiax
> colloquium commune tenent, duo fulmina belli. (364–65)

It is a small touch, but the meeting of these cousins who
will soon be foes continues the theme, which runs through

the entire poem, of kinsmen who are set at odds (Paris and his brothers, Helen and her husband, and others) while enemies conquer and marry (Telamon and Paris are alike in this respect).

After the week of hospitality the Trojans are ready to return home. Aeneas delivers a brief farewell (373–78), in which he acknowledges the state of affairs as Telamon has defined it (note that he twice calls Telamon *rex*, and by contrast simply refers to Priam by name without any title whatever). But however great Telamon's accomplishments, says the Trojan prince, Ajax will be the mightiest of them all. This comment takes us forward from the present moment of conciliatory rhetoric to the realization that another war lies ahead as the result of the legation's failure. Aeneas picks up on Telamon's command—*Priamo, Troes, mea dicta referte* (299)—with his last words: *Priamo tua dicta loquemur*. It is likely that Dracontius has assigned this role to Aeneas in imitation of the Buthrotum episode of *Aeneid* 3, where Aeneas likewise takes his leave of an exiled Trojan princess who had fallen to the lot of a conquering Greek prince. His words of farewell to Telamon, *felix in pace senesce*, carry an echo of the farewell to the inhabitants of Buthrotum, *vivite felices . . . vobis parta quies*.[40] It also has more than a formulaic value, since if Telamon grows old in peace, he will not be attacking Troy, and the Trojans can enjoy the same luxury.

With these words, the embassy departs from Salamis. Nothing whatever has been achieved, either for the stated goal of this embassy or for Paris. We have seen the inevitability of a second Trojan war, but in the context of a quarrel which will have no further relevance. Paris has played no part in this mission. The legates will report to Priam when they return (585ff.), but that is the only link between this scene and the rest of the poem.

We must return to the question of why Dracontius developed the embassy scene as he did. No doubt the rhetorical opportunities were an inducement, and he has exploited them enthusiastically. Dares, I believe, was available to him and provided such details as Antenor in the role of chief legate.[41] But there were two other considerations which shaped the scene.

First, I would venture to point to Dictys Cretensis' account of events following the abduction of Helen (*De bello Troiano* 1.4–9). The story has much in common with Dracontius' narrative, and I think may have suggested a design for the entire segment. After Menelaus lost Helen to Paris' attack on his city, says Dictys, the Greek king called his council and decided to send three legates (cf. Dracontius' *tres proceres*) to ask the Trojans to return his wife. Those chosen are Palamedes, Ulysses, and Menelaus himself. When they reach Troy, they cannot meet with Paris because—exactly as in Dracontius—he has been blown off course *to Cyprus* en route home. Dictys then follows Paris' adventures in the East Mediterranean including his treacherous slaying of Phoenix of Sidon, which leads to a battle on the beach with the local populace.

Meanwhile at Troy, Palamedes addresses Priam on behalf of the embassy. His arguments are arranged somewhat like Antenor's in our poem. He complains of the injury done the Greeks, warns Priam obscurely of the clash which must result from this action, and recalls previous quarrels between Greeks and Trojans (in this instance the rape of Ganymede). He closes with a contrast between the hardships of war and the *commoda* of peace and touches again on Greek indignation. Priam cuts him off even as he is speaking (not unlike Telamon's brusque response to Antenor) and points out that, since Paris is not in Troy, there is little point in pursuing the argument. Antenor then plays host to the legates and takes them to his home. Is this where Dares and/or Dracontius got the idea to have Antenor play a lead role in the embassy and to include a period of hospitality after the debate?

A few days later Paris returns to Troy with Helen, and there is acrimonious dispute among the Trojans whether to surrender Helen or support Paris (a topic which finds no place at this stage of Dracontius' story but recalls the earlier debate on allowing Paris to be admitted to Troy); but

suddenly a battle erupts within the Trojan populace, which
Dictys says was halted only *interventu procerum . . . duce
Antenore*. This language and Antenor's leading role coin-
cide again with Dracontius' account of the Trojan embassy.

I believe that Dictys' narrative has suggested to the poet
a sequence of events and even some aspects of the debate.
The references to Antenor, the three *proceres*, Paris' detour to Cyprus, and other details encourage this view.

But the two scenes are not designed exactly alike. There
is a second influence at work: Dracontius' love of structural
parallels within his poems. That has led him to construct
this segment along the same lines as the first part of the
poem:

a. Paris' dissatisfaction with his lot, which stirs him to
travel (to Troy/to Greece);

b. a debate involving three speeches (Paris, Helenus,
Cassandra/Antenor, Telamon, Polydamas) which include
the themes of a son claiming what he should have had long
ago (Paris' birthright/Ajax' property by his mother) and
pointed predictions of the fall of Troy;

c. a period of festivity which follows the dispute somewhat unnaturally;

d. a final speech accepting the earlier arguments and
putting a peaceful end to the scene (Apollo/Aeneas).

Dracontius' fondness for such architectural parallels has
led him to develop the scene more fully than the economy
of the poem requires, but such is his habit elsewhere as
well. It is jarring only because Paris has now played no role
in the poem—and Helen has not even been hinted at—for
nearly 200 lines. We will now be concentrating on our hero
for the remainder of the poem.

Storm at sea (385-434)

It was a time-honored device of epic to move the hero from
one adventure to the next by means of a storm driving his
fleet off course. The adventures of Odysseus are the earliest and most famous instance of this device which persists

through the life of epic poetry. It is interesting to note that the *Cypria* made use of such a storm as well, driving Paris, after his abduction of Helen, all the way to Sidon.[42] Dictys also reports that Paris went from Greece to Cyprus, and thence to Phoenicia (1.5), and we have seen already how Dracontius may have used Dictys. At any rate, it is safe to conclude that Dracontius did not invent the basic idea of a stopover at Cyprus but found it in the tradition and used it in novel ways, as was his wont.

There is no question, however, about Dracontius' model for the storm scene. He uses the storm from the *Aeneid* (1.83ff.): there, Aeneas finds himself at the mercy of a storm, laments his lot in life by wishing he might have stayed in Troy, and after the storm is driven to Carthage where he meets the queen who will cause so much grief for him. This is exactly the shape of this scene: Paris laments his new career as a sailor and is then swept off to Cyprus where he encounters Helen, fully as troublesome for the future as Dido. That Dracontius specifies the wind is *Africus* merely draws attention to his source the more clearly.

One significant difference between Dracontius and the earlier treatments of Paris' storm is the sequence of events. Previously, the storm had occurred after the abduction and was part of the adventure which brought Paris and Helen back to Troy. Now, however, as in Vergil, the storm is a prelude to the most significant event, the abduction itself, and to the trouble which ensues.

Indeed, the storm serves more than one purpose. It separates the dramatic events in Salamis from the scene in Cyprus, both in the sense of an entr'acte which diverts the reader and distinguishes the two stages of the action, and also in a more practical manner. Paris must obviously go to meet Helen unattended by the full Trojan delegation, and the storm is an easy way to free him from this company.

In this regard, we are inevitably reminded of the basic irrelevance of the Salamis episode. Paris had played no role in that scene and did not even appear to be one of the legates. This impression is confirmed now as the storm comes up,

obriguit per membra Paris, transire parabat
ad legatorum propria de nave carinas. (398–99)

Clearly the Salamis story and the abduction story were two
different narratives, and the poet is trying to get from one
to the other. We saw this same problem in *Medea* between
the Colchis and Thebes episodes. Here Dracontius must
rid Paris of the company and dispose of all links with the
Salamis episode in order to concentrate on the Helen story.
The story from Dares' tradition got Paris to Greece but became an encumbrance once Paris played no part in the embassy and still had made no progress on the abduction.

For these reasons the other ships of the fleet are blown
away from Paris' own, and he finds himself alone in the
storm. This brings on a fine description of the storm itself—among Dracontius' most successful lines[43]—and
Paris' mournful commentary on his lot.

We have heard Paris discontented before. In fact, every
move he makes is prefaced by grumblings about his situation, and this lament serves to advance the action in the
same way as lines 61ff. and 213ff. On Ida, Paris was tired of
being a shepherd, and longed to be a ruler; once he was accepted in the royal house, he wearied of the life of an idle
prince and longed to set forth as a sailor to seek adventure.
He has now found it, and now he wants only to return to
the peaceful existence of a shepherd! The poet's fondness
for employing parallel incidents or motifs to introduce suc-
cessive segments of a poem is all too evident here.

The lament itself is obviously modelled on Aeneas' cry of
despair and frustration (1.89ff.), but the poet has adapted
that model to the present situation. Paris regrets leaving
the carefree life of the shepherd, and his words seem specifically to cancel out the rejection of that life found in 61ff.
In a way, they reinforce the words of Apollo who commands
the Trojans not to despise Paris for his pastoral history (206–
10). Paris himself seemed eager to repudiate that past immediately thereafter, but now it holds far greater appeal,
and the god's assessment is proven accurate. The passage is

filled with Vergilian reminiscences, from both the *Eclogues*
and the *Georgics*,[44] and is suffused with affection for the
shepherd's life as well as horror at the prospect of death at
sea. A few lines will suffice:

> felici sorte creati
> pastores, quos terra capit, quos nulla procella
> concutit. haut ponti metuunt super aequora fluctus
> et rabidum pelagus temnunt latrantibus undis,
> sed celso de monte vident ut in arce sedentes
> pascua rura nemus fontes sata[45] flumina prata,
> per campos gestire pecus, pendere capellas
> praerupta de rupe procul dumeta sequentes. (402–409)

Yet at the end of this comparison the hero concludes that he
is glad not to be a *ruler*, which really takes us back to his
essential character and the choice, which has confronted
him all through the poem, between *pastor* and *dux*. As if to
underscore that these are the alternatives, Dracontius calls
Paris *pastor* as he lands on Cyprus (432).

Even as the storm scene is an entr'acte between Salamis
and Cyprus, so the prince's lament is a quiet pause between
two blasts of tempest which carry him to the island. The
storm resumes and interrupts him and deposits him on the
Cypriot shore. The shepherd-prince-ambassador-sailor is
ready to meet Venus' reward.

Cyprus (435–585)

It has been a long wait for Paris to get to meet Helen, and
we are two-thirds of the way through the poem before he
comes into contact with her. Much of what has preceded
appears to be unrelated to the actual abduction, and yet as
will be clearer when we consider the over-all structure of
the poem, the various elements contribute to a single architecture. Meanwhile, as we read the Cyprus episode,
certain features of plot strike us as familiar and even expected, having been encountered elsewhere in this poem
and also in *Medea*, and in other models.

Dracontius has borrowed freely as well as invented in this segment. The combination of originality and borrowing has led him into some peculiar contradictions. It is clear that Dracontius used a source which placed the abduction in Sparta, and when he decided to relocate the scene to Cyprus, he did not eliminate some details which make sense only if the scene is set in Sparta.

We should not be surprised that Paris arrives at the island during a festival of Venus, for we are constantly reminded of the way in which his actions impinge on the realm of the divine. But there are other models which play a part: Hippolytus and Phaedra meet in a festival of Aphrodite, and the meeting of Jason and Medea traditionally occurs in the temple of that goddess. But the most fundamental reason for the setting is that Venus is the one who has promised Paris his reward, and he is now to receive it: what better place than in the presence of the goddess herself?

I take this association with Venus' natal island to be the reason for the change of locale from the traditional setting in Sparta. The poet found encouragement for a connection with Cyprus in the fact that Paris is elsewhere reported to have visited Cyprus, as we have seen, *after* carrying Helen off from Sparta,[46] but nowhere else is the abduction itself set there. The advantages for the poet are two: he can bring out the connection with Venus not merely by having Helen act under compulsion of the goddess but by having her do so in the goddess' own birthplace; and he can more effectively set Helen alone and apart from her home surroundings, so that the decision to leave with Paris is more clearly her own. As an additional practical consideration, there are fewer persons around to dissuade or prevent her from this act.[47]

The poet's vague sense of geography has again led him astray. There can be no doubt the action is supposed to take place in Cyprus, and the recitation of Cypriot places sacred to Venus is conventional enough—except for *tacitas Amyclas*, which returns us at once to Laconia (even the epithet *tacitas* underscores the association with that laconic region):

Cypro festa dies natalis forte Dionae
illa luce fuit. veniunt ad sacra Cytherae
reddere vota deae quidquid capit insula Cypros,
quod nemus Idalium, quod continet alta Cythera,
quod Paphon exornat, tacitas quod lustrat Amyclas. (435–39)

There is perhaps more. The island of Cythera, off the Lace-daemonian coast, figures in Dares' account of the abduction (ch. 9); it seems that Dracontius has blurred the distinction between *Cythera* and *Cytherea* and combined the topography of the two areas, one pertinent to the prevailing tradition and the other pertinent to the birthplace of Venus. It is worth noting that these are the only occurrences of *Cythera* in Dracontius referring to Venus or Cyprus: elsewhere he uses either the Greek *Cythere* or the Latin *Cytherea* (indeed, he has just called Aeneas *Cythereus* in line 364). Such a confusion is likely only if Dracontius is working with a source which sets the action in Sparta, and it is all the more natural if he is using a source such as Dares where the epithet actually occurs at this point in the action. Finally, we may observe that Menelaus has gone to Crete (441), which also takes us back to the central Mediterranean instead of its eastern extremity.

The next lines offer further evidence that a Spartan locale lurks in the back of the poet's mind. The scene is inevitably influenced by Aeneas' arrival and reception in Carthage, in which word is brought to Dido at the palace that a stranger has arrived. The motif is repeated here with curious results:

nuntia fama ducis totam repleverat urbem
advenisse Parin Troiano sanguine cretum.[48]
audit ut adventum iuvenis Spartana decori,
mox iubet et famuli veniunt mandante Lacaena:
hospitio speratus eat, nam turpe videri,
regina praesente Paris ceu navita vilis
litus harenosum teneat. tunc hospes ad aulam
pervolat Atridis socia comitante caterva. (442–49)

Clearly Helen is inviting Paris to her home: indeed, the palace is expressly called *aula Atridis*. It would be understandable if a temporary residence of the queen were called her *aula*, but to call it the hall of Atrides takes us unmistakably back to Sparta. Note also that Paris is called *hospes* after being *pastor* so often in the past hundred lines or so. The necessary relationship of violated hospitality is being set up, even in this place away from the home of either party. Paris is not to be left like a common sailor camping on the shore: in much the same terms Jason was perceived when he first landed in Colchis (*Med.* 44, *ceu nauta*) and fell into the control of his fateful love. But most important, Helen is already in charge of the situation, and Paris, despite being the *praedo* of the piece, is at her command from the very start. The contrast contained in line 447 between *regina praesente* and *Paris ceu navita vilis* sets forth the whole picture.

Thus Paris hastens to the royal hall to accept the hospitality of the unknown queen. En route he observes the crowd of worshippers at the temple of Venus and bends his steps in the same direction. We may note that in the structure of the action, this visit to the temple has the same value and place as the digression in *Medea* which takes us away to the heavens to hear of Venus' plans and intervention (49ff.). Once again, and most fittingly here, the goddess breaks in on the action before the climactic encounter between the two lovers. In this instance, it is the mere presence of her temple and worshippers, as she is to play no direct role (the same is true of all the gods) in the economy of the poem. Thus in this humanized story her temple and the events around it are the equivalent of the digression to heaven in the other poem.

This detour to the temple of Venus brings Paris into contact with a prodigious display of bird omens, which spell out the disaster to come as clearly as if Venus herself had described it to Cupid. The use of birds for this purpose lends point to the poet's description of Helen, when she was first introduced in 440, as *Iovis alitis proles*. The off-

spring of the swan is to become entangled in a fate now
spelled out for us in kindred symbols: [49]

> interea nivei volitant per litora cycni
> flumine contempto, placidas hinc inde columbas
> molliter intendunt omnes per inane vagari,
> quas insanus agit rapidusque sequente volatu
> milvus insontes cunctas clamore fatigat,
> quas super accipiter volitans gravis imminet ales. (453–58)

It is excessive to have such a flock of omens, but we are
given a full translation by the augur who witnesses them.
Chance has brought him to the island—no doubt to be on
hand for precisely this event—and he volunteers the following interpretation. The doves obviously are the sign of
an impending marriage; the presence of swans betokens a
daughter of Jupiter as the bride (as was emphasized when
Helen was introduced as *alitis proles*). The danger signs are
equally clear: the kite which routs the doves is a token of
the death to come from this alliance (the omen is all the
more alarming for bringing a bird of the night out in broad
daylight); and looming over all is the fierce hawk whose
presence signifies the war ahead.[50] Thus the descendant of
Melampus interprets.[51] But there is perhaps more to observe in this omen. The swan has wandered away from the
river, by which it usually stays, to come to the shore: so
Helen has strayed from Sparta to this festival without her
husband. The meek doves (who must stand both for the notion of marriage and also, as the darlings of Venus, for Paris
himself) have wandered *per inane* even as Paris has done.
Both the relative intensity and energy of the two characters
and also their recent activities are shown in this omen.

Paris prays to Venus to fulfill the positive portion of this
prodigy and asks the augur to avert the alarming half (472–
80), incidentally tossing in the otherwise unattested notion
that Ganymede was the founder of the art of prophecy along
with one Polles, *cui pinna loquax dat nosse futura* (480).[52]
With this precaution, Paris now enters the temple of

Venus, where he is to meet Helen. The Vergilian model
plays its part once more: the meeting of that other Trojan
prince and his Carthaginian queen likewise took place in a
temple (in that instance the temple of Juno), from which
they repaired to the palace. Despite his regal presence,
Paris is again *pastor* at the very moment of his entry into
the temple (489), even as we see the queen coming to meet
him.[53] In this scene Paris is never called a prince by either
the poet or Helen.

Helen falls hopelessly in love and does so in the most traditional style. She questions Paris on his origins (although
her excitement in 441 had been stirred by the news that
the Trojan prince Paris had arrived, so she seems to know
enough already). In the middle of her questions her passion and modesty get the better of her and she falls silent.
Paris does not answer her questions directly but turns instead to skillful flattery of his beautiful hostess (511–14).
He manages to introduce both her beauty and Menelaus'
presumable negligence in treating a deserving wife so badly.

Helen responds in decisive manner, in view of his distinguished quality:

> est commune genus: pariter tua regna petamus,
> sis mihi tu coniunx et sim tibi dignior uxor. (533–34)

Like Medea, Helen wastes no time once she has made up
her mind.

Morelli claims that Helen's speech is similar to what Colluthus offers (*Rapt. Hel.* 265ff.).[54] But the whole scene is
very different in the two poets. In Colluthus' version Helen
does not know who Paris is; she makes the usual formulaic
inquiries about his background (as hosts have done since
Homer) but stresses that she does not know who he is. Paris
on the other hand announces that Aphrodite has promised
him a fair beauty named Helen, and he immediately proposes to her. He says nothing specific in praise of her beauty,
but talks at length of his own genealogy and merits (which
Dracontius has just told us Paris declined to do). The only

point in common is that in both poems the hero refers to his descent from Jupiter. Morelli's notion that Dracontius derived his version from Colluthus is patently erroneous. The fact that earlier authors did not describe in detail the meeting of Helen and Paris does not show any link between these two poets. Dracontius reflects the mainstream Latin tradition of the smitten princess, while Colluthus as usual follows the Greek side.[55]

As Helen takes charge, Dracontius breaks somewhat with the tradition of the submissive but helpful princess. While Paris was sweet-talking her, she was demure, but now she becomes aggressive, and Paris shrinks back into docility. Helen closes her case with two references to the fates as responsible for all that happens in any case (535, 539).

Once the princess has proposed, we do not even pause to hear Paris accept. The lovers speed toward the harbor in their haste to escape—from what? As with the departure of Jason and Medea from Colchis, Dracontius seems anxious to move abruptly from one phase of the action to the next without always taking enough care for the transition. There will soon be cause to hasten, but the emergency has not yet arisen. The poet has finished using one model or source and finds it difficult to move on to the next. The influence of Aeneas' meeting with Dido (and more remotely, the influence of Hippolytus-Phaedra) has shaped the scene up to this point; but now Dracontius is about to introduce a novelty, and his independence causes him a problem. His way of changing the pace is to have the woman become aggressive, again as in *Medea* (and *Orestes*, although there is a strong precedent in that story).

Helen's sense of urgency is not misplaced. Paris looks back to see a looming cloud of dust: it is Menelaus returning from Crete. This is yet another trace of the dominant version found in Dracontius' source, which placed the action in Sparta. For why is Menelaus arriving in Cyprus? He has not had time to hear of his wife's action, and has no genuine reason to come to Venus' temple on his own.[56] Nowhere else in the tradition does Menelaus come upon the couple as they are preparing to leave together. Dracontius has apparently introduced the incident chiefly as a source of suspense and to display the character of his two leading figures. The ploy does little to enhance Paris in the reader's eyes.

> tunc Paris adloquitur comitantem praedo rapinam:
> "occidimus, regina, pares, nos Graia iuventus
> insequitur gladio vestigia nostra sequaci;
> captatum pervenit iter quicunque satelles
> coniugis Atridis, subnixus et hospite turma,
> mox armatorum rapiens ad bella cohortes:
> et mecum fortasse cades, si tela sequentur." (544–50)

The poet is hardly convincing when he suddenly reverts to calling Paris *praedo* and Helen his *rapina*. Dracontius has inherited a tradition which views Paris this way, and he must reflect it at the moment of their departure. In fact, Paris' words remind us of Jason's hand wringing when Medea assumed control of their situation. His alarm is almost comical as he stands contemplating the impending assault, and his final line hardly restores his heroic chivalry. He thinks only of defeat and death, not even of resistance. A fine figure of a *praedo* indeed!

It is Helen who sums up the practicalities of the situation, and the contrast with Paris' mewling is pejorative in the extreme:

> tunc Spartana refert: "iuvenis, quid nostra retardas
> pectora colloquiis? Phrygibus tamen arma capessant,
> rex dilecte, iube, gressus celerare ministros
> imperio compelle tuo: properamus ad aequor,
> et vacat e iussis concurrens turba ministris." (551–55)

Her words are impossible to hear without being bludgeoned by the sarcasm of *rex dilecte* and *imperio compelle tuo*. The deference of a wife to her husband is used with devastating effect. Her initial *iuvenis* does more to suggest the tone and relationship. And yet just as we are sure we have seen the poet's real perspective on the situation, he continues with a preposterously unconvincing simile: Helen clings to the neck of her abductor even as Europa clung to the back of mighty Jupiter when he carried her away. There are certainly points of comparison between the traditional view of Paris the abductor of Helen and Jupiter the abductor of Europa: both are wife-stealers, and both carry their victims away across the sea. The image does much to enhance Paris' stature by ranging him beside the divine figure and suggesting tremendous power. It also casts Helen as weak and clinging, the victim rather than the field commander. The aptness of the comparison for the traditional Paris suggests that Dracontius found it attached to the story and kept it, despite having introduced a fundamental alteration in both the sequence of events and the character of his hero and heroine.

Note that Jason is likewise compared to Jupiter, and Medea to Europa, at the equivalent point in their story (*Med.* 314ff.). It was hardly more appropriate there than here, for precisely the same reasons. As we saw there, it fell flat because Jason was not even leaving with Medea but was to remain in Colchis for years. Perhaps Dracontius derived these comparisons, so untimely in their use, from a collection of such comparisons, and he lacked the discrimination to employ them suitably.

At any rate, the heroic moment is badly undercut as this latter-day Jupiter reaches the shore with his Europa:

> ergo ubi pervenit raptor turbatus ad aequor
> et licet exhaustus cursu vel pondere lassus,
> qui gratum portabat onus, tamen ipse Lacaenam
> litore non posuit, media sed puppe locavit. (563–66)

A panting *praedo* staggering beneath the weight of his victim—who prods him with sarcasm to get him to the ship at all—is not a spectacle to stir us to admiration. It scarcely allows us to take the poet seriously at this critical juncture in the action, and the suspicion arises once more that Dracontius' aim may be partly parody as well as traditional depiction.

As Paris and Helen move out to sea, Menelaus comes upon the scene, too late to catch them but in time to vent his distress from the shoreline. His reaction, it must be said, is hardly more heroic than the Trojan's:

> ut conspexit amens sulcari puppibus undas
> et thalamos gestare suos, collisus harenis
> ingemit et flavos extorquet vertice crines. (574–76)

We would expect rage as in all other accounts of Menelaus' discovery all the more in this case since he is on hand to witness the deed, but instead the poet has the hero weep as for one dead. The image of savage strength reduced to bitter tears is developed as the poet concludes with an extended simile (577–85) comparing Menelaus to a ferocious tigress: the beast loses her cub in the wild and a hunter has captured it. She tracks the path of the hunter's horse until she reaches the river and sees the man already safe on the other side, then collapses in grief at her loss. It is a curious simile, almost certainly designed by the poet himself, as it matches the situation he is describing with almost mechanical precision. But therein lies its deficiency: why is the cub captured rather than killed by the hunter, and is lamentation the response one would naturally assign to a tigress deprived of her young? Does one not think instead of rage and lashing tails and loud roars? It is a curiously tame sort of tiger. As for Menelaus, he has been reduced to the same kind of weak and passive figure as Dracontius' other male heroes when confronted by women of Helen's ilk. Once again Helen has been given sole possession of center stage, as both men shrink by comparison.

The simile serves another purpose. The abduction itself has now taken place, and we must shift the scene from Cyprus to Troy. The helpless anguish of Menelaus after their departure closes the relevant action, and the lengthy simile serves as a sort of entr'acte before the action resumes in Troy with another set of characters.

Troy (586–637)

Although there is an abrupt shift as we cut away to Troy for the last scene, the details follow the pattern observed in earlier segments of the poem. Indeed, our first glimpse of Troy is like a mirror-image of what we just observed in Cyprus. Priam looks for his offspring, and when he does not see him he weeps helplessly. The simile of the tigress who mourns the lost cub applies just as aptly to Priam as to Menelaus and stands between the two scenes as if to show their relationship. Both Priam and Menelaus look out to sea for Paris, one seeing him retreat and the other hoping to see him approach.[57]

The ships which do reach Troy are the embassy to Salamis, and the segment is introduced accordingly, but in a most perfunctory manner:

> interea Aeneas rediens legatio Troiam
> venerat et Priamo Telamonis dicta reportat.
> sed Paridem genitor postquam non vidit amantum. (536–38)

The detail is necessary to tie together the major portions of the poem, and give the embassy some relevance. But Priam shows not the slightest concern with the results, offensive though they were, of this effort to recover his sister. He is wrapped up in the loss of his son. Moreover, Antenor's report (590–96) is entirely on the storm and the fate of the young *pastor.*

Priam's grief seems genuine enough, as does Antenor's. The same cannot be said for the Trojan community in general. All share in lamenting the death of the prince, but not because they have lost a hero:

> non pro virtutis honore
> aut quod talis erat qui posset bella subire

aut ingesta pati vel summis viribus hostem
frangere . . .
sed regis quia natus erat fit planctus in urbe. (599–602, 607)

It is hard to blame the people for this attitude. Paris has
shown no real signs of heroic valor, and his only escapade
thus far has been to run off with another man's wife. He
took no part in the first Trojan war and will cause the next.
The poet goes even further in his blunt assessment of Paris.
Even if Paris were a mighty warrior, to match Hercules or
Meleager, so long as Hector was safe nobody would miss
him (603–606). But there is the problem: Paris' disappearance would seem to assure Hector's survival, as his return
will ultimately doom him.

>   nam quicumque memor Heleni mox dicta tenebat
>   laetatur gaudens et tantum voce dolebat. (608–609)

Our attention is sent back to Paris' first unexpected arrival at Troy, and to the prophecies now to be fulfilled. The
tangled skein of truth and falsehood catches everyone: the
people give voice to a false lamentation believing Paris
dead, which is what they want but cannot say so. In fact
their belief is false, and they will soon grieve to see him
return but must then feign joy. As a symbol of all this,
Priam builds a cenotaph at which to vent the empty laments of Troy.[58]

At this very moment Paris' ship comes into view. The
Trojans recognize it by the sails with royal insignia (615).
Paris has festooned the ship with the myrtle of Venus in
celebration of his marriage: this is an exaggeration at best,
for there has been no wedding. It is a perfect symbol of
Paris' attitude and of the source of all the troubles to come.

Paris once more arrives during a religious celebration,
this one mourning his own death. The lament is premature
but ultimately quite relevant, reflecting as it does the prophecies of Helenus and Cassandra. As at his first return, his
parents embrace and welcome him:

occurrit ad undas
Hecuba cum Priamo populi comitante caterva,
suscipiunt sponsam, dat cunctis oscula pastor
ad patrem Priamum gradiens matremque salutans;
dulcia colla tenent et vultibus oscula figunt. (619–23)

They had welcomed him thus in 107ff. We may wonder perhaps how convincing this show of joy can be, having just
heard that the mourning at his presumed demise was pro
forma. And Hector, straightforward as always, is profess-
edly unhappy to see his delinquent brother return with a
war bride. His feelings are conveyed through his constant
companion Troilus, who has dire visions of Death rampag-
ing through the Trojans. This not only repeats the close association between Hector and Troilus mentioned in the
first Trojan scene (84) but also offers a prediction to match
the prophecies of Helenus and Cassandra. Dracontius is
carefully building this second Trojan reunion on the model
of the first.

The procession this time is completed by Polites, whom
Dracontius presents in an elaborate simile as Troilus' shadow
(622–27).[59] The comparison is unsettling, as the poet refers
to a *larvalis imago*, thereby suggesting a specter more than
an optical shadow. We move ever closer to the world of
death.

motibus et falsis veras imitata figuras,
nil faciens quasi cuncta facit: sic quoque Polites (636–37)

seems to recall the empty and meaningless gestures of lamentation for Paris. This world of shadows, or shades, moving not of their own accord but in obligatory response to
external acts, catches perfectly the condition of the Trojans
who are impelled by Paris' reckless deeds into a war they
neither want nor deserve, and at the end they will all be
shades indeed.

One curious detail may be related to this impression that
we are looking at a shadow world: there is not a single verse

of speech by any character. The poet will report joy or apprehension, anger or feigned blessing, but we do not hear any of this directly.[60] Certainly this is in striking contrast to the first Trojan scene, where long speeches occupied 97 lines (about two-thirds of the entire passage), or Salamis with 106 out of 172 lines devoted to speeches (roughly the same proportion). The muted characters in this final scene are all the more removed from us, and unable to articulate, much less alter, the events now set in motion.

Epilogue (638-55)

The final 18 verses of the poem are both the completion of Paris' return with Helen and also an epilogue to the entire work. They complete the Trojan section by describing the ill-fated wedding, and yet the poet sets the lines apart both by stylistic signposts and by reentering the poem editorially as he has done in the prologue. The leap forward in time signalled by the opening pluperfect, *duxerat uxorem pastor* (638), and the repeated *iam* are both devices used to mark new sections of narrative.[61] We are being impelled toward the consequences of the poem's action, and the mixture of apparent joy and emerging disaster is harsher here than anywhere else.

The wedding is a travesty of the happy event it purports to be. Dracontius blends contradictory signals throughout the passage:

> duxerat uxorem pastor cum sorte sinistra:
> iam muros, iam tecta petunt, iam regis ad aulam
> intratur, sponsamque tegunt sua flammea pulchram,
> iam thalamis ornata sedet, saltatur in urbe,
> tympana iam quatiunt, iam rustica fistula carmen
> pastorale canit. lituus nil dulce remugit,
> fescennina silent et bucina bella minatur. (638-44)

The recurrent antithesis between shepherd and prince is used to good effect here. Paris is *pastor,* but the setting is

the palace and the city. Nevertheless, as befits a shepherd's
wedding, the rustic pipe plays its *pastorale carmen; saltatur in urbe.* The contradictory worlds and roles of Paris are
crashing into one another, and his presence is discordant
literally as well as figuratively. The swift alternation of
words suggesting happiness and foreboding points in the
same direction: *sorte sinistra . . . sponsam pulchram . . .
saltatur in urbe . . . nil dulce . . . bella minatur.* This has
been the underlying quality of every event in the poem:
what begins as a happy event carries the seed of destruction, and even conversely, apparent sorrow turns to joy.

The shepherd music fades and in our ears sounds the
trumpet of war. The Greeks are going to mobilize their
mille carinas (646).[62] Against this vision the poet delivers
his *sponsalis adlocutio* to the couple, and the traditional
blessing becomes a sorrowful realization that the visions of
Paris' prophetic kinsmen are now inevitable truths. Hecuba's dream of giving birth to a torch which would destroy
the city combines with the wedding torch just lit, and the
several portions of the poem are drawn together. Telamon
had suggested that the Greeks should claim Troy as the
dowry Hesione had never brought with her; now that idea
is applied to Helen in a crashing finale:

> ite pares, sponsi, iam somnia tetra probastis
> matris et ornati misero flammatis amore
> ostensam sub nocte facem, qua Troia cremetur,
> qua Phryges incurrant obitum sine crimine mortis.
> sanguine Troiano dabitur dos, clade Pelasgum
> ditetur Ledaea fugax per castra propago,
> orbentur superi, caelum gemat et mare plangat:
> crimen adulterii talis vindicta sequatur. (648–55)

The poet becomes our prophet as if to certify what the rest
of the poem has shown, and indeed to link it to higher
issues. He returns to his moralizing statements of the prologue and assigns the entire disaster to the adulterous union
just described as a wedding. As with *Medea,* the wedding
theme takes over the poem and brings the promise of ca-

lamity. The two poems are very close in their attitude toward the sanctity of marriage, the heroine who violates that sanctity (assisted but not really driven by the hero) and the disaster which follows.

Structure

The *Helen* displays a structure quite different from either *Hylas* or *Medea*, and yet employs many of the same devices for articulating its form. *Hylas* used repetition of opening lines, the repetition of basic actions and panels of equal length. *Medea* simplified this somewhat in having two pieces closely similar in both length and incident but repeated even the structure of the subparts from one half to the other. *Helen* is arranged like a drama in five acts, with the prologue and epilogue spoken by the playwright *in propria persona*.

The acts are not of equal length, although the three major episodes—Troy$_1$, Salamis, and Cyprus—are of very similar length:[63]

	Prologue	1–60	60
I	Troy$_1$	61–212	152
II	Salamis	213–384	172
III	Storm	385–434	50
IV	Cyprus	435–585	152
V	Troy$_2$	586–637	52
	Epilogue	638–55	18

This division of the poem shows the concentric pattern in which the separate incidents are arranged. The storm at sea is the middle episode, and the two developed scenes at Salamis and Cyprus stand on either side. Before the storm, Paris is overshadowed by the legates to Telamon, but after the separation caused by the tempest, Paris is the central figure. Encasing this triad of scenes are the two segments set in Troy, with the prologue and epilogue framing all. Dracontius makes use of this concentric effect by bringing

us back to the initial situation in the final scene: once again
Paris is returning unexpectedly to his family, and from this
reunion springs disaster. Everything that has happened
during the past five hundred verses has only served to fulfill prophecy and make matters worse.

The separate acts of the drama likewise reinforce one another because underlying the diversity of locale and dramatis personae is a similarity of basic incident. In this respect
Helen is very much like the other poems. Dracontius uses
a series or set of actions which can be variously combined
to suit the individual situation. It is interesting to observe
how these work in each scene.

In Troy$_1$ the components of the narrative are as follows:
Paris arrives amid religious solemnities; a speech of welcome is followed by speeches of prophecy which include
the prediction that the abduction of a woman will spell ruin
for all concerned. The gods intervene in the person of Apollo to bring about what is fated to happen.

Despite the apparently unrelated subject of the embassy
to Salamis, the underlying structure is similar. Paris arrives
with the legation, bringing an announcement not universally appreciated; after the welcoming speech come the
three speeches on the topic of taking away a woman.

Obviously the storm scene has little room for such inter-
play of characters and incident, but the Cyprus segment
combines the elements anew; we begin with the arrival of
Paris amid religious solemnities. He is welcomed. The augur's interpretation of the portents serves as a prophecy of
what is to follow. The speeches which follow, by Paris and
especially by Helen, are most assuredly on the topic of
taking the woman away. The gods intervene in the person
of Venus to ensure that the fated abduction occurs. This is
virtually the same sequence as in Troy$_1$.

We come to the second Trojan scene. The elements fall in
a different order but are clearly recognizable. The scene
opens with the arrival of the legation, and as in Salamis
they bring news of an unwelcome sort. In the midst of the
religious solemnities which follow the report of Paris' loss,

the prince himself arrives, having in fact abducted the woman. The welcoming speeches are balanced by the visions—amounting to prophetic announcement—of Troilus; his vision sees a personified Death, *saeva Mors*, intervening in battle to bring about *fata*.

This narrative technique is at once very simple and quite effective. The recycling of incident is more noticeable here than in *Medea*, perhaps because of the superficial diversity which is offset by the device. The reader is drawn into the action because of the familiarity of the structure. Thus the five acts of the drama are at once distinctive in setting, in size, in cast of characters, and in specific action, and yet are linked by the deep structure of their narrative syntax.

The suggestion of a five-act drama will finally take us back to the fact that our story was a standard item in the store of tragic plots. Even though Dracontius seems not to have used either Euripides or Ennius, he has nevertheless reflected this dramatic tradition. May we go further? We saw in both *Hylas* and *Medea* clear evidence that the pantomime—the most popular theatrical form of Dracontius' day—had influenced his manner of presenting the story. In *Helen* the "final act" is performed without any assigned speeches. Is this odd feature, apart from its immediate value in suggesting the silent world of shadows, a formal imitation of the pantomime again?

And if this is a drama, what other features may we note? Surely in both Trojan scenes the company of nobles in solemn procession sending up lamentation functions as a chorus. The parallel should not be pressed too far, but the effect is suggestive. Likewise, each act seems to be built around three principal speeches, as if delivered by the three actors—and in fact, the prominence of speeches is in itself a link with the dramatic models.[64] We shall see the fullest application of dramatic features to hexameter narrative in the *Orestis tragoedia*, to which we may now turn.

Chapter 5

Orestis Tragoedia

THE LONGEST OF the epyllia to be considered in this study is a poem which has attracted more attention than all the rest of Dracontius' so-called pagan poems combined.[1] Even its attribution to Dracontius is a matter of dispute, as the work is not preserved with the *Romulea* and is unattributed in the manuscripts. But since the conclusive detective work of Rossberg and Barwinski on internal features of style and language, the attribution has been universally accepted. We shall see ample evidence as well in the treatment of themes to endorse this conclusion.

The title likewise is a source of debate.[2] What does *tragoedia* mean in this case? That the tale is a grievous one filled with lamentable happenings, or that the poem tells a story previously treated in tragedy? None of Dracontius' poems shows more clearly the influence of drama in its structure and style. Obviously the Aeschylean trilogy should be the principal source and Rapisarda has argued at great length that we can see very specific echoes of the Greek tragedies throughout this poem.[3] This view is far from universally accepted, although nobody can deny at least a general similarity to the design of the Aeschylean plays.[4]

But there were several other dramatic treatments of parts of the Orestes story, both in Greek and Latin, and it is unlikely that Dracontius was familiar with all the relevant plays of Aeschylus, Sophocles, and Euripides. The influence of Latin sources such as Seneca's *Agamemnon* and the ever present mythographers surely played a part as well. It would be fruitless to spend all our time on *Quellenforschung* but the question becomes more important when we are invited by Rapisarda to see the *Orestes* as a Christian recasting of the Aeschylean trilogy: if that is true, then our impression of Dracontius' use of Greek sources will need modification, and so perhaps will our impression of his intent in the pagan poems generally.

How for that matter are we to relate this poem to the *Romulea?* That collection is now incomplete, and there is no clear evidence to affirm or deny that the *Orestes* was originally a part of the poet's only known collection of poems on pagan themes. We touched on this question in the first chapter, but we should bear in mind the implications for the *Romulea* if the *Orestes* turns out to be a poem of evangelical Christian intent, and belongs to a collection of poems for which such a claim has never been made. One question which remains unresolved is the relative date of the *Orestes:* Barwinski believed that it was among the earliest works of Dracontius, while others have seen it as a more mature poem, arguing for a significantly later date.[5] I believe that the poem is in fact earlier than the *Medea*, which seems to have borrowed one scene directly from it, and later than the *Helen*, to which it in turn seems to owe a major motif.[6]

As with each of the poems examined thus far, we shall need to consider the structure of the epyllion along with its debt to earlier accounts of the story. It is no surprise to see that there are episodes not found in any other version of the Orestes story, and that these are integrally related to the over-all architecture of the poem. This has been the poet's pattern in each case. The use of obscure or lost sources, the poet's own innovations, and the concern for structural effects work together to produce a unique rendering of a familiar tale.

It will be easiest to see these issues develop if we once again work our way through the poem. The basic divisions are the prologue (1–40) and three segments corresponding to the three plays of the *Oresteia*. For convenience I shall refer to these as the "Agamemnon" (41–426), "Orestes" (453–802),[7] and "Orestes furens" (803–974). Each of the three pseudodramas may be broken into five acts, giving

further witness to the way in which Dracontius conceived
the poem as a dramatic work.

Prologue (1–40)

This is a prefatory statement very similar to Dracontius'
other prologues. It gives us both an outline of the events to
be treated in the poem and also the poet's evaluation of the
events. As Aricò has noted, the prologue follows the triple
format described by Servius: *propositio* (1–12), *invocatio*
(13–24), and *narratio* (25–40),[8] although there is a significant amount of overlap between these parts.

> Gaudia maesta canam detestandosque triumphos:
> victoris pro laude necem, festiva cruenta,
> funeris effatus et lamentabile votum
> coniugis Iliacae, non quae iugularet Atridem,
> laurea regali rutilantia serta cruore
> et diadema ducis foedatum tabe cerebri. (1–6)

These lines will illustrate the general tenor of the prologue and its most striking characteristics. The enjoyment
of paradox and oxymoron so evident throughout Dracontius' poetry is carried to excess in this poem. It is partly
due to the inherently paradoxical notion of a justified matricide: the theme surely appealed to Dracontius for that
fact, as it provided wide scope for his rhetorical posturing.
But there is another element as well, I think. The use of
paradox is about the most common feature of Christian authors in meditating on the mysteries of their faith. Dracontius in both *De laudibus Dei* and *Satisfactio* makes unrelenting use of the figure, and a glance at any Christian
writer, Greek or Latin, of late antiquity reveals the same
taste. Christianity is a faith constructed on the awareness of
paradox, and the rhetorical training of antiquity taught the
use of paradox. The combination as we see it in Dracontius
is overwhelming.

A second feature seen in these lines is the moral or judg-

mental aspect of Dracontius' storytelling. Every stage of
the plot here, summarized in quick and allusive fashion, is
commented upon in moral terms. *Pietas/pius* are especially
frequent in the poem,[9] and almost every time a character
performs any action, there is an epithet of praise or blame.

And third, we may notice the poet's taste for the macabre
and the violent. This is a tale of murder and vengeance, but
there are various ways to present the facts. Dracontius is
more emphatic than necessary in his descriptions of split
skulls but thereby also reflects the unbridled tendency of
his age.

The opening 12 verses sketch the plot and impart the author's judgment on the events. The *invocatio* (13–24) concentrates more on the question of Orestes' guilt, the im-
pulses which drove him to his act, and the question of his
legal responsibility. This is naturally a topic of interest to
Dracontius the lawyer, and the account of the trial occupies
the last part of the poem. It is not merely the trial to come
which the poet has in mind: he himself is to present the
case by way of the poem, and his invocation of Melpomene
is closely linked with his role as advocate:

> te rogo, Melpomene, tragicis descende cothurnis
> et pede dactylico resonante quiescat iambus:
> da valeam memorare nefas laudabile nati
> et purgare foro quem damna‹nt impia facta›.[10] (13–16)

The appeal to Melpomene to step aside while the poet uses
other genres is reminiscent of the prologue to *Medea* (20ff.);
but we should note that the poet hopes to recall the story,
which the Muse should help him do, and also to *defend*
Orestes. This solid stance in favor of Orestes—strengthened by the constant paradoxes—determines his depiction
of all the other characters and is responsible for the two
striking innovations of plot, Agamemnon's visit to Iphigenia
(41–107) and the role of Molossus (803ff.).

The third segment of the prologue, *narratio* (25–40),
moves us from the poet's meditations on Orestes to the story

proper. In the same way the last part of the prologue to
Helen (31–60) set out the background for the story of that
poem. In this case we are introduced to Agamemnon en
route home from Troy. The poet stresses two points about
the king: first, his triumph in war, against which his immi-
nent murder is to be set; and second, his high goodness of
character.

His triumph is conveyed in the grandiloquent opening
words of the segment which ring like a trumpet blast as he
comes on stage:

> ductorum ductor, regum rex dux Agamemnon
> post duo lustra redux et post duo bella triumphans
> Martia bellipotens referebat classica princeps. (25–27)

The two alliterations of *ductorum/ductor/dux* and *regum/
rex* are intertwined in *redux,* emphasizing both his grandeur and his happy return home. The lines are clearly derived from Seneca's *Agamemnon* (39f.),[11] where the shade
of Thyestes ponders the horrors attendant upon the House
of Atreus, and Dracontius probably intended that somber
context to be recognized.

But this grand personage is also a loving family man and
pious. All his success he attributes to the gods and he plans
lavish gifts for them (30–34). He brings presents for the
family, all unaware of what awaits him. This too seems derived from Seneca's king:

> post gemina Phoebi lustra devicto Ilio
> adest, daturus coniugi iugulum suae[12] (*Ag.* 42–43)

who brings an unintended present to his wife's thirst for revenge. Here, Agamemnon ponders the many gifts for his
wife, never dreaming of her unworthiness, and for his children, whose youth and innocence are stressed by this gesture of a loving father bringing mementos of his trip. Orestes' youth is further emphasized by looking ahead to his
revenge:

plurima subridens genitor disponit Oresti

. . . .

non tamen aequa simul meritis animisque futuris. (37, 39)

The prologue thus gives us both Orestes and Agamemnon as entirely virtuous characters, and Clytemestra as unremittingly wicked. We know now how the poet will slant his story. As in Dracontius' other poems, the figures tend to the extremes: the wicked woman, the noble monarch, the dutiful son. Despite the lavish use of paradox, this is not an ambiguous telling of the tale.

"Agamemnon" (41–426)

i. 41–107

The most startling innovation of plot in the poem comes at the outset, as Agamemnon strays to the land of the Taurians en route home. There is no evidence that any other poet ever used (or even imagined) such an incident, and we are surely justified in regarding it as Dracontius' own invention.

The poet is inconsistent in his account of the reasons and circumstances of this event. At first glance, it appears that the fleet is driven off course by the winds, because of the anger of the god (we are not told which god is angry or why, merely *irato deo*). The device of the storm driving the hero to a strange land is a favorite of Dracontius, and it is a familiar, convenient means of accounting for a wildly improbable turn of events. But since the poet is also eager to show Agamemnon's piety, it emerges that the king intends to pay his vows to Diana:

> imperat indomitus praedam praeire Mycenis
> ipse secuturus post vota soluta Dianae (46–47)

Clearly the storm was not enough to prevent the fleet from going home, as only Agamemnon's ship is detained. Obviously this is a device to have Cassandra (the *praeda* of 46) arrive at Mycenae separately for the confrontation with

Clytemestra (133ff.), and also to leave Agamemnon unattended for his meeting with Iphigenia. Dracontius uses a similar ploy in *Medea* to leave Jason alone to encounter Medea, and in *Helen* to have Paris' ship alone reach Cyprus for the meeting with Helen. What vows Agamemnon owed to Diana we are not told, nor why he must redeem them in this land. But the action shows his piety, which is the poet's chief purpose.

As Agamemnon prays in the temple of the goddess[13] and presents her with a crimson robe (a distant reapplication, perhaps, of the famous crimson carpet in Aeschylus' *Agamemnon*), he sees his daughter. Although he reacts with a blend of amazement and guilt, it nevertheless appears that Agamemnon merely knew of the sacrifice of Iphigenia without performing or even sanctioning it himself.

The encounter between these two is reminiscent of Paris' return to Troy (*Hel.* 71ff.), in which a guilty parent likewise confesses his fault and is reunited with his offspring; and both scenes are indebted to the Buthrotum scene in *Aeneid* 3 as Aeneas and Andromache gaze at each other across the presumed gulf of the grave (cf. *Aen.* 3.310):

> vivis an effigies et imago volatilis extas? (67)

He is also puzzled that, if she is still alive, she is not home with her mother but instead is serving Diana at the ends of the earth. Iphigenia's explanation is consistent with Dracontius' desire to shift responsibility from Agamemnon to others. There is no mention of the fact that when Ulysses came to ask Clytemestra for Iphigenia on the pretext of a marriage to Achilles, it was Agamemnon who had directed him to do so. Instead, we hear only of Ulysses' treachery,[14] and responsibility is covered in a blanket of passive verbs: *nec vocor ad thalamos, sed victima trador ad aras* (80).[15]

Through the tender mercy of Diana, Iphigenia has been translated: but the kindness of the goddess will soon be called into doubt as Agamemnon appeals to her to let his daughter return home with him. His prayer (86–101) is very Greek, particularly Homeric, in its tone. Note the opening words, *plectriferi germana dei, Letoia Phoebe* with its Greek forms and the Homeric-sounding *plectriferi,* found nowhere else in Latin literature except Dracontius (cf. *Med.* 285).[16] The hymnic form lends a solemnity and effectiveness to the lines and enhances the liturgical aura of the occasion. We are reminded once more of the king's piety and his humility before the gods, particularly Diana:

> tu rapis ex aris animas et morte parata:
> pignora redde precor regi post funera patri, (93–94)

with the linking of *regi* and *patri* to show both his status and his paternal pride.[17] Despite this admirable prayer, however, Diana *crudescit in iras* and turns her face from his plea. No reason is given for the goddess' anger, although the poet obviously cannot allow her to accede to the request, since Iphigenia cannot possibly come home yet. With one of his characteristically abrupt conclusions,[18] Dracontius unceremoniously sends Agamemnon back to the ship and out to sea. Not a word of farewell or of explanation. The scene has served its purpose, and there is no graceful way to terminate it.

What is more, this astonishing addition to the plot is never mentioned again by the poet or any of his characters. Why is it that Iphigenia cannot leave now but can leave later with Orestes? And why does Agamemnon never mention to anyone that his daughter is alive and well?[19] We see again the compartmentalized mind of our poet. The scene is added for limited and discrete purposes, and has no organic link to the rest of the poem. However peculiar that these events should not come to light, they are irrelevant and intrusive in the rest of the story and are simply ignored.

This recognition scene *in Tauris* is a foreshadowing and a doublet of the canonical reunion scene of Orestes and his sister (862–86). Or perhaps we should say that the poet, having decided to include a meeting of Agamemnon and Iphigenia, had as his model the familiar Orestes-Iphigenia scene and simply worked from it in constructing this variant.

ii. 108–231

With this segment, we move into the range of events usually treated in the dramatic tradition: the news of Agamemnon's return with the fleet and Clytemestra's reaction to the news. It is almost as if the scene among the Taurians was an interpolation: even *interea* (108)[20] seems to follow naturally the last part of the prologue reporting Agamemnon's journey homeward. But as we shall see, the poet has good reasons for interposing the king's wanderings.[21]

This segment falls into three parts, the first and third dealing with Clytemestra and the second with Cassandra's prophecy. As in the opening scenes of both the Aeschylean and Senecan plays, the queen and people of Mycenae are awaiting the fleet's arrival. In these lines we hear of the arrival of the fleet without Agamemnon, and we hear Clytemestra and Egistus plotting to murder the king. But the absence of Agamemnon is not the only novelty in Dracontius' treatment of the scene. Each of the characters involved is portrayed differently from the traditional versions, and the entire story is pointed in another direction.

Clytemestra, for instance, bears no grudge against her husband for the sacrifice of Iphigenia (she later indicates her pleasure that one daughter at least is out of the way to reduce the prospects of revenge).[22] On the contrary, it is she who fears his anger, and the sole basis for her anxiety is her adulterous liaison with Egistus. As the fleet comes in, she goes to the harbor in dread:[23]

> captivos visura Phryges Agamemnonis uxor
> affuit, adventus metuens impura mariti. (114–15)

Her fear and guilt are vividly depicted by the poet, and she is in many ways the most interesting character of the poem.[24] She silently curses the crowd's joy at the safe return of the fleet although she outwardly joins in their expression of gladness (this hypocritical relationship with the people will be a motif of Clytemestra's role throughout the poem). As soon as she realizes that Agamemnon is not present, she concludes she has escaped punishment for her sins and heads off to tell Egistus of their luck. *Sed spes ibi fallitur audax* (132), since Cassandra speaks up to prophesy the tragic events ahead.

Cassandra has also been redrawn by Dracontius. She is not Agamemnon's concubine and therefore is not a point of jealousy for Clytemestra. She cannot be closely linked with him because such liaisons are the sole focus of Clytemestra's guilt, and of course Agamemnon must be free of any such blame. She is merely part of his *praeda* sent home with the rest of the booty. That she arrives separately from Agamemnon emphasizes how unconnected they are.[25] Instead, she is both the prophet of the violence to come and also an impetus to that violence by stirring Clytemestra and Egistus to action. As in Seneca, Cassandra welcomes the murder of Agamemnon as partial vengeance for the destruction of her land:

> salve regina Pelasgum
> ultio Dardanidum, captae solacia Troiae. (137–38)

Indeed, she prods the wicked couple to their crime (*quid dubitatis . . . perdite, ne pereat vestri cito fructus amoris*). The murder of the king is referred to allusively, the revenge and trial of Orestes more explicitly. And Cassandra is not killed by Clytemestra, but merely disappears from the stage after delivering her prophecies.[26]

Clytemestra is now impelled both by her own sense of guilt and by the urgings of the priestess to slay her husband. Her alarm grows along with her realization that she can perhaps avoid her just deserts after all. Spurred by these mixed emotions, she hurries home to tell her cringing paramour the news.

Egistus is weak and cowardly, in striking contrast to the

forceful character found in Seneca's play. Dracontius wished
to make all but Agamemnon and Clytemestra negligible figures in order to stress the fundamental contrast between
the two principal characters in this morality play. Egistus
engages in much hand-wringing and aspires at most to associate himself with the bold plans of the domineering queen:
in this we see the pattern found in Dracontius' other poems,
the powerful woman leading the subservient man into a career of crime.

Dracontius has underlined Egistus' unworthiness time
and again by calling him *pastor.*[27] The first occurrence of
this epithet is in Cassandra's vaticination, where she hails
him as *triumphalis domitor bone pastor Egiste* (139). Why
pastor, and why *bone?* It is possible that Dracontius is reflecting the Homeric epithet ἀμύμων by *bone;* or alternatively that she is being heavily ironic (*triumphalis domitor*
can hardly be sincere). As to *pastor,* I do not think the poet
is merely etymologizing on Aegisthus (goat-nursed): one
may wonder whether his readers would have spotted the
verbal play, especially in the debased form of the proper
name. The explanation surely lies in the comparison with
another wife-stealing shepherd whom our poet has already
treated. We have seen how Dracontius frequently called
Paris *pastor,* especially at those very moments when he
most needed to be *princeps* instead. Here the poet makes a
very special point of emphasizing Egistus' rise in the world
from the sordid circumstances of his origins:

> plumea cui praestant post pelles stramina lectum,
> quem post tecta casae regalis suscipit aula. (140–41)

This is remarkable since Egistus was after all as much of
royal descent as Agamemnon. But the moral point is made
more effective by presenting Egistus as a parvenu along
with his other deficiencies.[28]

The parallel between Paris and Egistus is striking. Both
are depicted as hot-blooded youths (Egistus is called *iuvenis* in 163 and 334, despite the presumable inappropriate-

ness of that term); both fall into liaisons with another man's wife, and the husbands so wronged are brothers. Both are depicted as spineless and vacillating, in both cases dominated by the woman in their lives. In fact, Dracontius draws the two together by comparison in Dorylas' prayer to Agamemnon's shade: [29]

> si gremio Paridis remanens est rapta Lacaena
> (nonne laborastis, Helenam ne pastor haberet?
> ecce, tuam nunc pastor habet!). (468–70)

As with Paris, *pastor* will recur to characterize Egistus at every turn, and will be in effect an editorial comment on his character. He is low in estate as well in moral stature, an interloper.

This pointed use of *pastor* as moral comment is so natural an extension of Paris' story and so unexpected in treating Egistus that I cannot avoid the idea that it appeared first in its more appropriate setting and was then echoed in the other. That is to say, it would appear from this motif that the *Orestes* is a later poem than the *Helen*. [30]

The long speech of Clytemestra (163–203) urging Egistus to action is a fine depiction of the *regina scelerata*. She begins in a state of great anxiety at her renewed expectation of Agamemnon's return: if he has done so much to avenge another husband's honor, what will he not do to avenge his own? Besides, he is now war-hardened and presumably insensitive to appeals for mercy. Our only hope then is to strike him down before he learns what is happening in his house. Note that Clytemestra refers to Agamemnon as *tyrannus* again (cf. 124 and 212); elsewhere the poet always uses this term censoriously to refer to Egistus usurping the rule. Clytemestra does her best to present Agamemnon as a cruel vindictive tyrant, herself and Egistus as undeserving victims of his wrath. And yet she is candid in explaining that she does not wish to lose the benefit of her crimes by being caught (179). To emphasize the odd perspective which portrays her as victim, she states again her

fears in grotesquely exaggerated terms: *formidine mortis /
territa sollicitor miserandi femina sexus* (184–85).[31] By this
she stirs Egistus to support her, as he faces certain death if
he does not. And as the savage murderess comes clearly
into focus, she ponders possible sources of punishment:

> non est quem metuas: brevis est et parvus Orestes,
> unaque natarum cinis est per templa Dianae,
> altera sexus iners recidens miseranda quid audet? (193–95)

Even here Clytemestra does not accuse Agamemnon of killing Iphigenia—for it is a boon to her plans that her daughter is dead, and it would thus be something to Agamemnon's
credit! The characterization of Electra as *iners* is nearly
accurate but foreshadows how the pair will carelessly let
Electra have her one crucial moment of activity in rescuing
Orestes (284f.); Menelaus is occupied with his recovered
queen, and the citizens of Mycenae will surely support the
king's murder (we are not told why).[32]

Egistus declares his willingness to assist in *tam grande
nefas* (another candid term) but clearly has no notion how
to proceed. Clytemestra now sets forth the traditional
scheme of the shirt with the top sewn shut by which she
can render Agamemnon helpless. She pictures with relish
the king encrusted in the gore of battle and needing a new
shirt.[33] After she traps him, Egistus is to pounce and kill:

> dum caput indutum cupit exertare tyrannus,
> egredere praeventor atrox violentus: Atridis
> finde secure caput cervicem colla cerebrum. (212–14)

The alliteration of 214 has the archaic sonority of a curse or
a ritual utterance.

Her fiery rhetoric does its work, and Egistus is stirred to
an empty display of bravery against an imagined enemy; he
is aptly compared to a venomous snake lurking until its
prey comes near (224–26). This show of vigor in turn stirs
Clytemestra's passion, and the scene concludes with the
pair in sinful embrace.

If we consider the overall effect of the changes which Dracontius has introduced in this scene, it is clear that he has had one purpose in mind: to produce a clear-cut fable of right and wrong. The pure and blameless king whom we met in the previous scene is set against the adulterous wife and her base lover, who conspire to murder the king at the moment of his righteous and joyful return. The hesitant man and the calculating, ambitious queen show something irresistibly reminiscent of Macbeth spurred against his hesitations by his ruthless wife to commit murder and so gain the throne. But all the characters in this poem are cast as simple representatives of moral types. As in the other poems we have examined, there is the fairy-tale quality of both character and plot which allows us to see the hero and the villain with a view uncluttered by subtlety or ambiguity. Perhaps this desire for a simple scheme has accounted for the disappearance of the nurse who played an important role in the equivalent scene in Seneca's play.[34] We now have two tableaux of equal but opposite force in the good king and the wicked conspirators. The confrontation of good and evil can now follow at once.

iii. 232–83

The contrast between the king and the conspirators is bluntly depicted: Agamemnon's ship arrives even as the adulterous couple pursue their pleasures. This segment comprises three parts: the arrival of Agamemnon (232–48), his murder (249–70), and a reflection on the crime by the poet (271–83).

Agamemnon presents an awesome figure as he steps from the ship. He is still covered with the gore of battle, which only serves to enhance his grandeur:

> bellorum maculis rutilabat, sanguine pulcher,
> grandis in aspectu, pugnarum horrore decorus. (240–41)

Moreover the poet likens the king to Jupiter in his triumph over the Giants, his head adorned as with a crown of stars, and pouring forth flames of glory.[35] It is a startling contrast to the gory warrior's clothing just described, but both aspects will have their relevance: the gore of battle is to be replaced by the blood of the king himself, and the crown on his head is dashed by his murderer in an act both real and symbolic.

Agamemnon shows again what an affectionate family man he is as he greets his eager children and looks about to find his wife. But she is busy in the palace: the conspirators have taken their respective posts, Egistus hidden in the closet with the axe and the queen in the chamber with the fateful tunic.

From the splendor of his public appearance, the king passes within the palace to be greeted by his loving wife. She urges him to exchange his *cultus minaces* for her gift:

> en tibi vestis adest nostro contexta labore,
> aurea purpureo radiantur fila colore. (251–52)

Here clearly is the Aeschylean crimson symbol offered to Agamemnon; as with the carpet, the crimson signifies not royalty but blood. He replaces one blood-hued garment for another (note *perfundit* as the queen puts it on his head). The queen specifies that the shirt is of her own making: this is her trap in every way. We may think of an ironic perversion of Penelope who whiled away her time—and fended off suitors—by weaving a shroud. So this shirt will be a wrapping of death for Agamemnon.

Once she has entangled the king in the tunic, Clytemestra calls Egistus to slay him, and Dracontius gives a vivid, macabre description of the attack, as Agamemnon's skull is split open by the axe. The account owes much to Seneca's version (*Ag.* 875ff.), including the simile describing the twitching, fallen victim as like a ferocious boar caught in nets by hunters (265ff.); but the final line is of distinctly Vergilian cast, looking back to the slaying of Priam (*Aen.* 2.555ff.):

> sic Asiae domitor consumptus fine cruenta. (269)

Egistus as he bobs and weaves with the axe, *dextra vi-*
brante, recalls the snake to which he was compared when
preparing himself for the murder (224).

The debt of Dracontius to the dramatic versions of the
story is obvious at every turn; among the more striking adaptations of the tragic form to narrative is the moral lament
by the poet in his own voice following directly on the murder. It is clear that this meditative entr'acte represents the
function of the chorus in the dramatic form. It marks the
major action of this part of the story and provides a pause
for reflection as well as a comment by the author. Dracontius' style in these lines is rather more elaborate than in the
straight narrative portions, as if to suggest the heightened
language of the choral passages in tragedy. His theme is the
unreliability of the gods and of fate:

discite felices non umquam credere fatis! (278)

The gods raise men up at whim and they punish or destroy them in the midst of their prosperity. Hardly a novel
thought, but it is striking in this poem because the gods
play virtually no part in the story. Dracontius has focused
his attention on the human participants in order to show
how praise and blame attach to men for what they do. The
reflections on the uncertainties of life as caused by the
heartless whim of the gods contain several echoes of other
Latin poets on this subject; it is probably pointless to see
a debt to the general tenor of Aeschylus' meditations as
found in various parts of his plays (Rapisarda): what is remarkable is their placement in this poem. I suspect the
passage reflects instead the poet's adverse view of the pagan
gods who normally drive the action. We have seen Dracontius' attacks on the worship of the pagan gods in the closing
lines of the *Medea,* and there is a similar passage concluding the *Orestes* (963ff.; cf. below).

It is probably impossible to disentangle Dracontius'
sources for the version of the murder which he presents.
There had always been considerable diversity in the tradi-

tion as to the precise place where Agamemnon was killed, and the relative role of the conspirators.[36] Servius reports as one strand of the tradition that *in ipso ingressu, id est prima die qua domus suae limen ingressus consilio Aegisthi ab uxore vestem accepit clauso capite, qua implicatus adulteri manibus interiit* (*ad. Aen.* XI.267). This agrees with our poet—and is apparently alone among extant references in doing so—that the murder took place in the palace but not at a banquet or in the bath. But Servius attributes the plan to Aegisthus, and suggests some delay not reported in *Orestes*. If Dracontius was working from the source reflected in Servius, he has altered the picture at least to the extent of assigning the lead role to Clytemestra (which is, as we have seen, consistent with his treatment of women generally). Servius elsewhere (*ad Aen.* IV.471) reports a tradition exactly like that which Dracontius presents: *hunc Oresten Electra, soror eius, post occisum ab Aegistho* dolo Clytemnestrae *matris Agamemnonem subtraxit.* Either Dracontius knew and followed the source implied by Servius, or he settled for himself on a scheme already used once before.[37] The murder is sometimes committed by the queen alone, sometimes by Egistus alone, and frequently by the pair together. Dracontius has chosen to have both involved because it will be important that both share the blame when punishment is meted out by Orestes and Pylades.[38] It is an excellent indication of the two characters that Clytemestra plans the scheme and shows the brazen hypocrisy, while Egistus merely strikes like a snake from his hiding place when it is safe to do so.

iv. 284–349

The fourth act of Dracontius' "Agamemnon" is relatively brief, and contains little action, but it is important in setting up later developments in both Mycenae and Athens. There are three moments in this act: the rescue of Orestes (284–304), Clytemestra and Egistus plotting their next move to secure their new power (305–37), and a lament by the citizens of Mycenae for their fallen king (338–49).

As in the dramatic tradition, Orestes has played no part in the story thus far (except that Cassandra has foretold his role as avenger). Clytemestra dismissed him as a threat, calling him *brevis et parvus* (193), but of course he must be removed from the scene now. There was considerable variation in the tradition about Orestes' life before his return to avenge his father: how old was the prince when he left Mycenae; who sent or took him away, and to what place of refuge?[39] It is not necessary to review the many strands of tradition on the fate of Orestes, but one or two items are of interest to the study of Dracontius' version.

The dramatic tradition was united in having Orestes go to Phocis, where he was cared for by King Strophius and where he met (and was raised with) Pylades. Homer has him return from Athens, where we may presume he spent his period of exile (*Od.* 3.304–10).[40] The age of the prince was less clearly thought out: certainly Orestes returns as a young man, normally about eighteen years old, but in some versions he was sent away very young,[41] while in others he was a young boy rather than a baby. Dracontius' Orestes says he was eleven years old (572). Homer specifies that Orestes' exile lasted seven years, and Dracontius preserves an odd version of that tradition (cf. 455: 7 years and 8 months).

And who sent or took him? Aeschylus has Clytemestra tell Agamemnon that she has sent Orestes to Strophius (*Ag.* 869–70), but in more versions he is rescued from the queen by Electra or a nurse or servant. Sophocles combines the two by having Electra deliver Orestes to the paidagogos. What then of Dracontius?

> clade repentina premitur Pelopeia virgo,
> sed tamen ultorem patris servavit Orestem:
> faucibus eripiens germanum Electra parentis
> inposuit puppi secumque adduxit Athenis
> et bene sollicita studiis sapientibus addit. (284–88)

This will be Electra's only appearance in the poem except for a curtain call in 960. She vanishes from the story as quickly as Cassandra after performing her one essential act, and will have no part in the return and revenge. For this reason, she does not send her brother away but takes him herself, so that she too can be out of the picture and leave the regicides to indulge their power and wickedness untrammeled even by a harmless girl—we recall that Clytemestra had dismissed Electra as *iners recidens miseranda* (195). There is no faithful retainer at this point in the story, although Dorylas in the later phases picks up on the role.

Why does Orestes go to Athens? Dracontius may be preserving the Homeric tradition, but I do not think that is the decisive reason. Rather, we may observe that in the *Aegritudo*, Perdica is also a student in Athens before his fateful return home. It would appear that this was a feature in the poems invented by the poets from their connection with the rhetorical schools.[42] This is what highborn young men did when they left home, and Athens was the great center of learning to which heroes and princes naturally went. The details of Orestes' life as a student may even contain some idealized recollections (or wistful reconstructions) of Dracontius' own school days.

In Athens, Orestes' classmate is Pylades, whom we may imagine that he met at school. Aricò assumed as a novelty in our poet's treatment of the story that the two youths were already friends in Mycenae, instead of meeting in the place of Orestes' exile; but there is no warrant in the text for this assumption. Dracontius simply has Orestes meet Pylades at school instead of at the court of Strophius. Dracontius expressly tells us that they were brought together by their studies: *iunxerat hos studium sollers et gloria linguae* (292).

At any rate, the two are inseparable in study and at play, and the poet gives a charming picture of their mutual enjoyment in a leisured life in the gymnasium, at the hunt, and in every other pursuit (292–301). The comparison with Castor and Pollux (302–304) is an apt one, for it includes the willingness to share death as well as life, and to this risk they will be called when they return to Mycenae.

As is Dracontius' practice on many occasions, we are shifted abruptly from this scene in Athens back to the wickedness of the palace in Mycenae, just as in 108 we were whisked away from the good king to the plotting lovers. One almost has the feeling of moving from one panel of a painting to the next: the juxtaposition is effective but startling. In this scene Egistus has assumed the trappings of his usurped throne but now seeks Orestes to eliminate him as a threat to his position. There is a lacuna following 309, but the sense is clear enough. Egistus wants first to find the prince and then to find the wealth to sustain his tyranny. But Electra has providently taken with her the treasure of Troy brought home by her father (290), and so Egistus is left without resources, having squandered the wealth of Mycenae already.

The scene is a vivid depiction of the character of Egistus and Clytemestra. Once again Egistus is blustering but ineffectual. He needs wealth to sustain him in his rule, but cannot find it for himself and falls at once into despair as he had done in the earlier scene when plotting the murder. *Aestuat impatiens, quod regni nomen inane / offendit* (313–14); and once again it is the queen who takes control (note *callida* in 316 for pointed contrast) and solves their problems. Her speech in 321–34 is a very unflattering picture not only of Clytemestra but of all women: for the poet has her assume that she can manipulate the wives of the wealthy simply by bribing them with her jewelry. Her sensuous tastes and greedy instincts are projected onto all her sex:

> nam principis uxor
> cuiuscumque libet, licet extet pulcra pudica,
> censibus his ornata nitens placare maritum
> aggreditur:
> . . . .
> mollibus artifices iungens amplexibus artus,
> et faciet nobis sublimes sexus amicos. (323–26, 329–30)

As Clytemestra's fear and guilt recede into the background, her passion and her greed reassert themselves as foremost

in her character; and as Egistus is reassured, he displays
once more his reckless ambition for power. The first scene
of these two plotting ends with them gratifying their passions (230–31). This scene ends with Egistus indulging his
dreams of unlimited rule.

The final component of this scene is another "choral"
passage, this time a lament by the citizens of Mycenae. It is
reminiscent of the chorus in Aeschylus (*Ag.* 1531ff.) as the
Argive elders cry out in accusation and despair. That is at
the end of the play, but we are still one scene from the end
of Dracontius' Agamemnon. The final scene is pure invention by our poet, so that in following the Greek model,
the final chorus is reflected here. As with the gathering of
the servants at Agamemnon's tomb, with which the second
phase of the trilogy opens, there is little doubt that Dracontius is trying to create the effect of a chorus, and the
structural correspondence between Aeschylus and Dracontius is too close to be accidental.[43]

v. 350–426

Following immediately after the choral effect of these lines
comes a distinctly epic touch as the poet invokes the Muse,
marking a moment of particular importance as we enter the
last act of this portion. As the lament of the Mycenaeans
looked back over the events just reported, now the invocation of the Muse turns our attention ahead in anticipation.

There are once again three subparts: the actions of Dorylas (350–81), the behavior of Clytemestra and Egistus as
rulers of Mycenae (382–418), and a brief comment by the
poet *in propria persona* (419–26).

The first of these is apparently the invention of Dracontius, although he is combining traditional elements in the
process. After Orestes had been carried to safety, Egistus
had sought him without success (cf. 305ff.), and the threat
to his life persists. A family servant named Dorylas now un-
dertakes to close off the hunt for the prince by bringing a
false report that Orestes and Electra are dead. There is no
basis for this figure in the tradition, and the only previous

occurrences of the name Dorylas[44] have nothing to do with this story. Dorylas *libertus Atridis / et pueri nutritor erat fugientis Orestis* (352–53), and thus corresponds in some degree to the paidagogos who rescued Orestes in the Sophoclean version; but here his role is not to remove the prince but merely to prevent his further persecution in exile. He is an old family retainer, rather like the figure of the nurse. It is misleading to cast him simply as the *paidagogus* of the exiled prince,[45] for it is his bond to the slain king as well as the young prince that dictates his actions.

The false report of Orestes' death is an element drawn from the tradition, although it is Orestes himself who performs this function in Aeschylus (*Ch.* 675ff.). In Sophocles, however, Orestes has the paidagogos deliver the news (*El.* 40ff., 600ff.), and that is closer to what we find in Dracontius. Thus in Dorylas, Dracontius combines the paidagogos who rescued Orestes and the false report of the prince's death delivered by Orestes himself (or at his bidding) at the time of his return to Mycenae seven years later. But why has the poet assigned these functions to an entirely new character? Is this merely another instance of his alleged passion for novelty?

On the contrary, Dracontius has two quite specific purposes in creating Dorylas. First, the children must be made safe from their mother's continuing pursuit:

> dic mihi, Musa, precor, qua re materna noverca
> quaerere neglexit pueros et tradere captos
> patris in occasus? (350–52)

Egistus had sought them in order to take their wealth, but Clytemestra is a more deadly foe. Only this false report that the children are dead will fend her off. It is an intensification of the queen's wickedness that she should not only slay her husband in order to pursue her adultery, but that she should then pursue the children even when they are out of her path.

The second and more important function of this development is to allow full play to the vileness of both Clytemestra and Egistus once they are sure that retribution will not come to them. This has been the theme of this entire poem: the endlessly wicked queen and her endlessly ambitious lover. Even as they were alarmed, when we first saw them, by the prospect of the king's return to punish them and responded by plotting his death, so now the prospect of the prince's return to punish them leads to attempts to eliminate him as well. Now we see the results of their belief that they are beyond revenge.

Dorylas conceives the plan to announce that the ship carrying Orestes and Electra from Mycenae has gone down. There is, as Quartiroli puts it, a *gusto avventuroso* about the plan: the story of the son lost at sea only to return years later is a common feature of romance plots at all periods.

After a prayer to the gods of land and sea (357–62) for assistance in his piously dishonest plan (there is no relief from the use of paradox in this poem), Dorylas lends credibility to his story by wading into the water to get wet; and then emerges from the waves to cry his news. The figure rising from the sea we have seen before in both *Hylas* and *Medea* and reminds us of our poet's fondness for such aquatic settings, perhaps with a connection to the Carthaginian taste for aquatic mimes.[46]

His speech (367–78) is of a strongly dramatic cast. There is even the suggestion of stage directions in the way Dracontius leads into it.[47] Thus even when he is creating a scene from his own imagination, he is affected by the conventions of dramatic forms, perhaps even borrowing phrases from tragedy.[48]

As the bearer of welcome news, Dorylas is heaped with gifts by the royal couple, *quod gaudia ferret / mentibus incestis*. With the last threat of reprisal gone, the *regina proterva* summons the citizens to hear her proclamation of the new order. Clytemestra's speech (384–411) is a splendid piece of characterization and shows Dracontius' rhetorical powers at their best.

The queen has completely redefined the murder of Aga-

memnon, and describes the event as a political upheaval.
Like the exchange between Clytemnestra and the chorus in
Aeschylus (*Ag.* 1395ff.), she openly reviles Agamemnon
(but not Cassandra in this case) and justifies her actions;
but of course there is no appeal to the loss of her children,
whom she regards as well disposed of in any case, nor any
justification in terms of revenge for suffering as a mother.
She calmly turns the tables and accuses Agamemnon of
squandering the manpower of Mycenae by his mad war
policy. Her audience consists of the long-suffering survivors
of a violent king's rule:

> eximii proceres Danaum populique pusilli,
> quos Agamemnonii per ferrea lustra triumphi
> non mersere neci, sed adhuc superatis inanes
> visceribus vacuis, exhausto sanguine fuso:
> quod vos sic minuit saevis Bellona duellis
> regis culpa fuit. (384–89)

As Clytemestra in Dracontius is a more aggressively political creature, her perspective is set in terms of power and
rule, and the personal vengeance becomes a political re-
form. Her hypocrisy is so complete that she accuses Agamemnon of depriving sons of the affections of their fathers.
So cruel a man deserved to die as he did: the murder is
then the execution of justice. And *sua proles iacuit modo
vindice fluctu* (393): the recent news of the drowning of the
children is likewise a vengeance from heaven upon them.

By contrast with this violence, Clytemestra presents herself as the source of peace. There is a hypnotic quality in
her words as terms for rest and quiet accumulate:

> spondeo iam requiem, placidam sperate quietem:
> otia pacis erunt, nulla nocturna cubantem
> classica sollicitent . . . (394–96)

until we wonder whether the citizens are being lulled to
sleep or to some more permanent state of rest. And yet

there is an alluring vividness about Clytemestra's description of peace which is somehow at odds with the ruthless goal of her speech. It seems so heartfelt that it comes through from the poet's heart despite the character to whom the words are assigned. Rapisarda suggests that the lines arose from Dracontius' yearning for peace in a turbulent and violent world of the Vandal overlords.[49] This may account for the apparent intrusion of a biblical phrase: *curventur falcibus enses* (398) is surely a reminiscence of the great prophecy in Isaiah 2.4, "They shall beat their swords into ploughshares, and their spears into pruninghooks."[50] The yearning is Dracontius', though the speech is Clytemestra's.

The people are urged now to turn to enjoying life and to hope for a natural death, a decent burial, and an enduring grave.[51] These are all unspeakably ironic from the lips of the woman who has denied each of these hopes to her own husband and children.

After a final slur on the memory of Agamemnon (*crudelis et impius hostis*), Clytemestra announces that she is to marry Egistus, who will be as it were the Citizen Robespierre of Mycenae: *civis Egistus erit* (contrast *rex Agamemnon erat* in the previous line). We are given an account at once of how Citizen Egistus behaves, and it is predictably deplorable (412–18).

As in each scene involving the lovers, the arrogant, unintelligent bully Egistus is set off against the wily and passionate Clytemestra. Whereas she was able to formulate clever oratorical devices to deceive the people, he merely struts his imagined divinity[52] and behaves toward the servants as only a lowborn escapee from servitude could. The general tenor of the passage recalls the arrogant posture of Clytemnestra at the end of Aeschylus' *Agamemnon*.

To conclude the first major portion of the story, the poet reflects again on the appalling events he has depicted (419–26): who could have believed that such things could happen? Egistus was more feared, *bubulcus* though he was, than the mighty Hector; and the poet's epitaph for the good king is a gloomy ending indeed:

ius Agamemnonium fuerat: post Pergama capta
verbero plectibilis comes armipotentis Achillis. (425–26)

These lines are in effect a final choral passage to end the
"Agamemnon."

The reshaping of the story in the hands of our poet is
characteristic of his interests and his artistic tendencies.
He has simplified the characters to pure types of good and
evil, and has made the entire story revolve around two
issues: the sin of adultery and the nature of royal authority.
The good king is vanquished by two types: the adulterous
wife and the lowborn pretender to the throne. What Dracontius has lost in subtlety he has perhaps regained in the
vigor of his depictions. There is a satisfying sense of reaching a definite stage in the action. Evil is absolutely in control, but good will surely return. On this Saturday matinee
note, the first part of the poem concludes.

"Orestes" (453–802)[53]

The second phase of the poem, which I have called the
"Orestes," is of virtually the same length as the "Agamemnon" (376 lines), and likewise falls into five recognizable
"acts." Moreover, the recognition of these acts allows us to
see some interesting parallels of structure between the two
major divisions.

Clearly, the "Orestes" is analogous to the *Choephoroi*
and is similar to that play in presenting the return of Orestes and the slaying of Clytemestra and Egistus. But Dracontius also shows a different approach to his material and a
different economy for the story as a whole. In particular,
we must note how much happens before Orestes ever gets
back to Mycenae: whereas all the Greek plays on the theme
begin with the arrival of Orestes and are set entirely in
Argos, Dracontius' hero only reaches Mycenae at line 682,
nearly two-thirds of the way through this segment. The
poet spends more than 200 lines preparing us for the event
by having the characters thrash out the arguments for and

against so drastic an act and by imposing the matricide upon Orestes as a sacred duty from beyond the grave. There is then a commensurately abrupt treatment of the story once the hero returns.

The role of Electra has been eliminated entirely, which makes the intrigues in Mycenae both unnecessary and impossible. The Greek dramatic tradition placed heavy emphasis on the role of Electra. The mythographers basically preserve the tradition of the drama, although in Apollodorus there is no reference to Electra in his first statement of the matricide.[54]

Counterbalancing the loss of Electra are the role of Dorylas and the appearance of the ghost of Agamemnon. These are devices which the poet himself almost certainly invented—we have seen that Dorylas is a modification of other elements not intrinsic to the story—and shaped to fit parallel events in the "Agamemnon."

Thus we see in the Dracontian "Orestes" two familiar tendencies from the poet's other works. First, the streamlining of the plot so as to make the principal characters more readily recognizable as types by the elimination of obscuring side issues: the poet wishes to set up the starkest possible contrast between Orestes and Clytemestra, as he had done between Agamemnon and the queen. And second, the invention of new incidents which will lend structural symmetry to the poem as a whole.

i. 453–514

The passage of time marks the transition from one play to the next; continuity is provided by focusing on the *pastor* and his deplorable behavior on both sides of that time lapse. Dracontius has an odd detail: *fruebantur amore / annorum septem spatiis et mensibus octo* (454–55). This is both pointlessly precise and without basis in the rest of the tradition (generally, the term of Orestes' exile is seven years). I suspect Dracontius may have misread or misremembered Homer, *viz.*, the very passage which agreed with our poet by having Orestes return from Athens rather than Phocis:

ἐπτάετες δ' ἤνασσε πολυχρύσοιο Μυκήνης
κτείνας Ἀτρεΐδην, δέδμητο δὲ λαὸς ὑπ' αὐτῷ.
τῷ δὲ οἱ ὀγδοάτῳ κακὸν ἤλυθε δῖος Ὀρέστης.
(Od. 3.304–306)

The scene opens with the faithful band of servants gathering at Agamemnon's tomb to lament his death. Despite
Aricò's doubts, this is surely a reflection of the opening of
the *Choephori,* where the chorus comes in similar fear and
sorrow to make offerings at the king's tomb (75ff.). In our
poem the chorus displays its grief without speaking, its
urge to weep overcome by its fear of the tyrants, so that the
effect is rather like a mime. It is Dorylas who stands apart
as the leader of the chorus and speaks on behalf of the rest.

His long speech (462–99) serves both to summarize the
events to date and to look ahead to the second crisis, the
slaying of Clytemestra. He invokes the shade of Agamemnon to rise from the tomb. This is a prominent aspect of the
rest of the poem: the action is driven in both the "Orestes"
and in the "Orestes furens" by the vengeful shades of
Agamemnon and Clytemestra. Dracontius is perhaps affected by the prominent place which such specters have in
Senecan drama (cf. the shade of Thyestes at the opening of
his *Agamemnon,* and the shade of Tantalus who opens the
Thyestes)[55] and certainly by the taste for the supernatural
and the macabre common to his own time.

Dorylas' speech takes the form of a prayer, following the
conventions seen, for instance, in Medea's invocation of the
chthonic powers (*Med.* 436–46): invocation of the spirit of
Agamemnon, listing of his attributes, citing of past faithful-
ness, and finally specification of the favor being asked. This
is indeed the standard form for such prayers at all stages of
Greek and Latin literature but is normally used to invoke
divinities, not ghosts. It clearly puts Agamemnon in the
category of a god rather than simply a dead king and lends
further authority to his pronouncements when he responds.
The parallel with the invocation of the Furies also points
up how Agamemnon is to function: he, like Clytemestra in
the final segment, is a vengeful Fury.

But another sort of precedent is invoked. Dorylas refers
to the ghost of Achilles, who rose up to demand the sacrifice of Polyxena—by Agamemnon. The story is attested
from the *Iliupersis* onward,[56] but I believe Dracontius
had before him Ovid's recounting (*Met.* 13.440–79), as he
has used other details from that version elsewhere in this
poem.[57] As Achilles was stirred to demand the death of an
innocent woman as pacification of his shade, how can Agamemnon not demand the sacrifice of the woman who murdered him (479–82)? The motif will reappear in Orestes'
own reaction to his father's demands (622). It is not altogether clear what Dorylas is asking Agamemnon to do. Is
the king's shade itself to compass the death of Clytemestra,
or is Dorylas asking the ghost specifically to stir up Orestes
(of whom he makes no mention)? In terms of the subsequent developments Agamemnon will obviously go and
move Orestes to action, but Dorylas makes no such suggestion at this stage. Rather, he merely expresses the helpless
grief of the Mycenaeans and pleads with the powers beyond the grave to avenge somehow the murder of the king.
For this reason, the focus of the prayer shifts from Agamemnon to the Furies:

> di, regitis quicumque chaos crudele barathri,
> rumpite tartareas proscisso gutture fauces,
> mittite virgineas funesta in tecta cerastas! (483–85)

This will be a familiar place for the Furies to visit, notes
Dorylas, as they have already spent more than enough time
here in connection with the crimes of the House of Tantalus. Dracontius' debt to Statius is evident throughout the
prayer, as he reflects Oedipus' anguished plea to Tisiphone
and the Furies in *Thebaid* I.[58] But we can certainly also see
the similarities with Medea's invocation of the Furies, notably in 488f. (*Med.* 457–59). As Dorylas builds to the climax
of his prayer, he calls on the Furies to add torture to whatever Acheron may already provide:

> non sat erunt quaecumque reis tormenta paratis. (499)

Agamemnon's response from the depths of the earth is impressive but uninformative. He chides Dorylas with disturbing his grave instead of promoting his rest and recapitulates the crimes of his wife. The chief contribution of Agamemnon's remarks is to provide an assessment of Clytemestra which balances her description of him in 384ff. We have not heard any criticism of Clytemestra from Agamemnon since he arrived home laden with gifts for his presumably faithful wife. This scathing evaluation from the grave makes up for that lack. The poet plays with the echoing effects of *ultor/ultor adulterii/adultera/nec inultus* to link crime and punishment and lend a ritual solemnity to the ghost's utterance. The same eerie effect is achieved by Agamemnon's triple use of the name of Cassandra (512-13), urging the mourners to believe what the priestess had said. Inasmuch as Cassandra has foretold both the murder of the king and also the eventual revenge by Orestes, this is a statement which, like the rest of this scene, looks both backward to the "Agamemnon" and forward to the action of this segment.

After these highly theatrical declamations by Dorylas and the ghost, the poet marks a clear break in the action by a line of stage directions:

dixit et abscedunt omnes linquendo sepulchrum, (514)

in which the effect of a dramatic model is unmistakable. The poet has cleared the stage for the next scene, which will take us to Athens.

ii.515-626

Orestes is now a young man.[59] The flitting shade finds him asleep after exercise in the palaestra (attesting to his vigor and fitness to undertake revenge), with his inseparable friend Pylades. So closely linked are the two youths that their very breathing is intertwined:[60]

flatibus alternis perflans commercia somni
lassus uterque fuit, (518-19)

and this interdependence is carried even further as the ghost of Agamemnon appears to both of them at the same time (*ambobus visus Atrides in somnis*). I know of no parallel to this phenomenon of a ghost or a dream appearing to two persons simultaneously, as Orestes likewise *stupet attonitus* (555). Dracontius has apparently used this as a way of showing how Orestes and Pylades are essentially two aspects of a single personality, and this will become evident in other ways as the scene proceeds.

Agamemnon's appearance is reminiscent of several spectral apparitions, the most famous being the shade of Hector as he came to Aeneas (*Aen.* 2.268ff.).[61] In each case the purpose of the hero's appearance is to stir the sleeping recipient of the vision to action at a critical time. It was customary to describe the dead hero as he was when he died, and Dracontius has played this for all it is worth:

> tristis iners tremulus, gemitu suspiria rumpens;
> pallida puniceo perfuderat ora cruore
> et tremulas languore manus; cervice vacanti
> et pede vincla trahens quibus est abstractus ab aula. (523–26)

The lines show the same morbid taste for the gruesome as we saw in the account of the murder itself and will see again when the queen dies. No other poem of Dracontius shows this quality to nearly the same degree: it is an index of the horror with which the poet regarded his theme and perhaps a hint of the violence in the world in which he lived. We recall his earnest description of peace by contrast with these horrors (394ff.). The slaying of a king was not an unknown event in Dracontius' time, and palace plots and savage retribution likewise occurred. But at the same time, the visitation of a ghost was a theme so popular in both art and literature that Dracontius felt a challenge to emulate his predecessors with even more horrific effects.

Agamemnon's speech is a lawyer's performance, filled with principles and precedents. The ghost's aim is to rouse his son and to justify the action to which he is prompting

him. I believe that Vollmer has distorted the speech by the
insertion of lines 427–52, and I would place them instead
following 749, where their argument fits as it does not here.
For Agamemnon actually delivers a well-balanced oration,
moving smoothly from one topic to the next, and the ex-
crescence of a 26-line catalogue of exempla not only disrupts that even flow but also—and what is more important—speaks counter to the point he is otherwise making.

His indignation at first is aimed at Egistus, the usurping
pastor, for his luxurious existence on a stolen throne, his
voluptuous ways, and his pleasure at the presumed death of
the prince. Can Orestes stay idle in Athens while this situation prevails at home? Agamemnon first demands action as
a king, and then as a husband. He urges Orestes and Pylades to take up arms *in bella domestica* and with that turns
his thoughts to Clytemestra. He must argue that Orestes
will be justified in killing his mother,[62] and the argument
comes hard from so virtuous a figure as this particular Agamemnon. But the thought moves cleanly from 539–40 to
541ff. You will commit no crime in punishing your mother,
for you will be executing one who is already polluted by
hideous crimes (539–40). Indeed, your slaying of her, done
out of *pietas*, will not only prove your own status as your
father's son by avenging his death, but will actually purify
your mother of all her sins: *crimina purgabit matris de tempore prisco* (543). This is a single thought which can ill en-
dure being interrupted for 26 lines, especially for examples
which are less than germane. Consider the content of these
lines.[63] It is generally assumed that the first point of the
catalogue is to amplify Agamemnon's comment that Orestes
will be justified in killing Clytemestra, and the first example seems on the surface to look in that direction: Tamyris the Massagete queen slew Cyrus but did so in vengeance for her family and thus was justified. This is a
somewhat feeble parallel to Orestes killing his mother, the
only link being the vengeance for one's family; as Tamyris
was killing an enemy and no relative, the key point, the justification of matricide, is quite unaffected. The succeeding

illustrations move steadily further from any such theme, and all the instances adduced are *women* who acted in remarkable ways. Moreover, Clytemestra is addressed directly for most of the second half of the catalogue: we could regard this as an apostrophe by Agamemnon to the absent queen, but it is certainly more natural to regard the lines as addressed to Clytemestra in person, and therefore in another place.

To resume the king's arguments: Orestes will show himself to be a true son by avenging the crime of adultery (Agamemnon does not speak of the queen's role as murderer). He must be *pius ultor et heres*. Moreover, the Greek servants are all on Orestes' side so that he may rely on support in his task.[64] (Note how we have returned to the plural now—*ite pares animi* [547]—for the recovery of power will be a shared venture as distinct from the lonely burden of matricide.) Agamemnon seems to reveal an inherited characteristic in his description of the servants' eagerness:

> ore fremunt famuli, qui carpere dentibus optant
> corpus Egisteum vel vivum. (549–50)

We return to the Thyestean curse.

Orestes and Pylades awaken and are astonished that the dream could have appeared to them both at once.[65] The debate which follows (557–615) reveals the character of these two youths in interesting ways. It is startling to realize that not until line 557 does Orestes utter his first words of the poem. He will now dominate the action of the poem to its conclusion, at least in being the most prominent figure; but he is not at first a very imposing hero, as this debate shows. His first lines reveal both his indecisiveness and his tendency to let his emotions rule him: indeed, the poet seems to pile up words for emotional urges until he runs out of breath:

> "dic mihi, frater" ait "dic iam modo, quid sit agendum.
> pectora cor sensus animum praecordia mentem

conturbat pietas dolor anxia maeror origo
affectus natura pudor reverentia fama." (557–60)

His lush sentimentality and his hesitant nature are precisely the qualities most likely to deter him from so unnatural a deed as matricide, and in this way the horror
of his task is borne in on us. Orestes recalls that Clytemestra carried him in the womb he is now called upon to
pierce, nursed him at the breasts he must now attack, suffered as every mother does the pains of raising a baby. It is
an almost ludicrously overdrawn picture of the sacrifice of
motherhood, applied to the woman who after all made him
flee for his life at the age of eleven. The irreconcilable
duties to living mother and dead father are too much for
Orestes, and he decides that he will slay only Egistus as a
sacrifice to his father's *manes:* Clytemestra's punishment
will be to lose her lover. His words show how badly he
underestimates and misunderstands his mother: he calls
her *muliercula,* a drastically inadequate term for such an
adversary.[66]

Dixerat haec dubius. It is as if we are seeing two diametrical models of the human personality. Pylades strikes
back with near savagery in reacting to Orestes' maundering: *dentibus infrendens suspiria traxit ab imo / pectore
longa ferox.* Dracontius seems to be developing the one
role which Pylades plays in the *Choephori:* to encourage
Orestes when he hesitates to kill Clytemestra (*Ch.* 899–
903). His words are violent, sarcastic, confident and ruthless, all in contrast to Orestes: are we then to go back
to Mycenae to pardon and not to punish? Pylades returns to
Agamemnon's argument that Orestes must prove himself to
be his father's son by avenging his father's suffering. If not,
the ghost will surely walk again, and Pylades imagines what
speech the dead king might deliver the next time he haunts
Orestes (595–601). Surely Egistus could ask for nothing
better than to leave Clytemestra behind to avenge him by
murdering her son, which she would not hesitate to do.
Orestes must be either an avenger or a victim.

After further exhortations, Pylades pledges his support to Orestes in the ordeal ahead. And he shows his practical side as well as his *thymos* by recommending that he go ahead to reconnoiter at Mycenae and alert the servants to expect the prince's return.

Pylades' speech is a complete success. Orestes is so moved that he is now almost impossible to restrain, and he prances about in swashbuckling gestures, gnashing his teeth and stabbing at invisible foes. This scene is clearly reminiscent of the feeble Egistus who likewise, stirred by the dominant Clytemestra, suddenly shadowboxes in boundless confidence (222–23). Dracontius has made the two scenes parallel: Pylades and Clytemestra are both dominant and practical in laying out the plan to murder their enemies; Orestes and Egistus are alike driven by passion (albeit vastly different passions) and are ready to follow the advice of their partners. We may suspect that the poet was more intent on handling the two scenes in parallel manner than in drawing morals about contrasting characters.

Orestes is compared to Pyrrhus after Achilles' ghost had appeared to demand the sacrifice of Polyxena (we recall that Dorylas had cited the same precedent in invoking the king's shade, 476). It is an apt parallel here, for both princes have seen the ghost of their fathers requiring the death of a woman to put the shade at rest, and Pyrrhus was a particularly ferocious figure: witness his ruthless slaughter of Priam at the altar (*Aen.* 2.526–58). Moreover, Pyrrhus will appear again in this poem, to be slain by Orestes, and so the reference to the son of Achilles prepares us for that confrontation.

iii. 626–81

There is no change of scene or of time to mark the next phase of the action, but *ergo* (626) has a resumptive effect after the comparison of Orestes to Pyrrhus with which the debate concludes. This scene is a transitional passage, which links Athens and Mycenae by dwelling on the process of getting from one city to the other, thereby creating some suspense; and it also links the earlier phases of the action with the current situation by bringing Dorylas back for one final function.

Orestes and Pylades set out by night to return to Mycenae. The poet compares the young heroes to Diomedes and Ulysses in *Iliad* 10 (the *Doloneia*). The value of the comparison rests not only in the fact that they are stealing through the night on a dangerous mission. There is the same distinction in temper between the Homeric figures as between our heroes: *fortior Oenides, sollers Laertius heros* (637). The reference to Odysseus moreover points to an aspect of Orestes' situation which will find further emphasis as we proceed: like Ulysses, he is the rightful ruler presumed lost at sea, who must return by stealth and kill the usurpers to regain his position (Dorylas is to that degree analogous to Eumaeus the faithful servant who facilitates the homecoming).

It is not clear what Dorylas is doing on the road to Mycenae. As he meets the travelers, he asks the formulaic questions about their origin, names, and destination, but they try to pass him by in silence. He recognizes Orestes, however, and embraces the long lost prince, amazed that he is still alive. There is something unconvincing about this whole scene: if Dorylas was coming to look for Orestes, why is he surprised to find him alive? If he is not looking for him, this is a very clumsy coincidence to cope with a necessary meeting. Why does Orestes not recognize the man who saved his life and was his old *nutritor?* The picture does not hang together well, and so we must simply take it as a mechanism for advancing the action. It smacks of the coincidental encounters in faraway places found sprinkled through the plots of the romances, such as we have already seen in the meeting of Agamemnon and Iphigenia.

The meeting does have practical advantages, such as allowing Orestes and Pylades to learn of the situation at Mycenae and to make more specific plans. Dorylas' report of conditions at home is concentrated on the moral situation: the degeneracy of Egistus and Orestes' *polluta mater.*

There is no report of the populace suffering from this situation: the reaction is outrage, and the plea is for punishment on the guilty rather than release for the innocent. Dracontius has chosen to use the adultery as the outward proof of the sins—of all kinds—in the guilty couple. His condemnation, and that of all characters, looks to this fault almost exclusively.

Dorylas reports as well the assiduous lamentations at the grave of the king and Agamemnon's promise that justice will come (he adds, with charmingly ingenuous surprise, "even though Cassandra said it would happen, Agamemnon promised that it really would!").[67] He appeals both to Orestes' sense of duty and to his emotions, and we see again the twin aspects of personality embodied in the two young men. The dichotomy appears again in their reactions to Dorylas' news. Orestes is ready to dash into Mycenae, while Pylades shows his prudence in sending the old man ahead to alert the servants. This is the plan which Pylades had offered before they left Athens and merely provides a mechanism for carrying it out. Dorylas hurries off[68] and whispers in a few ears; the news is passed to all and the stage is set for the arrival of Orestes.

iv. 682–728

The transition to the fourth act is strongly marked. Not only is there a change of scene as the hero reaches Mycenae, but the poet describes the break of day at that moment. Nature participates in the renewal which Orestes' return brings. Not only is the rising sun a symbol of hope and a reversal of the moral darkness brought on by the crimes of Thyestes, but it also sheds relentless light on the sins of Egistus. Orestes makes a theatrical entrance at the walls of the city, which he had left "as an infant,"[69] and pauses to declaim his salute:

> dextram cum voce tetendit:
> "salve, prisca domus, patriae salvete Mycenae,
> execranda prius, sed post veneranda manebis
> sanguine si matris cineres satiabo paternos." (686–89)

This from the man who has skulked in the shadows to reach a place held by his enemies: but the entire plan of secrecy is ignored now, and both Orestes and Pylades simply proceed to confront their adversaries. There would seem to be little point in secrecy anyway, as Orestes is recognized at once by all the servants.[70]

Pylades continues to provide the initiative and even gives orders to Orestes that the doors be locked (note again the parallel to Odysseus as he begins his revenge on the suitors). The doors clang shut, *crepuerunt classica Mortis*. Egistus and Clytemestra had been confident of their position all these years, and *securus* is frequently used to describe their attitude. It carries a nicely ironic echo also of *secures*, by which they obtained that position and by which they will now lose all.

They are stunned by the sound of impending death, and their reactions are in each case characteristic.[71] Egistus is terrified, and if 701–703 are his lines rather than the queen's, he falls back on blustering and claiming credit for what Clytemestra had promised the people (peace in our time).[72] The lines are peculiar for either to deliver, as they now claim that the victory in Troy was what made Greece safe—Clytemestra had earlier used the war as the chief grounds of accusation against Agamemnon. The usurpers' memory of their own propaganda is weak. Clytemestra's reaction is likewise characteristic: she lashes out in imperious fury at the servants.

When a servant girl announces that Orestes has returned, she is not believed. Obviously this is Orestes' entrance cue—but instead, enter Pylades. He is a dreadful figure, likened to Ajax as he pursued Hector (*Il.* 7.205ff.). Note how the poet distinguishes once more between Pylades and Orestes, for the prince will not be given a heroic simile at his appearance. Pylades is wrathful fury, but Orestes is righteous vengeance. So Dracontius has carefully distributed the action, with Pylades confronting Egistus and Orestes left to face his mother in the next scene. The chief effect of this is to isolate the matricide which is to be tried in the final segment of the poem.

The division of fates for Clytemestra and Egistus corresponds both to the distinction between the roles of Orestes and Pylades and also to the distinction between the crimes of the two culprits. Clytemestra has consistently been seen as the more guilty of the two because of her role as planner, and the fact that it is her husband whom she has murdered. There is thus a climactic arrangement in the revenge scenes which gratifies both our theatrical and our moral demands.

Pylades acts as if with full regal authority: he pronounces sentence on both and decrees that they are to die separately. There is a crude and predictable justice in the sentence—Egistus is to be knocked off the throne he has usurped and treated exactly as Agamemnon was treated:

> carnifices frangant durissima[73] membra secures
> et pereat pastor qua regem morte peremit. (721–22)

The poet indulges once more his taste for the gruesome as we hear of the zeal with which this sentence is carried out by the servants. True to the decree that Egistus is to die as Agamemnon had done, the usurper even twitches in agony as his limbs are severed (cf. 264). Moreover, the execution is performed in the same spot in which the king had perished. There is a sense of definite, even if tedious, poetic justice in the whole matter, although *carnifices secures* reminds us of the base nature of the criminal, as does the contrast *pastor . . . regem*.

v. 729–802

In many ways, this is the most important segment of the poem, for it contains the event toward which all the rest have been tending and from which the rest of the poem will proceed. It is the scene which brings together the two most important figures, and the one in which the moral issues are foremost. Here we may see the greatest similarity to the Greek tragedian's purposes; and indeed the similarity to drama is enhanced further by the short speeches which they exchange (nearly all 5 or 6 verses) creating an effect equivalent to stichomythia.

Clytemestra is in the same situation as in the first segment of the poem: after an initial alarm when punishment
seemed inevitable, she believes that she will not suffer
after all (*secura* 730; cf. 700). This time, however, the tables
are turned. Orestes enters like Agamemnon, as a conquering prince returned home—not as a victim. His aspect is
like Pylades, *truculentus, immanior hoste, terribilis*, and
his rage against his mother conveyed by the same basic
questions (*impune . . . sperasti regnare?*). And as Pylades
has executed Egistus in the same manner as Agamemnon
died, so now Orestes will kill his mother in the same spot as
the king.

Clytemestra bares her bosom and appeals to Orestes as
the mother who nursed him: this is taken ultimately from
Aeschylus (*Ch.* 896), but recalls precisely the nature of
Orestes' own fretting (566–69) as he imagined this moment. The queen's frantic words convey both her panic and
her characteristic willingness to say anything she thinks
might help her:

> per haec, puer, ubera, parce!
> per superos patremque tuum, per cara sororis
> pectora, quae nostro te tunc rapuere furori,
> et per Pyladen, quod plus est, testor amicum. (740–43)

Her appeal says nothing about the charge itself, but merely
relies on sentiment, and as we have seen, Orestes is a sentimental soul. But he has recovered from such weaknesses
now, and his reply to his mother is a stern one. Against
her catalogue of sentimental appeals he sets illustrations of
other women's behavior. The speech deserves scrutiny because it seems to be at odds with information found elsewhere even in this poem; and I believe that the wandering
lines 427–52 should be placed within this speech.

Orestes' main point throughout is that Clytemestra
should not have slain Agamemnon despite whatever reasons she may have felt justified the act. In 747–49 he gives
two illustrations of women who might have had cause to
slay men but did not. The first is surprising:

Ilias ingemuit domini Cassandra ruinam.

This of course refers to the death of Agamemnon who, in the older tradition, had not only captured Cassandra but had made her his concubine, and at his death she wept. But in Dracontius, as in Seneca, the Trojan captive is filled with joy at the king's death, by which Troy is avenged for his victory. Orestes' point is consistent with the older versions and shows one who had more than enough reason to kill Agamemnon, yet did not. And second, Orestes cites Andromache, who was enslaved after the death of Hector and handed over to Pyrrhus her conqueror; and yet even with this hideous fate, she did not strike down the source of her suffering. Both, it will be noted, are not Greeks but Trojans.

It is in this context of women who have responded to strong provocation or urging that I believe the catalogue of 427–52 should follow 749. Consider what would ensue. Dracontius gives further examples of women's behavior in these lines. The first is Tamyris, queen of the Massagetae, who took a ghastly and celebrated vengeance on Cyrus (cf. Herod. 1.205–15). She slew a king, to be sure, but there was no wrong in her act because she was avenging her son who had taken his own life when captured by the king.

> praecidit regem Tamyris regina Getarum,
> sed nil turpe gerens vindex fuit illa suorum.[74]

This is an apposite illustration to fling at Clytemestra, but ill chosen as a justification of Orestes' matricide (which is the necessary function if the lines come after 540). Second, Orestes adduces Medea, who admittedly murdered several members of the royal house, but did so in the wild grief of losing her wedded love.[75] She acted to punish the *paelex* Glauce and was thus defending marital bonds, not the reverse.

The next few lines are unnecessarily obscure in other editions because of faulty punctuation. They should be presented as follows:[76]

impia Lemniades sumpserunt arma puellae
atque maritali foedarunt sanguine lectos,
sed Veneris furor acer erat; facinusque nefandum
quod Scythicae gessere nurus: in crimine tanto,
barbara turba fuit. (432–36)

Third, then, are the Lemnian women, who illustrate not
regicide but mariticide. Dracontius can at least note that
they were driven by *furor Veneris*, although that is a weak
excuse at best since Clytemestra can presumably make the
same plea. The fourth crime is obscure: who were these
Scythian women, and what was their misdeed? Apparently
nefandum is to be taken literally in this case, but the context would strongly suggest slaying husbands again.

We thus have three pairs of exempla: two who refrained
from killing a king, then two who indulged in it, and two
who killed their spouses. But all six examples thus far are
summarized in *barbara turba fuit*. Here are barbarian
women, of whom we may expect less restrained behavior,
and yet some of them showed restraint, and the rest had
some justification.

But *you*—and Orestes turns now to Clytemestra—you
are a Greek and a queen from the homeland of the law
(*legum fecunda creatrix*), whose husband was a king and
the avenger of adultery: but you have committed both
adultery and mariticide and are worse than the barbarians.
It would have been better to emulate the Greeks in the
matter of wifely conduct, and with this Orestes brings in
two final examples at the other end of the spectrum:[77] Alcestis, who so far from encompassing her husband's death
prevented it by offering herself in his stead; and Evadne,
whose loyalty was so great that she even slew herself on her
husband's pyre to be with him in the next world.[78] There
are many examples, concludes Orestes, of what *honestus
amor* is (452), but you—and we rejoin the text with 749—
have instead laid your lord low with the connivance of a
common herdsman.

In this way the speech is neatly constructed, moving in
four pairs of examples through the main points of his indict-

ment. The whole passage has an air of the exercise about it
and may indeed have been adapted from some earlier composition. This would incidentally explain why several of the
examples are at odds with what the poet himself says elsewhere; and that is a feature of both parts (747–49 and
427–52) which may further argue for uniting them.

Orestes ends by claiming to act under the commands of
Pylades (a fine illustration of Pylades as Orestes' *thymos*)
and of a sister—whether the absent Electra or the presumably dead Iphigenia we are not told.

Clytemestra sees that appeals for mercy will avail her
nothing, and she shifts the grounds of her plea. At least let
Pylades slay her, with the same sword as Egistus and atop
the body of her paramour, whom she rather ungraciously
calls *nostri criminis auctor* (758). Her explanation has been
misunderstood:

> mixtus uterque cruor testabitur omnibus umbris
> consortes scelerum quia sors manet una malorum. (759–60)

The scene is a variant on the *Choephori*, in which Orestes
threatens to kill Clytemestra atop the body of Egistus as she
valued him more highly than her own husband (*Ch.* 904f.).
Here it is the queen who requests it, and Orestes who refuses to accommodate her. Rapisarda saw this as evidence
of Clytemestra's penitence at the point of death: she wants
to go with Egistus to the underworld in order to warn the
shades of the penalties awaiting sins such as hers. This
moral focus is present in Orestes, but not in Clytemestra,
who—in a perverted echo of Evadne—wants simply to
join her lover in the next world by perishing atop his body.
She wants the shades to know that they shared a fate, not
that the wages of sin is death, which is presumably a shal-
low lesson to those already dead.

Orestes is equally aware of the symbolism, and perhaps
the practical results, if his mother dies in conjunction with
Egistus, and he will not mingle their blood on the same
blade, nor allow their bodies to fall together. Instead, he

insists that she be taken to the tomb of her husband to be
executed as a sacrificial offering to the shade of Agamemnon.
This seems to be an interpretation developed by Dracontius
and would certainly appear to run counter to the Christianized understanding of the poem advanced by Rapisarda.
There is rather the tone of an anguished Achilles sacrificing
victims to the shade of Patroclus:

> accipito inferias quas offero. victima iusta est:
> macto Clytemestram matronam regis Egisti
> atque (utinam non!) ante tuam. (769–71)

Throughout the poem Egistus has been *pastor,* or at best
civis; now Orestes with heavy sarcasm calls him *rex,* and
Clytemestra is his *matrona.* After a final prayer from Clytemestra (modeled, Rapisarda claims unconvincingly, on
Prometheus' prayer in *PV* 87ff.), which ends on the note of
the thankless child, Orestes strikes down his mother. Dracontius tries his best not to describe the deed directly, and
in fact does not ever say that Orestes struck the blow. Instead, the prince turns his face, *quod potuit pietas, vultus
avertit Orestes,* and nature does the same. At the beginning of this confrontation the sun came out to reveal a new
day, but now it hides its face in horror at what it has shown.
This is the second time the sun has refused to appear because of the crimes in Mycenae, the first occasion being
the deeds of Thyestes,[79] and with that comparison we are
brought to realize the enormity of what Orestes has done.
However justified and encouraged he may have been up to
now, his deed remains unnatural and revolting, the devour-
ing of his kinsman as surely as Thyestes' meal.

The dying queen is overcome by sudden *pudor,* and
draws her garment down to cover her feet, *metuens ne
mortua nuda iaceret.*[80] It is an unexpected gesture, which
has been interpreted as the penitent sinner acquiring that
sense of shame which she had lacked until now and presenting an image of that new grace: "così su Clitenestra si
posa la carità divina."[81] But the scene is in fact borrowed

from Ovid: Polyxena acts in precisely the same manner as
she dies (*Met*. 13.478–79):

> tunc quoque cura fuit partes velare tegendas,
> cum caderet, castique decus servare pudoris.

Quartiroli was more perceptive:[82] this is an exceedingly
vain woman who finds herself helpless before her enemy
and takes the only action she can to bestow dignity on herself. She fears for her reputation at all times, and we have
just heard her speak of how the shades in Hades will regard
her. Now she worries, unreasonably but in a manner common to persons in disasters, about minor details. The *pudor* is not a Christian category of conscience, but the traditional Roman concern. The moment of her death is sharply
visualized by the poet, including the red blood splashing on
her white limbs as she thuds to the ground like her husband and lover before her. There is something almost admirable about her reluctance to surrender her life: *tandem
iussa mori vitam cum sanguine fudit*.

The hunt is over, and the two warriors return home like
lions sated with killing cattle. It is a brief simile (796–97),
cruel and effective after the baroque scene we have just
witnessed.

As we come to the end of this second phase of the trilogy,
there is another equivalent to a chorus to mark the moment. The citizens of Mycenae assemble to greet their de-
liverer and new lord. It is remarkable that Dracontius
should have a divided response among the folk, nowhere
else reported in this way:

> pars dolet Atriden, set pars dolet altera matrem,
> nemo tamen facinus verbis culpabat apertis,
> nec fuerat quisquam qui non damnaret Egistum. (800–802)

The ambiguity reflects both the final smidgeon of rehabilita-
tion we saw in Clytemestra, translated into residual admiration among the citizens, and also the unpalatable condition

in which Orestes now finds himself. The Mycenaeans will regret the death of both their king and queen, but nobody has the slightest regret for the removal of the unspeakable Egistus. The confrontation between Clytemestra and Orestes has shown us a genuinely interesting, and impressively depraved, criminal and an avenging angel in full fury. At the end of that confrontation, the wicked queen has gained some little measure of our sympathy in dying, and the angel has fallen into grievous sin by performing his sacred duty. The two figures loom so large as against Egistus that the poet is able to despise him without qualification.

Thus the "Orestes" ends with the elimination of Clytemestra and Egistus, and with the citizens of Mycenae gathered around the palace to learn their fate. This is precisely parallel to the end of the "Agamemnon"—the death of the king and the citizens gathered to hear from their new ruler what will become of them.

"Orestes furens" (803–974)

At this point in the story Dracontius finds himself in something of a difficulty. Obviously what remains to be told is the *Eumenides* or its equivalent; but he has so downplayed the divine element (as distinct from the ghosts) that it would be a redefinition of the world of the poem to introduce the Furies as the prosecutors in the third segment.

What is missing then is a mechanism by which Orestes will be tried and purged of his guilt. Who is to accuse Orestes? Dracontius has solved the problem by indulging a tendency we have seen in other poems, namely, presenting a more or less comprehensive version of the hero's story. The result is a final segment which is teeming with incidents from the Orestes myth. Dracontius has drawn on the other homicidal experience of Orestes, the slaying of Pyrrhus, and has used that as the springboard for the rest of the story. This entails the betrothal to Hermione and—in this version—the intervention of Molossus. Dracontius also throws in the visit to the land of the Taurians, so that

the total effect is much like the account of Paris in the
Helen: a garland of the hero's major adventures festooning a
central theme.

This part of the poem is much shorter than either of the
previous segments and is much more episodic. Eventually
the threads are drawn together, but we are given a unique
rendition of the Orestes myth.

The "act" structure is less developed in this portion as
well, and in particular there is nothing corresponding to the
choral pauses we have seen in the other parts, at least until
the final reflections by the poet in the epilogue (963–74).
But there are still five recognizable segments.

i. 803–19

We have seen already how nature participates in the events
of moral significance in our story, and the beginning of this
third tragic narrative is another example. The day whose
dawning marked the return of Orestes is now over, and the
night signifies the darker times ahead for all concerned. At
midnight comes the report that Hermione, Orestes' be-
trothed,[83] has been carried off by Pyrrhus. The accounts of
this abduction, its justification and results, are dreadfully
confused in the sources[84] but nowhere does this sequence
of events appear. We should not look too closely at the chronology, which traditionally requires Orestes to be affianced
to Hermione before the Trojan War (though he was, like
Telemachus, a mere infant at the start of that war) so that
Menelaus' promise to Pyrrhus will be a second giving away.
No more should we expect consistency in a story which
usually has Pyrrhus abduct Hermione after Orestes is mad,
and, in the most extreme versions, after Hermione is already married to Orestes and bearing his child.[85]

In Dracontius' telling, however, Orestes is deprived of a
fiancée he never had time to acquire, and the abduction occurs immediately after he regains his heritage. He is not
yet mad, although there may be a trace of the traditional
sequence in *furit* (809).

Why would Dracontius rearrange the tradition in this

manner? It is probably wrong to imagine, as Quartiroli does, that our poet found the version in some lost mythographic source.[86] We have a wide variety of sources, and none of them points in this direction. Moreover, the solution is really tailored to Dracontius' own narrative demands. Orestes has been carefully vindicated in his actions to date, and the moral ambiguities concerning both Agamemnon and Clytemestra have been removed. There is, in that sense, nothing to drive the action of this last part of the poem. No other version of the myth suffers this want. Moreover, it fits with the tastes of our poet, in showing a *gusto romanzesco* in the adventures imposed upon the hero. Here we have another prince abducting a princess, a hero going off to rescue her, meetings in faraway lands, chance reunions, and so on. These we have already seen in Paris and Helen, Telamon and Hesione, Jason and Medea.

There is a hint of Hercules as Orestes learns of the next task before him: *nos alius vocat ecce labor.*

We seem to be suddenly in the flow of a series of adventures rather than in a unified story. But in fact, Orestes is being plunged into a reworking of his family history, as he is cast once again as the avenger of adultery (a major theme of Ovid's version). This time he is himself the aggrieved victim—he has grown up to take his father's place: *nam decet ultorem patris sibi quoque mereri* (814).

But this high-sounding talk rings hollow as we see Orestes track down Pyrrhus entering a temple and slay him at the altar. Dracontius has used Vergil's language to describe the deed (*obtruncat ad aras*),[87] a harsh phrase which Vergil himself had repeated from Pyrrhus' sacrilegious murder of Priam in the carnage of Troy (2.663). There is no explanation of Pyrrhus' act, or even an elaboration of it which might make Orestes' sacrilege seem more understandable. We may feel that Pyrrhus has been repaid in kind, as is the general law of this poem, but the crime on Orestes' head is no less severe for that. Even worse, he returns home *elatus caede secunda,* and the sin of this slaying seems to spill back onto the grim duty of the first killing.

The episode is brief and ends very abruptly. The quick shifts from one theme to another and the sparseness of the narrative create the impression that Dracontius has inserted this event because it served a purpose but that it has not engaged his interest. The consequences of the murder will loom later on, but for now the matter is simply dropped.

ii. 820–61

When we looked at the "Agamemnon," we noted that the first scene, of Agamemnon's visit with Iphigenia, seemed almost intrusive in the sense that the poem would have flowed smoothly from the end of the prologue to the beginning of the second scene and thereby kept the traditional sequence. The same effect is observable here: if we were to go directly from 802 to 821, we would find the traditional sequence closely preserved. In 802, Orestes has just claimed his victory over his mother, and in 821f. he is visited by the fury of his mother. The Pyrrhus episode seems all the more intrusive for its lack of development and the abruptness with which it begins and ends. But as with the detour to the Taurians in 41ff., the poet has integrated the story into the larger plot. The price Dracontius pays, however, is that the madness of Orestes comes not as an immediate consequence of the matricide, but only after Orestes is settled on the throne with two murders under his belt.

In keeping with the general treatment of the divinities, it is not the Eumenides themselves who haunt Orestes but Clytemestra with the attributes of a Fury:

> astitit ante oculos genetrix sua non ut inermis,
> sed faculis armata rogi, subcincta cerastis.
> ignibus admotis resolutos orbibus angues
> ingerit in faciem iuvenis, mortale minatur. (821–24)

That Clytemestra herself should haunt Orestes is not new with Dracontius, since Vergil had already summoned such a dream for the desperate Dido (*Aen.* 4.471–73) although

in that passage the Furies themselves also sit *in limine*.[88]
Clytemestra has all the attributes of Tisiphone the arche-
typal torturer (cf., e.g., Tib. 1.3.69; Ovid *Met.* 4.780ff.). I
do not know what Quartiroli had in mind by her comment
that having Clytemestra haunt Orestes "rende più intima
l'atmosfera della pazzia,"[89] but that is unlikely to have been
the primary intent of the poet in adopting this version. It is
a "humanized" rendition, and a streamlined depiction of a
complex idea—both features common in Dracontius' poetic imagination.

The ghost of Clytemestra takes a very high tone for one
with her record. Because of the unique sequence which
our poet has adopted, Clytemestra is able to charge Orestes
with both her own death and the slaying of Pyrrhus, as
these will likewise be conjoined in the trial. And whereas
the Furies pursued Orestes because his crime was simply
and elementally wrong, a violation of the most primitive ta-
boos, Clytemestra is in effect weighing the precise extent of
his sinfulness by compiling a list of charges, and the effect
is discordant because of her own character.

As she attacks him with the flame,[90] Orestes tries to fight
back against the insubstantial foe—a picture perhaps derived (as Aricò suggests) from Euripides' *Iphigenia in Tauris* 296ff. It will also recall, however, the previous scenes in
this poem of Orestes battling the invisible enemy (616ff.).[91]
He fends her off by showing her the blade with which she
was killed, but her task is already done, and the madness is
implanted. Dracontius cannot restrain himself and gives
three illustrations of madness in other heroes. But even despite this pedantry,[92] the pace of the scene is very rapid,
with the repetitions of *perfurit . . . ut furit . . . ut furit*.
The madness takes the form of seeing his mother everywhere (*matrem . . . matrem . . . mater*): even his friends
and servants appear to him with her countenance, and
everywhere he finds the fire and the serpent which were
her instruments of torture. The only person who does not
terrify and delude Orestes is his alter ego Pylades.

The other form of torture is that Orestes may not eat. In

the midst of royal banquets he is starving—he is in fact re-
living the punishment of his ancestor Tantalus, with the implied judgment that he is similarly guilty.

Obviously this scene of a spectral appearance must be
viewed beside the equivalent (second) scene in the "Agamemnon," of the king's shade visiting Orestes. In both
cases the prince's dead parent stirs him to ungovernable
emotions and impels him to action (specifically a voyage).
In both he has settled into an untroubled existence only to
be driven from it by a voice from the dead; in both he relies
on Pylades to guide him and in both he shows his spirit by
swinging at the empty air with his sword. The depiction of
Orestes' madness is very fine[93]—Dracontius is at his best
in such scenes—and keeps before our eyes both his helplessness in the grip of this frenzy and the guilt which has
prompted it.

iii. 862–86

The story is now catapulted forward by another novelty of
plot which we may in all probability assign to Dracontius.
Molossus, the son of Pyrrhus by Andromache, comes to
avenge the death of his father. Elsewhere, when Orestes is
taken to trial by a human accuser (leaving aside, that is, the
unique situation of the *Eumenides*), it is either Clytemestra's father Tyndareus or Egistus' daughter Erigone.[94] Once
again, it is fruitless to speculate on what lost source may
have secured as Dracontius' inspiration, for the situation
he presents is distinctively suited to the poem and was his
own idea. His fondness for patterns and repetitions has
yielded a mirror image of Orestes: a prince come to avenge
the death of his father. The figure is a familiar type and
needs no development, which is precisely what Molossus
gets. He is at this point a mere mechanism to drive the next
phase of the action. He will have his day in court shortly.
Meanwhile, it is to escape Molossus that Orestes leaves
Mycenae and goes to the land of the Taurians. Thus the
three strands of the story are pulled together—the matricide and subsequent trial, the adventures *in Tauris*, and
the slaying of Pyrrhus.

Orestes is more adept at getting into trouble than getting out, but he can apparently rely on his friends to rescue him. On a previous occasion he was rescued by his sister Electra and taken to Athens where he met Pylades. This time he is rescued by Pylades and sent to the Taurian shores where he meets his sister Iphigenia. He leads a very patterned existence.

As we would expect by now, Dracontius' Orestes *in Tauris* is different from the traditional version in several respects. It is given in a very spare narrative, presenting the whole story in precisely twenty verses, and so there are few explanations. This makes it all the more remarkable that the poet has introduced so many unusual features into a brief segment of his story. Yet I believe that virtually all the novel features are Dracontius' own, precisely because they fit the other details of his new version so carefully. For example, consider the fact that Pylades does not accompany Orestes on this journey but merely sends him (as he imagines) to safety. Two considerations come to mind: first, there is now nothing for Pylades to do in the encounter with Iphigenia. The poet strips down the scene until it matches the simple one-on-one encounter of Agamemnon and Iphigenia. Second, as noted, the stated purpose of the visit is not linked either to Orestes' madness or to retrieving the image of Artemis. Unfortunately, this removes any reason for Orestes to find himself at the other end of the world. The narrative structure at this point is arbitrary but functional: it gives no explanations, but merely has those things occur which the narrator wants to have happen.

> Pylades Orestem
> tollit et externas subtractum mittit ad oras.
> litora contigerat. (865–67)

Orestes is immediately seized and bound for sacrifice, and now the novelties come thick and fast. Although Euripides' Iphigenia was careful to explain that she did not perform the sacrifices herself (*IT* 617–24), Dracontius is equally explicit that she does wield the knife. The differ-

ence again may seem slight, but it raises in the most direct
manner the prospect of yet another family member slaying
a kinsman (one sister saves his life, the other takes it). The
result of this impending death is another surprise, some
part of Orestes' sanity returns: *expulsus terrore furor*.[95]
This eliminates the role of Apollo, as we might expect
by now.

With all these changes, we still have not had the recognition of brother and sister. Now that Orestes has regained at
least part of his senses, he calls on the name of Agamemnon
(like Croesus on the pyre invoking Solon), which naturally
astonishes Iphigenia:

> hostia, dic, quis eras, aut cur Agamemnona clamas? (875)

Orestes ignores the grim implications of the imperfect *eras*
(*ego sum miserandus Orestes*) and half the suspense is over.
It rests with Iphigenia to extricate her brother from his
peril (like Electra before her), but the simplicity of the
structure provides an advantage at this point: there is no
Thoas to deceive with the ruse of washing the cult figure.
Yet Iphigenia must account for her sudden action in sparing
the victim. She pretends he is unsatisfactory, *sanguine
corda carent, non est haec hostia grata* (881),[96] and he is
released; when the acolytes are dismissed, she identifies
herself to her brother.

Two actions remain, and both are surprising. Orestes was
only partially restored to sanity by his terror at knife point,
and Iphigenia exercises what sounds suspiciously like magi-
cal rites by night to cure him. Note that it is not so much
a purification by the gods but a cure from his madness by
the incantations of—dare one say it—a witch. Apollo is not
involved at any stage. More striking is the way in which
this Iphigenia looks like a Medea working her charms by
night. Indeed, these final lines will remind us of Dracontius' *Medea* in another way as well. We saw in *Medea* (360ff.)
how the poet brought his story of the events in Colchis
to an abrupt end, even including the murder of Medea's
brother apparently because it was a part of the traditional

narrative and was simply left in despite its irrelevance. In precisely the same fashion, this adventure among the Taurians throws in a traditional item:

quem nocte precatu
purgat et *ablata* migrat cum fratre *Diana*. (885–86)

It was how the story ended, from Euripides onward. Unfortunately there has been no mention of the statue, and there has been no role for the gods which would make the statue relevant. There is no role for Athena either, for this human-oriented situation now requires no *deus ex machina*.

We should perhaps return for a moment to Barwinski's objection[97] that Diana is content to allow Orestes and Iphigenia to leave now but prevented Agamemnon from taking her with him earlier. The dynamics of that inconsistency is clear enough. As the vestigial reference to the statue shows, the story here has been pruned to eliminate the goddess and concentrate on the brother and sister as responsible for their own fates; the earlier episode is parallel in many ways, including the surprise arrival of Iphigenia's kinsman, a scene of her at the temple, the recognition, and the hasty departure. The quick allusion to the angry goddess in 104 is a parallel to the mention of Diana in 886, but in the earlier instance she performs a function which is not only traditional in the Taurian narrative (albeit with Orestes), but which she alone can perform. In its own odd way, the role of Diana in 104 is as much a vestige as the statue in 886.

iv. 887–938

We saw in the "Orestes" how Dracontius did not move at once to the traditional events—beginning with the return of Orestes—but occupied more than half of his account with preparatory matters. So also we come only now, in the fourth scene, to the trial, having occupied the interim with other matters, which will point to the issues to be raised in *his* version of the trial.

That the trial took place in Athens was a standard part of

the tradition,[98] but it comes oddly in this version which makes no use of the Areopagus as a vehicle of divine justice. We may well doubt, however, whether Dracontius gave thought to the possibility of a change of venue. It was, after all, where Orestes had gone in the earlier portion of the story, and no doubt represented the center of Greek life to the poet. But the trial sounds more like a case heard by a Roman court than by the Areopagus:

> legibus exhibitum mediis induxit Athenis;
> conscendere patres templum praebente Minerva. (889–90)

Certainly we are operating in the realm of Roman law, as Molossus' comments on punishment show, and we should imagine the scene as a Roman trial rather than even a loose imitation of the trial presented in Aeschylus.

Dracontius is at his best in this scene, as it gave him a grand chance to deal with the world of the law to which he was devoted. The scene consists essentially of the two speeches, by Molossus (892–908) and Orestes (911–37). It would be pleasing to imagine that Dracontius modeled these two lawyer figures after specific characters of his own experience, for both are convincing depictions of courtroom manners and tactics.

Molossus is all business, a man who relies exclusively on the law and its provisions. Even his opening address to the magistrates reflects this: *proceres, legalis origo.* Contrast Orestes, who begins by addressing *sapientes, lumina cordis* because he bases his argument on wisdom and emotion more than on law codes.

We would expect Molossus to concentrate on the murder of Pyrrhus—for why else would Molossus be prosecuting the prince?—but he speaks primarily of the matricide, to which he has no connection, and the result is a weak case. It could be argued that this is a flaw in Dracontius' conception of the trial, that he has combined two quite separate charges which ought to be considered separately, but I suspect it should be seen as a weakness in Molossus' approach which Dracontius has built in so as to make the prosecution's case shaky and allow for an acquittal. At any rate, Molossus turns at once to Orestes' violation of sacred and profane law in the death of Clytemestra, for which the only possible response from the court is death. As the *fact* that Orestes slew his mother is uncontested, Molossus proceeds to anticipate *reasons* which the defense might allege to exculpate him: *sed adultera forsan/mater erat.* In that case she could indeed be put to death, but Molossus thus ties in the second charge: surely Pyrrhus was not another Egistus that he deserved to die on holy ground? The shift is his one clever move, comparing Pyrrhus to the one figure who has had no sympathy from anyone (cf. 802), and moreover referring to Pyrrhus as *eversorem Asiae*—a considerable exaggeration in itself, but a rhetorically effective one, since the phrase was last used in describing none other than Agamemnon at the moment of his death (275).

A second line of defense is anticipated: that Clytemestra was not only guilty of adultery but also of murder. Granted there was no doubt that she had to be punished, but it did not rest with her son to take the law into his own hands. We need not conjecture that Dracontius had to rely on Euripides to provide this argument (*Or.* 500ff., where it is offered by Tyndareus),[99] which in fact merely amounts to asserting the competence of the court to hear the case and the authority of the law over private vendetta.[100] Not only is this one fundamental issue of the poem—the devastating effects of revenge in kind—as well as a fundamental issue of the Roman legal tradition, but it is a courtroom ploy as old as the law itself and could surely have occurred to a seasoned pleader like Dracontius without prompting from Euripides.

The punishment Molossus proposes is entirely Roman and quite specifically for the murder of Clytemestra (it is the sentence for *parricidium* which Molossus discusses):

cuius in exitium sat erit non culleus unus. (906)

Roman law provided for parricides a peculiar and archaic punishment: that after a lashing they should be sewed into

a sack with assorted live animals and thrown into the sea.[101]
But that is not enough: Molossus requires that Orestes suffer the same fate as all the other victims in Mycenae before
him, but even more gruesomely and deliberately:

> partibus abscisis sibi sit de morte superstes,
> tempore sed modico vivax laniando cadaver. (908–909)

The extreme tone of Molossus' proposal, amounting to a
savage continuation of the law of vendetta, finally makes
his whole presentation suspect and sets up the contrast
with the earnest and restrained Orestes.

The prince's plea is attuned more to the dictates of the
heart and of the gods than the mere terms of a law code.
He is a smooth performer; we can hear the genuine courtroom pleader in Dracontius: *gaudeo securus quod apud
vos causa movetur* (913).

As Molossus had begun his speech with the matricide
rather than the death of Pyrrhus, so Orestes curiously begins with his second crime. It is hardly a cogent line of legal
argument: surely the judges have wives, or can remember
being young and in love. Orestes wisely does not pursue
this any further, but it shows the sentimental, emotional
character he has exhibited throughout the poem and is a
nice passing appeal to their hearts.

The rest of Orestes' defense deals not with his actions
but with the manifest support which he enjoys from the
gods. He is grateful to the gods that they have restored his
sanity, and by their gift he can distinguish right from wrong.
This places his actions in the realm of the sacred, reflecting
the will of the gods, so that

> non de lite mea sententia vestra ferenda est,
> sed de iure deum, qui me purgasse probantur. (912–22)

It is only fair to point out the inaccuracy of this claim,
however ingenious it may be in taking the whole case away
from the prosecution. First, as we have seen, Dracontius
actually eliminated the action of Apollo in restoring Ores-

tes' sanity; second, even if this ability to discern right from wrong has come to him by the healing power of the gods, both the matricide and the murder of Pyrrhus occurred before his madness, so that a plea of temporary insanity is irrelevant.

The accusation against Orestes is thus cast as an impious act, since Molossus must accuse the gods themselves of sin. But Orestes can foresee objections as well as his opponent: if the gods favored him, why was he driven mad in the first place? Orestes' answer can only be called a prevarication:

cura doloris erat, proceres, nec poena reatus:
taedia sollicitant animos mentemque fatigant. (932–33)

The visit of the vengeful shade of Clytemestra was never presented as a delusion or the product of Orestes' fevered imagination: she was as real as the ghost of his father. A more modern, psychologically oriented reaction to the scene might resolve the difference by internalizing the vision, but it would be unreasonable to impute such thoughts to the poet. Orestes is simply asserting what we must regard as false—that he has not been accused by powers beyond the human realm.

Orestes concludes by setting both killings in contrast with the actions of those he killed:[102] if Clytemestra deserves to be avenged—as this trial shows—then how much more so Agamemnon? And Pyrrhus likewise was already a criminal, Orestes again the avenger after the fact. The only dissenter from this view is *unus iners*, who has ranged himself against the *ordo deorum*. The judges must therefore choose not between Orestes and Molossus but between Molossus and the will of heaven. The case has changed from an evaluation of Orestes' piety to a display of Molossus' impiety. It is a brilliant redefinition of the issue, and if this is an indication of how Dracontius himself worked in the courtroom, we can understand how he gained the prominence he enjoyed.

The point of the whole story has been the conflict between duty and piety in Orestes as pertaining to the killing of Clytemestra, and any derailing of the reader from that train of thought is a disservice. Thus even Molossus focuses his arguments on the legalities of that case, and Orestes focuses on the divine perspective of that deed; in both speeches the slaying of Pyrrhus makes only brief and tangential appearances. From that angle it can be readily seen that the linking of the two murders is an awkward solution at best, leaving Molossus to prosecute a case in which he has no stake, and Orestes turning the charges back against an opponent who should not even be in the courtroom.

v. 939–74

The final segment of the poem brings both the "Orestes furens" component and the epyllion as a whole to a conclusion. There are in effect two verdicts delivered: first on Orestes by the court and then on the gods by the poet.

Consilium petitur, facta tractantur Orestis. Dracontius reproduces the situation of the *Eumenides:* the vote is equally divided, and Minerva acquits Orestes by her support. In fact, nearly all students of Dracontius have misrepresented the relationship between our poem and the *Oresteia* here: it is normally claimed that Dracontius has introduced a novelty in that Minerva's vote yields an absolute majority, whereas Aeschylus has Athena produce a tie by her vote, which then entitles Orestes to clemency. But the matter is far from settled with regard to Aeschylus.[103] Athena announces (*Eum.* 735) ψῆφον δ᾽ Ὀρέστῃ τὴν δ᾽ ἐγὼ προσθήσομαι and promises νικᾷ δ᾽ Ὀρέστης κἂν ἰσόψηφος κριθῇ (741). Then when the votes are counted, she declares that he has prevailed since the votes were equal (752–53). This is a perfectly ambiguous situation: has Athena voted with the jurors to yield a tie, or have the jurors deadlocked, and the announcement of her vote in 752 produced a majority? Certainly Dracontius' account is consistent with one of the two reasonable interpretations of the lines. The tradition is otherwise mixed. Some sources refer only to a tie and an acquittal,[104] others mention Athena's intervention as producing the tie,[105] and a few specify that her vote yielded a majority.[106] We have no reason to suppose that Dracontius abandoned the *Oresteia* at just this moment to follow Aelius Aristides or a scholiast and should assume that he continued to follow the most famous depiction of the trial ever penned. He may or may not have understood the passage as Aeschylus intended it, but there are still many—indeed the majority—who take the passage just as Dracontius has described it.

Why else would Dracontius have inserted this single incursion of divine action into the poem? A tie vote in itself would have been sufficient to acquit Orestes both on the basis of the Greek tradition and also as a principle of Roman law.[107] The intervention of Minerva must therefore be preserved in the story because it is a part of the dramatic version, and because it allows the poet to attribute the release of Orestes to *clementia caeli* (949), which was after all the basis of Orestes' own defense.

Thus the final prediction of Cassandra (151) is fulfilled: *"purgandus Orestes" dicitur* (945–46), and the judges deliver their opinion. It is not a verdict, since that has been rendered in the vote itself: this is the judicial *sententia*. Dracontius has captured nicely the flavor of judicial expression in these lines (947–57): the judges weigh the competence of the court to hear the case and conclude they lack such competence since it amounts to passing judgment on the gods and challenging a verdict already rendered by the gods in their *perfecta potestas*.[108] They therefore dismiss the matricide with the words *clementia caeli / non sinit audiri*: this court has no jurisdiction in heaven. The judges then establish the view that passing judgment on the gods is a bad idea by citing precedents:

> non erat inpunis Paris arbiter ille dearum,
> Teresias nec erat iudex inpune Tonanti. (952–53)

Thus the poet has acknowledged the fact that Orestes' killing his mother was an act outside the power of human law to forgive, an act which can only be countenanced by ex-

plicit indulgence from the gods; and yet Dracontius has incorporated that acknowledgment into the framework of a
legal opinion such as the Roman law employed. This is a
more complete absorption of the decision into the human
realm than is conceivable in the framework of the *Oresteia*
with its gods debating the case and pronouncing the verdict, and it is consistent with the attitude found throughout
the poem that the actions of man are to be measured and
explained by the yardstick of accepted human law, but that
the law is an extension of a larger order.

There remains the charge of murdering Pyrrhus, and the
judges' *sententia* is terse and unequivocal: *raptor obit Pyrrhus iusto mucrone peremptus* (954). This is more like the
verdict of a court, as it touches a matter over which the
court has jurisdiction. Yet when the opinion goes on to clar-
ify the knotty question contained in the indictment—that
Pyrrhus was in a temple when he was cut down—there is
further evidence that the judges have yielded in the face
of Orestes' general line of argument that he acted throughout in accordance with the will of heaven. Since the gods
can do as they please, they could certainly have punished
Orestes themselves if they had so wished. In the absence of
such action on the part of the gods, this court assumes they
condone the defendant's conduct. Thus the last item in the
charge, sacrilege, is dismissed. All elements of the charge
are accounted for, and the case is closed. *Actum erat.*

The ensuing scene is played out in courts everywhere,
and we can easily imagine such celebrations outside the
courts in Dracontius' own day. The solemn blessings on the
Athenian land that conclude the *Eumenides* are replaced
here by the *patronus* surrounded by his family and cli-
ents—a sister on each arm, the faithful Pylades, and *populi
clamore faventes*. All return in joy to Mycenae to live, we
assume, happily ever after. This recasting of the happy
issue out of all Orestes' afflictions takes us away from the
world of the tragic tradition and back once more to the atmosphere of the romances.

What does correspond to the final choral song of the *Eumenides* is Dracontius' epilogue (963–74). But whereas the Aeschylean chorus invokes the now civilized Eumenides and hymns the blessings which justice brings to Athens, Dracontius' concern is precisely the opposite. His invocation of the gods is a cry of desperation at the horrors he has depicted. The language of his invocation will remind us of the opening lines of the *Satisfactio*, addressed to a different deity in whom Dracontius saw more hope of rescue from tribulation than the divinities he has treated in this story. The use of a prayer to finish his tale is a device he has also used in the *Helen* and the *Medea;* both of those epilogues were likewise filled with apprehension. In this instance the prayer is simple, despite the elaborate form in which it is cast: let there be no more suffering such as this story has depicted. The poet reminds us once more of the crimes which illustrate this wickedness: the Lemnian women and the Danaids, the Thyestean feast, and others too appalling to recite. This is no song of hope, following upon the vindication of Orestes, but rather an anguished cry following upon the whole story with its larger implications (note that the list of crimes sends us back to the second portion of the poem, overleaping the absolution of the trial).

Lines 972–73 have been generally misunderstood, I think:

> ecce Mycenaea triplex iam scaena profanat
> Graiugenum famam.

There has been confusion here trying to guess what three crimes the poet has in mind. Rapisarda guesses Tantalus' slaying of Pelops, the deeds of Atreus and the killing of Clytemestra, others have their own lists of three crimes; but *scaena* need not, and does not, mean *scelus.* It is the triple stage-spectacle of Mycenae: and that is the *Oresteia,* which Dracontius has just reproduced (*ecce*) in this poem. And that story *profanat Graiugenum famam,* for it is a record of crimes which, though pardoned, remain unspeakable. The happy curtain call of the cast in 958ff. is the ending of the *Eumenides*, translated into the setting of a Roman courtroom, but that happy moment is subordinate to the poet's meditation on the whole story. The epilogue is more like the exodos of *Choephori* (1065–76), which speaks of all the disaster befalling the House of Tantalus and wonders whether there will ever come an end to the afflictions sent from heaven. Aeschylus presents an answer of hope rooted in the civilizing power of justice; Dracontius clings to his alarm, rooting his fears in the nature of the gods. The *clementia caeli* which brought about the acquittal of Orestes appears in this light to be less than is needed, however blessed the relief which it brought may have seemed at the time.

Dracontius' prayer is the same as the one at the end of the *Medea:*[109]

> vestro iam parcite mundo
> atque usum scelerum miseris arcete Pelasgis. (973–74)

The language, the prayer, and the mood are all relentlessly pagan. If this is the Christianized version of the story of Orestes, Dracontius has suppressed his Christian hope. The condemnation of the gods may spring from a Christian perspective, but it is not presented in a form which allows us to hear the poet's faith in God, only his disbelief in the gods.

Summary

After considering each part of the poem, it may repay our attention to pull together briefly some of the conclusions to be derived from the study of this epyllion. Although the *Orestis tragoedia* presented a different set of devices and a somewhat different format from any of the other epyllia, we may still see characteristic features of Dracontius' art in his handling of his material.

First, it is clear that the poet has used the *Oresteia* and followed it with care. As the analysis has shown, the epyllion reproduces the structure of the trilogy so thoroughly that the innovations of incident are recognizably modifications of Aeschylus for identifiable purposes. Apart from Aeschylus there is no full-scale treatment of the story of the *Oresteia:* the return of Orestes was frequently treated, the return of Agamemnon more than once, but the unified story from the return of Agamemnon to the purification of Orestes is found in Aeschylus and in mythographic sources, and nowhere else except in Dracontius. Aricò dismisses this correspondence with the glib observation that since all treatments of the story except Homer are after Aeschylus, Dracontius is bound to reflect the Attic poet, and there is no reason to think of direct influence,[110] but this ignores the fundamental point that these are the *only* two such treatments extant or known.

As to the possibility that Dracontius may have relied on mythographic materials, one can only say that they have preserved none of the details which I take as suggesting direct influence. When we can compare Dracontius with Hyginus or Apollodorus, there is never any reason to think that Dracontius could have found in these sources the features which he shares with Aeschylus. A clear instance is the lament of the servants at Agamemnon's tomb to open the *Choephori/*"Orestes."

Second, we have seen numerous traces of Senecan tragedy in the language and even the handling of themes:[111] the hostile Cassandra who rejoices at the death of Agamemnon, for example, and such verbal echoes as *Orestes* 25 and *Agamemnon* 39f. I think the influence goes far deeper than isolated borrowings: Dracontius has conceived each of the dramas which make up his trilogy along the lines of Senecan drama. Each is divided into five acts, as we have seen, and those acts tend to consist of a few major speeches more reminiscent of the rhetorical display pieces of Senecan drama than any stage-oriented composition. Moreover, several of the "acts" end with some equivalent of a choral passage such as demarcates the Senecan acts. The following attached chart will show how the poem is distributed—following the divisions used above—together with the notation of the choral equivalents. Sometimes these are speeches or passages offering the kind of lyrical or editorial comments one associates with the chorus, other times it is the presence of a corps such as the citizens of Mycenae (e.g., 799ff.) or the servants.

There is more. Dracontius has even observed the three-actor rule. There is no scene in which more than three persons speak:[112] it would be very simple to distribute the roles of the speaking parts among three actors if one were to imagine a dramatic reading of the poem.

Aricò discusses the importance of the speeches without apparently realizing exactly why they are so important.[113] There are some 45 speeches in the *Orestes* ranging from one word to 41 lines[114] and comprising just over half the text (498 of 974 lines). As Aricò notes, these are used, in addition to their obvious functions, for the moralizing comments of the poet, and above all to present the characters themselves directly. This is precisely because the poet conceives of the poem as essentially a drama, not as a narrative genre, and therefore, the speeches are the central material. The narrative merely sets the stage and moves us from one speech to the next. Once we view the speeches in this way, we can recognize the flaw in Quartiroli's analysis of them: she lamented that there were no short speeches, and that the lengthy rhetorical performances bogged down the dramatic effect and impeded the action. But the speeches in Senecan tragedy are of precisely this sort: typically an act will contain a modest amount of dialogue and will rely on a few major declamations of brilliant effect which nobody could mistake for stagecraft. Dracontius, working in a medium which is already heavily rhetorical and not attempting even to reproduce in workable form the illusion of a play, can indulge to the full this congenial feature of the Latin dramatist he so admired.

Third, if we consider what other sources Dracontius had

Prologue: 1–40

Orestis Tragoedia as Trilogy

	Agamemnon	Orestes	Orestes Furens
I	Agamemnon in Tauris 41–107	Agamemnon at tomb 453–514 Chor: servants	Murder of Pyrrhus 803–19
II	Cl and Eg plot to kill Ag 108–231	Ag. Or and Pyl plot to kill Cl and Eg 515–625	Orestes driven mad by Fury of Cl 820–61
III	Murder of Agamemnon 232–83 Chor: poet's reflections	Or and Pyl set out for Mycenae 616–81 Chor: servants greet Or	Orestes in Tauris 862–86
IV	Or and Pyl flee, Cl and Eg plot 284–349 Chor: Myc citizens lament	Or and Pyl return, murder Eg 682–728	Trial of Orestes 887–938
V	Cl and Eg rule 350–426 Chor: Myc citizens	Murder of Cl, Or rules 729–802 Chor: Myc citizens	Resolution, exodos, epilogue 939–74 Chor: poet's prayer (epilogue)

and used, and to what extent his unique version of the
story is due to these sources, we are faced with a dilemma.
The list of literary treatments of his theme, or at least of
parts of it, is a long one, and it is obviously foolish to think
he used or even knew all of them. Did he, for example,
know or make any use of the *Electra* of either Sophocles or
Euripides or the latter's *Orestes? non liquet.* He almost
certainly knew Euripides' *Iphigenia in Tauris*, and there
is no particular reason why he could not have known the
other plays as well, but it is pointless to insist. The range of
Hellenistic and Republic Roman tragedy is a lost cause—
lost to us and in all probability lost to him. At any rate, if we
were to conjecture that some of his novelties were derived
from Hellenistic-Republican plays now lost, we would need
to overcome the problem that there is no evidence that
they contained these features, either in remnants of the
plays or hints of their influence in any other work in the
intervening half millenium.

The use of Seneca's *Agamemnon* is guaranteed, and there
is probable cause to see echoes of the *Troades* and *Hercules
furens*, perhaps also *Thyestes*. In any case, Dracontius was
deeply affected by Senecan drama, even though it is risky
to see specific imitations in any given line.

At the same time, Dracontius is very far from adopting
Seneca's version of the *Agamemnon*,[115] even when he di-
verges from Aeschylus; it is clear that he felt free to modify
his story in all parts of the poem without necessary reference to either Aeschylus or Seneca. To what then should
we attribute the changes? To what sources, and to what
purpose?

As to sources, argument from silence is always dangerous, but when a scan of all reasonable options gives not
even a hint that there is a hidden candidate, it becomes at
least probable that the silence is significant. I see no appropriate source from which Dracontius is likely to have derived his novelties of incident and characterization, and I
am convinced that such features as Dorylas' character and
the visit of Agamemnon to the Taurians are inventions of

the poet himself. This notion is greatly strengthened by
the functions which we have observed for these novelties.
They appear without antecedent, and they serve particular
purposes where the poet has inserted them. The ever-
popular lost mythographic source is a red herring in these
instances, and in the next chapter we shall see to what extent this may be true of novel features in the other epyllia
as well.

On the question of purpose, I return to the point raised
at the outset of this chapter. It is clear enough that the
poet's moral indignation is aroused by the story he has to
tell, and he has missed no opportunity to excoriate the sins
of Clytemestra and Egistus while extolling the virtues of
Agamemnon and Orestes. He has turned the story of Orestes into a parable of virtue and vice rather than a myth of
the establishment of justice. I suspect that Dracontius'
choice of emphasis in all the epyllia, but most systematically in the *Orestes,* is influenced strongly by the intention
to measure conduct against the standard of the Law of God,
i.e., the Ten Commandments. Here all the poet's interests
converged, his zeal for the law and his deeply held faith.
The story of Orestes becomes a means of contrasting what
his faith taught and what the pagan world countenanced.

In fact, if we consider the prescriptions of the law against
the performance of the characters, it seems that the principal themes of the epyllion tell of violations of that law.
Some obviously loom larger than others: the adulterous relationship of Clytemestra and Egistus is the central focus of
their characters, and the punishment of their sin is a constant theme of both the poet and the king. We have seen
how Dracontius recasts Agamemnon in order to clear him
of any irregular behavior and to let Clytemestra's adultery
become all the more offensive by contrast.

As to "Thou shalt not kill," there are violations aplenty
and the other major driving force in the poem is the punishment of murder. Again we note how Agamemnon is cleared
of even accidental involvement in the apparent death of
Iphigenia, while Clytemestra is depicted as bloodthirsty and

gratuitously violent. The trial of Orestes for the slaying of Pyrrhus and Clytemestra underscores both the accountability of even the noblest characters and also the difference between justified and unjustified taking of lives.

Closely linked to the topic of matricide is the injunction of the fifth commandment, "Honor thy father and thy mother." We recall Orestes' elaborate anguish at the prospect of taking vengeance on his mother, and the fact that it was only an overwhelming sense of duty to his father which impelled him to accept the obligation. The first commandment is perpetually reinforced by the poet's harsh words on the folly of worshipping the gods, a point which he made in both the *Helen* and the *Medea*. Certainly there is ample covetousness in Egistus: his ambition for the power of Agamemnon, as embodied in the king's wife, is what stirs him to action in the first place. And even the prohibition against graven images, which may seem quite irrelevant, may explain in part the rather intrusive reference to the statue of Diana (*ablata Diana*) in 886.

In short, Rapisarda was right to see in this poem a Christianized retelling of the Orestes story, but its aim is not to articulate the Christian message implicit in the tale itself but to point out the unredeemed quality of the story by measuring characters and actions with the yardstick of Christian standards.

Chapter 6

Dracontius and the Tradition

AFTER LOOKING at the four narrative poems separately, let us now draw together some of the features which characterize Dracontius' work. In doing this, we must bear in mind that the epyllia come from various times in his poetic career: the *Hylas* is surely an early composition, and the *Medea, Orestes,* and *Helen* are very probably from his mature period. But the principal features of his art were apparently developed early, and the later phase shows refinement of style, not a change of artistic patterns.

Structure and Myth

Several of the most prominent aspects of these poems spring from Dracontius' fascination with pattern. He has not hesitated to tamper with the stories and their characters in pursuit of symmetrical effects. The results of this approach may be seen in the structure of scenes, in the depiction of character, in the actions which the characters perform, and even in the shape of individual lines.

Dracontius has frequently streamlined the action of his myths by eliminating subordinate (or even major) characters, with the result that the action is played out as a confrontation between two principal figures. We have seen how, in *Medea,* the poet cut out the Argonauts from the action in Colchis and likewise left out any significant role for Creon and Glauce in Thebes, so as to leave Jason to face Medea alone; similarly, the meeting of Orestes and Iphigenia is a stark scene, with no Pylades, no Thoas, and no intervening gods. And even in *Hylas* the context is simpler

207

than in the traditional versions so as to allow us to concentrate on the one or two figures on stage at any moment. One reason for this procedure is surely to make the issues inherent in the scene stand out more clearly. Dracontius is generally aiming at some moral comment or judgment (whether he spells it out or allows it to emerge from the story), and this is most effective when there are no subordinate issues intervening between the poet and his readers.

The scenes themselves are set in parallel or balanced arrangement. The four panels of *Hylas* offer a good illustration of the benefits to be derived from this approach: each of the characters is set beside and against each of the others. Equal, or nearly equal, numbers of lines impose a symmetry of proportion and an orderly pace of narrative which further enhance our awareness of these relationships. A variant on this structure appears in *Medea*, with its two massive blocks of virtually equal size, each containing subparts, which likewise match from one half of the poem to the other. All four epyllia show extraordinarily careful structures, and what is remarkable is that no two patterns are quite alike. Dracontius has shaped each poem according to its individual purpose and has not merely settled for an easy paneling or symmetry.

A related feature is the way in which Dracontius has manipulated the actions which the characters perform. He tends to work with sets of individual narrative moments, which he arranges in differing patterns: note in *Helen* how each scene involves basically the same set of actions but is assigned to various characters and presented in varying order. Sometimes this is emphasized by repeated lines (e.g., *Hyl.* 94, 141), sometimes by repeated epithets from one character to another. In *Medea* the parallels are constructed by having characters involved in the same situations: Jason's arrival in a strange land leads to the princess falling in love with him, which leads in turn to the rest of the story laid out in parallel fashion.

In the interest of such an approach, the story may be altered. The introduction of Agamemnon's visit to the Taurians anticipates his son's later journey, and conversely Orestes' encounter is shaped to some extent by the depiction of Agamemnon's visit.

There is a price to be paid for this manipulation of both plot and character. In many cases Dracontius has reduced the major figures to types or even caricatures—the blameless king, the wicked queen, the loyal son, the murderous witch. He may invest them with flamboyancy in their rhetoric and extravagance in their actions, but they generally have few if any individualizing traits. Even Clytemestra, whom we saw to be the most complex character in the *Orestes*, is essentially a collection of qualities associated with the malignant purposes she represents. Egistus is a mere lay figure elaborated to the point of revulsion: his wickedness is eventually quite unimpressive for being so unrelieved and lacking in subtlety. Dracontius seems to have fixed upon a single looming characteristic for each of his principal characters. He has then used the person to illustrate the trait, rather than endowing a convincing personality with a given quality. We are very close to the morality play in these poems.

Indeed, the impression of typicality in single figures implicitly extends to entire classes. We have seen how Dracontius' women are all stronger than the men they confront and conquer. In almost every case this strength is expressed in a greater initiative for wickedness. The disastrous enterprises in which the heroes find themselves are all either initiated or completed by the women. There may be several explanations for this phenomenon. Quartiroli[1] conjectured that the dominance of women was a feature derived from the romances, drawing a line of tradition from the Hellenistic poetic interests in the erotic, and focusing on the aggressive heroine, such as Catullus' Ariadne or Vergil's Dido.[2] This may well have affected the tradition in broad terms, but Dracontius seems to have gone further than his predecessors and used far more systematically the motif of the woman as a source of trouble. Moreover, it is linked to stereotyping of the hero as pusillanimous, which is not a necessary part of the older attitude. Dracontius appears to be deliberately undercutting the heroes and their achievements and replacing them at the heart of the action with women whose purposes and methods and morals are thoroughly reprehensible. How admirable can the traditional feats be if in the last analysis they are the crimes of women? Likewise the gods are harshly depicted, where they are not actually ignored. We have seen how *Hylas* exposed the gods to ridicule, and how in the *Orestes* they do not even perform those acts which are clearly associated with them in the tradition. Three of the four epyllia end with prayers which amount to indictments of the gods and all their works.

This tendency to generalization—the wicked woman, the vicious god, the sham hero—is probably the result of the poet's Christianity. There is a paradoxical aspect to this. Dracontius has dealt with stories which must surely have played a crucial role in his education and which he must have loved dearly as he met them again and again in the great works of the Graeco-Roman literary tradition. And the rest of the *Romulea* also deal with traditional themes or forms. Dracontius was a fervent student of the pagan past, to which he most keenly felt himself to be heir: this is obvious from the fact that his Christian apologetic works are in precisely the same style, and employ the same tropes, even the same similes and figures. There is no rejection of the pagan tradition as a source of inspiration for both subject and style. And yet there can be no mistaking the negative element in his handling of the familiar myths. Dracontius was functioning at two levels. His choice of subject came naturally out of his education, his reading, and the culture which he had absorbed so deeply and which gave him his voice as an artist. But at the same time his faith shaped his reactions to these myths into a sturdy disapproval, of which in many ways he may not even have been fully aware. He saw Medea and Clytemestra, Hylas and Jason, Paris and Helen from a Christian perspective, and his imagination shaped them accordingly. They became not only the great stories familiar to all, but also object lessons. Hence the lesson they taught dictated the character they had, and the result is a tendency to create flat figures embodying single qualities.

Both the structural principles and the moralizing purposes identified thus far allow a fresh look at Dracontius' manipulation of his sources. When his stories are set beside the more canonical versions, we see that he combines elements which appear irreconcilable (e.g., the list of stories in *Orestes* 427–52 as compared with his own use of those stories elsewhere). It would seem that he was not concerned to present consistent versions of even the most familiar stories but was willing to alter them for differing purposes in different poems. This shows a willingness to intervene in the casting of a story—Dracontius did not regard the myth in any sense as a given. The numerous novelties of plot must be seen from this perspective. They are evidence of Dracontius' engaging his material in order to make it serve his purposes. The innovations nearly all occur at crucial moments in his story and are related to a moral comment he wants to make or to the sharper delineation of a character as embodying some particular quality (Agamemnon's blamelessness, for example). For this reason I am convinced that the novelties should be attributed to Dracontius rather than to untraceable lost mythographic sources.[3] He is drawing new lessons from the myths, and like his predecessors he felt free to give the myth the shape which would make those lessons clearer.

As in all such sewing together of parts, the seams are occasionally visible. Our poet sometimes abandons a scene or a source too abruptly without pausing to tuck in the loose ends. In *Medea* we saw how the transition from Colchis to Greece was abrupt and clumsy, including the slaying of Apsyrtus for no reason except that it was in the tradition (which Dracontius had just repudiated), and likewise how Orestes and Iphigenia stole the image of Diana although it had neither function nor place in the new version he had just created. Sometimes the weakness is not so severe and involves mere abruptness without actual inconsistency: consider Paris' departure from Cyprus or the ending of the Salamis episode.[4] In general terms, Dracontius' transitions are among his least felicitous touches. He either lingers or leaps, with unhappy results either way.

The Visual Arts

The salient features of Dracontius' art may be compared with tendencies in the visual arts of late antiquity from the beginning of the fourth century into the Byzantine era. These tendencies may be summed up in the idea of greater regularity of structure and loss of individualization.

The change in structure may be seen most readily in the realm of architecture. L'Orange showed how the transition from the classical tradition to the practices of the later principate amounted to a nearly complete redefinition of the relationship between the enclosing structure and the enclosed space.[5] The earlier conception of an integrated building, in which each part played a specifiable role in relation to the whole, included a diversity of parts and functions which made the total structure rich, intelligible, and subtle. In the era marked off by the introduction of the tetrarchy, this relationship is disrupted, and instead we find a tendency toward a massive total structure which dominates the parts. The Palace of Diocletian at Split is a clear example of the idea: a massive, blocklike structure with repetition in a somewhat mechanical fashion of the main conception in the subparts.

Another element of the change is the simplification of the main lines and a more obvious use of supporting members: L'Orange illustrates the tendency with the basilicas of the early fourth century. Accompanying this simplification of the main structure is a reduction of subordinate detail especially in the interior space. The net effect is to make the interior space more unified because it is less differentiated, and from this comes a vagueness, a vastness, which L'Orange described as "the insubstantial, intangible interior filled with light and shadow."[6]

These same effects may be observed in the structure of Dracontius' poems. His epyllia, as we have seen, display a strong overall arrangement, in which the subparts repeat the main lines on a smaller scale—consider the pattern of the *Medea* or *Hylas*. But we have also noticed how the development of individual incidents lacked sharpness, and the component parts are not always well integrated into the overall structure of the narrative. The architecture of the poems, like that of the official buildings of the later Empire, is more concerned with larger effects than with the careful integration of all subordinate parts with the large-scale design.

Another way to approach this question is by considering the development of portraiture in this same period. The remarkable tradition of portraits, which preserve so many vivid faces from the earlier phases of the Empire is suddenly and startlingly disrupted, and by the end of the third century we find ourselves confronted by stylized, frozen faces from which has disappeared all feeling of a living individual. The conception of an integrated picture has broken down, and the artists instead present a collage of features conceived separately and depicted separately. The result, as L'Orange puts it, is a pointillism which reduces realism but allows other kinds of inner vision to emerge, focusing on the spiritual values, the "pneumatic personality."[7] One is tempted to suggest that the approach to a large composition by way of minimal parts built up is most conveniently seen in the mosaics which will be so important an expression of religious and imperial authority in the fifth and sixth centuries. The significant point is the discontinuity between the details, which are cast within the limits of their own purposes, and the picture as a whole. The goal of this later portraiture is to capture the essential personality, or rather the essential character. This is related to attributes such as the majesty of an emperor or the sanctity which attaches to his office rather than his idiosyncrasies as a person.[8]

If we turn to Dracontius' depiction of character—his portraits of his personae—we see a comparable phenomenon. We have observed how the poet's creations display two qualities: their typicality and their inconsistency. By this I mean that the overall depiction of a character tends to show the features typical of the rank or the role, such as, Agamemnon as the king or Medea as the witch. The animating, idiosyncratic features which make a distinctive flesh-and-blood figure are not developed: we seem to be looking at a persona in the full sense, a mask of a role rather than a personality. In this respect the poetic creations are like the plastic arts. At the same time there are discrepancies in the details as if the several parts of the depiction do not fully belong together. We have noted how the story sometimes leaps from one phase to the next without integration or even presents internal inconsistencies: the apparently pointless killing of Apsyrtus by Medea at the seam between the halves of the story, or the inconsistency between the mythological catalogue in *Orestes* (427ff.) and the poet's own accounts elsewhere. He is developing these details in their own place and on their own terms, without regard for how they fit together. In this respect, too, our poet may have the tendency described by L'Orange, to assemble features rather than depict a unified person. I do not mean that the introduction of these inconsistencies is a deliberate act of disintegration by the poet, but merely that their presence was tolerated, perhaps not really even noticed, because the poet was looking to other more important purposes.

And third, we should consider the selection and presentation of actions by the characters. The artistic tradition shows how strongly the actions of all individuals—chiefly emperors, saints, and heavenly figures—are depicted as frozen in the midst of hieratic, ritual acts. Such events as the *Adventus* of the emperor, which has been thoroughly analyzed recently,[9] bring out the timelessness of sacral characters and actions, the entire ceremonial universe in which the imperial houses sought to depict themselves as existing.[10] The Arch of Constantine shows rank upon rank of figures posed in symmetrical patterns which display

their relationship and their dignity rather than their actions. Narrative has been replaced by the timeless representation of those qualities which narrative would merely
have reduced to a particular time and place.

The mosaics of San Vitale in Ravenna illustrate in another medium how the depiction of specific situations may
be equally absorbed into the generalized portrayal.[11] The
twin "Palatine" mosaics showing Justinian and Theodora
presenting the Chalice and Paten for the Liturgy combine
hieratic gesture and artificial symmetry of arrangement
with the clearly distinguishable features of the prelate
Maximianus, even more distinctly drawn than either Justinian or his Empress. The effect of these scenes is no less
eternal than the biblical and heavenly scenes elsewhere in
the Church. It is significant that once again we see the Imperial House in a procession, an *Adventus*.

Dracontius' poems fall chronologically between these
two monuments and show the growing influence of this
style of depiction transferred to the literary realm. The
poet does not develop actions even in his narrative but
tends to present a series of poses, like panels, marked by
speeches and set apart, as we saw in the *Orestes,* by abrupt
shifts having almost the effect of going from one picture to
the next. The actions themselves are frequently of a ritual
or ceremonial nature: consider the arrivals of Paris at Troy,
or the legation to Salamis, or the arrivals at Cyprus or
in Tauris. The *adventus* of Agamemnon at Mycenae (*Or.*
232ff.) is a prime example already in Aeschylus of the power
and meaning of a king's solemn arrival.[12] In Dracontius such
moments of arrival, identification, and assertion of one's
status are a principal means for the poet to convey his views
on the characters. The procession at Troy when Paris first
arrives sounds rather like the processions seen in imperial
monuments from Constantine to Justinian, with the priests
and heroes of Troy behind the king (cf. again the priests and
the armed troops behind Justinian in San Vitale).

Thus the actions of Dracontius' personae are intended to
display their character more than to advance the narrative,

and we are led to visualize a series of frozen moments rather than a progressing story. Those actions share the ceremonial content as well as the hieratic form seen in the visual arts of the time.

Sources and Influences

But naturally, the strongest single type of influence on Dracontius' poetry was the previous poetic tradition. What sources did he rely on, and what influences was he under as he developed his peculiar vision of the myths?

First, it is obvious that our poet was familiar with the Latin poetic tradition from the Augustan era onward. There is no surprise in this: both in choice of theme and in language he is continuously in touch with the mainstream of Latin poetry, especially the hexameter poets. Vergil exercised the most extensive influence, and the Silver epic poets played a considerable role as well, chiefly for the rhetorical effects so pervasive in all poetry of the Empire. Lucan and Statius are next in importance for our poet, with Silius and Claudian also contributing.

But other parts of the Augustan corpus are less sure. Even in the case of Tibullus, to whom Dracontius is regularly said to be indebted, the one echo is slight and unconvincing,[13] and the same may be said for Propertius.[14]

The picture is quite clouded for Roman Republican literature. Lucretius is quite definitely represented, but most of the other apparent echoes of Republican poetry could well be culled from excerpts or at second hand. Dracontius pretty certainly knew Catullus' poems,[15] although there is less recognizable influence than one might expect. The one case in which I believe modern scholarship has been unduly optimistic is Ennius. The survival of Ennius' tragedies into the fifth century is highly unlikely,[16] and as we observed in the *Helen*, such fragments of evidence as we have on Ennius' play do not suggest a direct influence anyway, certainly not in manner and probably not in plot. In any case, the gulf between Ennius and Dracontius is no less cultural than chronological. Even if he had known the plays, Dracontius would have found them forbiddingly foreign. This is also the observation which Aricò made about Dracontius using Euripides, but oddly enough the argument has less force with the Greek dramatist than the Latin. Euripides was in many ways a more "modern" poet than Ennius, more attuned to questions of psychological analysis and above all attuned to the study of crime. He is closer to our poet in all ways except chronology.

It is thus better to think of Dracontius as familiar with only a couple of Republican poets and then more extensively acquainted with the Augustan poets (with some gaps) and far more so with the post-Augustans.

With Euripides we may turn to the question of Dracontius and Greek sources. Again, the earlier studies of our poet have frequently denied him any knowledge of Greek literature, but that is surely a false view. The *Orestes* shows unmistakable evidence that Dracontius followed the *Oresteia* itself, not a desiccated précis in some mythographic text. And a poet who can follow the *Oresteia* is presumably able to use almost any Greek text he can lay his hands on. The congruity between Dracontius and Apollonius probably suggests direct familiarity (admittedly it does not require it), and the details in Dracontius which are otherwise attested only in the Greek scholiastic tradition at least allow a similar conclusion. If any part of the West were to preserve this degree of familiarity with the Greek texts, it would naturally be Carthage, at least until the advent of the Vandals. As noted earlier, it has long been an article of faith that the knowledge of Greek vanished from North Africa when the Vandals arrived, but such a disappearance is in many ways an unreasonable scenario. The Vandals had no more reason deliberately to eradicate Greek learning than Latin, and the attitude of the barbarians to Roman traditions was tolerant enough. In any case, we can come back to the *Orestes* itself as evidence that for Dracontius at least, the Greek texts were not a closed book.

Certainly tragedy was the other principal genre, besides

epic, to inform Dracontius' poetry. The thoroughness with which he incorporated the features and conventions of tragedy into his *Orestes* is quite remarkable. And yet it was Roman, and specifically Senecan, tragedy which served as the formal model for this generic blending, while the Greek sources provided elements of plot and conception. In *Orestes*, as we have seen, the adaptation went so far as to accommodate the five-act structure, the chorus, and even the three-actor rule. It is not impossible that Dracontius intended these declamatory versions of tragic dramatic stories to be given recitations. If Senecan tragedies, outwardly designed as they were for stage performance yet clearly unsuited to such a use, could be given recitation performance, there is nothing inherently improbable in the notion that the Dracontian poem might likewise be "performed."

The impact of tragedy may be seen as well in the overall structure of the *Helen*, which is clearly constructed in five scenes, even though it does not apparently derive its contents from any specific tragedies. The *Medea*, on the other hand, deals with a topic closely associated with tragedy but shows little evidence of structural similarities.

Along with these two poetic traditions rhetoric has influenced Dracontius most profoundly: not merely the use of rhetorical language such as is pervasive in all sorts and conditions of Latin literature, but the actual practices of the rhetorical schools and the very forms of the *controversia*. Two of the *Romulea* are actual *controversiae* in hexameters, and there are parallels to this activity in the *Latin Anthology*.[17] But even in the narrative poems, the devices of the rhetorician are seen everywhere. The speeches of the characters are frequently designed like small *suasoriae* or *deliberativae*, and the pairing of speeches on nearly every occasion reminds us not so much of the epic as the law courts. The flamboyant, indeed excessive, use of sound effects such as alliteration and even rhyme have an almost Gorgianic effect.

This link to rhetorical training may have had another impact as well. We have seen that Dracontius was powerfully

attracted to the tragic tradition and has even constructed a
hexameter equivalent of a tragic drama. Why did he not
simply write a proper tragedy? It has been argued that the
day of drama was past, and that avenue was simply not
open to Dracontius.[18] But Aricò sees evidence that tragedies were still performed, and thus by implication could be
composed, in fifth-century Carthage.[19] It is clear that a
tragedy composed in this era was not intended for staging
any more than its forebear the Senecan drama. The form of
presentation, if any, would be recitation, and we return to
the possibility that at least some of these epyllia may have
been performed. In that case, the format most likely to be
employed for display performance is the same as the other
rhetorical exercises preserved for us in Dracontius' work—
the hexameter poem. This is the link between the exercises
which had shaped Dracontius' skills, the rhetorical style
which he made his own, and the epic tradition from which
he derived his inspiration. The hexameter was his mé-
tier when he turned to the articulation of poetic themes,
whether tragic or otherwise.

The form of dramatic presentation which enjoyed greatest favor in Dracontius' day was, as noted, the pantomime,
and we saw that this genre exerted influence at several
points in our poet's work, most prominently in *Hylas* but
also in *Medea* and perhaps in *Orestes* as well. The pantomime had been popular in all parts of the Empire for
a long time, but it is particularly understandable that it
should appeal in those areas where the link with the Latin
literary tradition was weak—that is, in those areas heavily
populated or controlled by persons with little knowledge of
Latin. Obviously the Vandals fell into this class, and the
pantomime had a far greater appeal for that element than
complex achievements in Latin. It is true that except for
the court of Thrasamund, the Vandals apparently showed
no great interest in any cultural achievements, but the accommodation of nonliterary elements in entertainments
was a long-standing practice, and if any form of public
amusement of a nonviolent sort caught the attention or

even tolerance of the Vandals, it is likely to have been the pantomime with its broad and unmistakable style of communication and its unsophisticated level of intellectual challenge. The impact of this form on Dracontius shows his openness to all kinds of cultural activity, and not merely the high-level literary texts.

The fifth strand to be identified is the romance, by which Dracontius often seems to have been influenced in a general way, although there are no specific details to which one can point as definitely derived from the romances (there is further evidence of their influence in the *Aegritudo Perdicae*). What one notices is the taste for the plot elements so prevalent in the romances: the disruption and eventual reunion of families after fantastic adventures, travel to faraway places, preferably by being kidnapped, coincidences that would leave Sir Walter Scott agape, narrow escapes and exotic customs and pirates, and the action set on the human level rather than the divine. Perhaps it is accurate to say that the romances created widely shared expectations as to the scope of incident, the style of character, and the shape of plots, and Dracontius reflects these expectations in his poems without specifically drawing on identifiable models.

Another evidence of his openness to a variety of cultural impacts is the apparent impress of the folktale observed in *Medea*. The effect which the Germanic strain may have had on Latin letters in the Vandal context is untraceable simply because of the lack of evidence: the illiterate Vandals left no literature. But as we saw, the novel morphology of the Medea tale is not likely to have arisen within the Graeco-Roman context, and if it comes from any external source, that source is presumably the Germanic tradition. There may be other instances of this influence which have gone unnoticed, even within Dracontius' poetry.

Finally, we may note the other subliterary materials to which Dracontius had recourse. We saw that he was aligned with the mythographic compilations in more than one instance, in the sense that he presents a version of a

myth not original with him but represented elsewhere only
by the mythographers. It would be rash to conclude that
his debt is to the mythographers we happen to have at our
disposal: most often the correspondence between Dracontius and Hyginus, for example, is partial, and we must
think in terms of more complex traditions. But apparently
the mythographers' general preference for a comprehensive rendering of a hero's exploits has had its influence on
our poet, and Dracontius probably had such surveys in
mind when he concocted his poems.

The works of both Dictys and Dares occasionally bear remarkable resemblances to what we see in Dracontius, and
I think it quite probable that both works were familiar
to him: the resemblance between Dares' account of the
embassy to Telamon and Dracontius' *Helen* is too great
to ignore and too peculiar to relate to anything else we
know about.

The third strand of subliterary materials is the scholiastic.
We have seen some evidence suggesting that Dracontius
was at least familiar with specifics known to us only via the
scholiasts, both Greek and Latin. Again, it would be foolish
to link Dracontius to any particular scholiastic text, but his
use of such materials is a high probability.

Chapter 7

Aegritudo Perdicae

AFTER OUR STUDY of the mythological poems of Dracontius, we may learn something of his place in the poetic tradition and the extent to which his art is distinctive or shared by looking at the contemporary composition of an unknown writer: the *Aegritudo Perdicae* (*AP*).[1]

Unusual and interesting problems are presented by this work. As art, to be sure, it is formidably rough, but there is much in the story and its sources which will repay inspection, as well as in the poet's manner of presenting his tale. Among the questions are the links with other branches of literature, the treatment of sources, and the poetic qualities of the poem.

In its present state the *AP* consists of 290 verses, although there are certainly lacunae following verses 12, 23, and 73, and almost certainly the damaged verse 98 was followed by several lines which are now lost.[2] The poem did not originally run much beyond 300 lines. It survives only in codex Harleianus 3685 (fifteenth century), the work of a copyist who does not inspire confidence.[3] Because of those features which suggest that the poem should be dated to the same period as Dracontius, scholars have from time to time ascribed the poem to Dracontius himself, but the ascription is surely erroneous.[4]

The Story

The subject of the epyllion is the fateful passion of Perdica for his mother Castalia. After a brief prologue, the poet introduces his hero heading home from Athens where he has

been a student. For some reason, Perdica neglects to worship Venus and Amor, and from this omission flows all that
ensues. When Perdica and his companions stop to rest by a
spring in a grove, Venus sends Amor to exact revenge. As
Perdica sleeps, Amor assumes the form of Castalia and appears to the prince in a dream. The youth is stirred to great
desire, but because of his long absence from home he does
not recognize the face of his mother.[5] Upon reaching home
he is appalled at the desire he has entertained, and after a
sleepless night of pondering his incestuous urge, by morn-
ing he has begun to pine away from guilt. His mother in
alarm summons the leading physicians, including Hippocrates. All are puzzled until Hippocrates happens to be
checking Perdica's pulse when Castalia enters the room.
The prince's racing pulse tells the doctor everything, including the absence of any remedy; and he departs. Castalia tries to comfort her son: she can arrange for a match
if only he will identify the lady. Perdica turns away in
anguish.

That night Amor continues to torment his victim. Castalia
then summons all the fair maidens and matrons in town
to pass by her son's couch in hopes of identifying his beloved, or diverting his passion to an attainable object. All,
of course, in vain. The poet invokes the Muse and describes the worsening symptoms. Finally Perdica in despair
determines to end his life more swiftly than by emaciation
(if he can find a means for which he still has the strength).
When he begins to consider hanging, Amor is perturbed
lest he be trapped inside Perdica and perish with him. This
lends resolve to the lover, and the poem ends with Perdica
composing his epitaph.

The Tradition

The mythological trappings are at odds with the appearance of two historical names, and this blend of history and
mythology is a crucial feature of the epyllion. In fact, the
story as told is derived from two quite separate threads of

purported history, and it is then adapted to the conventions of mythological poetry.

The first trail of evidence leads to Perdiccas II of Macedon (ca. 450–13 B.C.). Hippocrates was his contemporary, and there is nothing inherently improbable in the report that the great physician was called to the Macedonian court. The anecdote of immediate relevance is, however, peculiar. Soranus in his life of Hippocrates tells how Perdiccas, after succeeding to the throne upon the death of his father, fell in love with Alexander's mistress Phila.[6] Hippocrates was summoned by the people. He diagnosed the difficulty as residing in the king's mind, recognized the source of Perdiccas' passion, and spoke with Phila. The sight of her inflamed the king: she should stay out of his sight. Thus the king was restored.

The similarities and differences between the anecdote and this poem are readily apparent. Foremost among the differences is that Soranus' Perdiccas is enamored of his dead father's mistress, and thus his passion carries no such burden of guilt as Perdica suffers. Perdiccas is already king, and his mother does not enter the picture; and Hippocrates is able to effect a cure. All these differences are significant, yet there is no doubt that the basic story is the same as in our poem.

There are two other representations of Perdiccas which are important for our understanding of the tradition. One is a small bronze figure now in Dumbarton Oaks, discovered in France, and first published in 1845.[7] An emaciated half-nude youth sits on a stool, his left hand extended with the wrist bent. His right foot is swollen, misshapen, and unshod. Inscribed into his garment with a punch are the names ΕΥΔΑΜΙΔΑΣ and ΠΕΡΔΙΚ. The forms of the letters prompted Longpérier to assign a date in the first century A.D., probably in the Augustan era. Chamoux was inclined to date the figure itself earlier, perhaps even in the early fourth century. That is surely too early a date for the work, but it could well be from the Hellenistic era. Martin Robertson also regards the clumsy inscription as later than the figure, and even if the statue is of Augustan date, he considers it to be a copy of "a Hellenistic, perhaps an Alexandrian, work."[8]

Obviously Longpérier could not know of the *AP*, and could not make the link between the figure and the story. But even since the *AP* was published, the association has been rejected, most notably by Richter,[9] who pointed instead to Aristophanes *Aves* 1292: Perdix is the name assigned to a lame man, and the scholiast tells us that Πέρδικος σκέλος or Περδίκειος πούς became proverbial for clubfoot.[10] Richter regarded the bronze as an ex voto by Eudamidas who had a clubfoot, a Πέρδικ[ος σκέλος. Chamoux settled the question by comparing the figure with a mosaic from the tomb of Cornelia Urbanilla at Lambiridi (Algeria), dating from the late third century of our era. The mosaic depicts an equally wasted youth in exactly the same pose, but his outstretched wrist is held by a physician who is clearly Hippocrates.[11] In the mosaic, there is no clubfoot. Thus the pose of the bronze is explained, including the position of the left arm,[12] and the identity of the youth is definitely settled as Perdiccas. The story of Perdiccas as a young prince (rather than an older king) and the intervention of Hippocrates including the revelation from the pulse, can thus be traced back beyond any extant literary source, and probably into the Hellenistic era.

We should probably note that the mosaic is also from an African context, whence comes the preponderance of later evidence for the story. In addition to the texts already cited there are a half-dozen lines preserved in the *Latin Anthology*, and presumably also of Vandal African date:

> Eximius Perdica fuit, qui corpore eburno
> fulgebat roseisque genis, cui lumina blanda
> fundebant flammas, crocei per colla capilli
> pendebant variosque dabant sibi saepe colores.
> fulvus poples erat, niveus pes. omnia habebat
> quidquid avet iuvenis: solus vincebat Adonem. (220R)

As the verses occur in the *Anthology* between comparable pieces on Narcissus and Cupid, it is reasonable to assume that they do not refer to a contemporary figure but to a mythological person. Baehrens conjectured that they might be a fragment of a lost epyllion on Perdica,[13] but the balance of the expression (opening with *eximius Perdica* and closing with *solus vincebat Adonem* after summing up with *omnia habebat*) sounds like a complete poem.[14] They do show the further popularity of the story, and its status as a mythological topic rather than a historical anecdote.

The last text to be adduced is Claudian *carmina minora* 8, which has long been misunderstood. It is entitled *De Policaste et Perdica:*

> Quid non saevus Amor flammarum numine cogat?
>   sanguinis en fetum mater amare timet.
> pectore dum niveo miserum tenet anxia nutrix,
>   illicitos ignes iam fovet ipsa parens.
> ultrices pharetras tandem depone, Cupido:
>   consule iam Venerem, forsan et ipsa dolet.

These verses had always been regarded as presenting the reverse of the usual myth, i.e., that Policaste fell victim to a desire for her son. In an ingenious article, G. Ballaira showed that in fact the story here is basically the same as in *AP*.[15] The verses have accompanied a painting or mosaic (an idea already proposed by Birt), which incidentally gives even further evidence of the popularity of this theme in the later period. It has always been assumed that the *anxia nutrix* of 3 was the *mater* of 2, even though this presumably results in a very young Perdica and a uniquely bizarre attraction.[16] Ballaira, by comparing the account in *AP* and also Ovid's treatment of Myrrha (*Met.* 10.298–502), where the nurse is a crucial figure, argued that *mater* and *nutrix* are separate characters. The picture would then have a central group of Perdica collapsed in anguish on the breast of his old nurse; his mother Policaste stands off to one side afraid to come near or show normal affection, as it only serves to terrify the boy (cf. *AP* 188: *"mater" ait "discede precor, plus uris amantem"*); and, I would conjecture, Cupid on the other side with his weapons, balancing Policaste.

This shows that the version found in *AP*, Perdica in love with his mother, was already developed by the beginning of the fifth century and was illustrated on wall or tomb. Clearly it had also been fully mythologized by then.

The mythological treatment is significant, for at some point the tale of Perdiccas the prince became intertwined with the myths about Perdix the partridge.[17] Names are a particular puzzle here: Perdix was either the sister of Daedalus and mother of Talos (Kalos) or else his nephew, the son of his sister Polycaste.[18] In either case, the nephew is the ingenious young inventor of the saw, compasses, and so forth, who incurs Daedalus' jealousy. Daedalus hurls the boy off the acropolis, and the mother hangs herself in grief. The Athenians built a shrine in her honor. But according to one branch of the tradition, most fully told by Ovid (*Met.* 8.236–59), Minerva took pity on the boy and rescued him by turning him into a partridge.[19]

The only apparent point of contact between this story and Perdica is the similar—but not identical—name. The chronology of the association between the stories is not clear. Ovid says nothing of an illicit relationship, nor does Hyginus. But in the later stages, Perdix' irregular passion has become the focus of the fable. Fulgentius (*Mythologiae* III.2) offers a version which is clearly much closer to *AP* in crucial ways:

Perdic[c]am ferunt venatorem esse; qui quidem matris amore correptus, dum utrumque et inmodesta libido ferveret et verecundia novi facinoris reluctaret, consumptus atque ad extremam tabem deductus esse dicitur. primus etiam serram invenit.

Perdica is consumed by passion; there is no mention of Daedalus, although Perdica is still the inventor of the saw. In fact, the jealousy and murder have vanished, and have been replaced by the romantic features of the Perdiccas story. Most important, Fulgentius agrees with our anonymous poet in that the hero's name is Perdica and the object of his passion is his mother. Fulgentius is followed, as in so much else, by the Vatican Mythographers.[20]

But then, Fulgentius sanitizes the myth by treating it as an allegory of agriculture:

. . . hic primum venator fuit; cui cum ferinae cedis cruenta vastatio et solitudinum vagibunda errando cursilitas displiceret, plusquam etiam videns contiroletas suos, id est Acteonem, Adonem, Hippolytum miserandae necis functos interitu, artis pristinae affectui mittens repudium agriculturam affectatus est; ob quam rem matrem quasi terram omnium genetricem amasse dicitur. quo labore consumptus etiam ad maciem pervenisse fertur. et quia cunctis venatoribus de pristinae artis opprobrio detrahebat, serram quasi maleloquium dicitur repperisse. matrem etiam Policasten habuit quasi policarpen quod nos Latine multifructam dicimus, id est terram.

Thus the tale of Perdiccas the Macedonian prince has become the myth of Perdix the partridge who was a farmer and loved Mother Earth.[21]

We should return for a moment to the bronze figurine. The one detail which puzzles all who study this piece is the deformed foot. Obviously the deformity was introduced for a reason: what was the artist trying to say? One possible solution is to regard the feature as a reference to the most famous "swollen foot" in antiquity, that of Oedipus, whose misfortune was exactly that which befell Perdica. Is it possible that the deformed foot is the artist's way of identifying the reason for the young man's emaciated state: a second Oedipus, who loved his mother? This would account neatly for the foot, but would have the very surprising effect of moving the extreme version of the story back into the Augustan or even Hellenistic period, before we encounter the far more restrained "historical" version of Soranus' anecdote.

Alternatively, one may return to the proverbial reference to Perdix as clubfoot, implied by Aristophanes and elucidated by his scholiast. By this explanation we may conclude that the artist knew of the use of Perdix as a proverbial name and used it here as a sign to convey the identity of the figure: clubfoot means Perdix. The names, however, are not quite the same, but if Robertson and Chamoux are correct in believing the clumsily punched names to be later than the figure, then this confusion may account for the fact that the inscription is not complete. Whoever added the name (Eudamidas?) wavered between Perdix and Perdiccas, the one seemingly guaranteed by the deformity and the other by the theme: he paused after ΠΕΡΔΙΚ and never completed the inscription.

If this was the case, we can see a convergence of the Perdix and Perdiccas threads already in the Hellenistic era, and it would be unreasonable to insist that there was no literary treatment of the story in that period as well, even though none survives.

The second line of historical report concerns another Greek prince with ill-placed affections. Far more frequent than the tale of Perdiccas is the story of Antiochus I, who fell in love with his stepmother Stratonice.[22] Our sources are somewhat remote in time from Antiochus. The earliest seems to be Valerius Maximus (V.7 *ext*. 1), with references running through the second century and then reappearing in late sources such as the *Suda*. There are imitations and echoes down to the Renaissance.

The Antiochus-Stratonice tale has a slightly larger cast of characters with clearly developed roles. There are four figures to observe: the king who has remarried, the lovely new queen, the prince who falls victim to her innocent charms, and the wise physician who sets all to rights. The focal point of the tale is always the cleverness of the doctor or the selflessness of the king. In all accounts the following elements appear.[23] Antiochus falls hopelessly in love with Stratonice. He cannot satisfy or shed his desire, and cannot tell anyone what is troubling him. As he wastes away, his father summons the physician Erasistratus. The doctor accidentally notes that Antiochus' pulse races when Stratonice is near and devises a solution which requires deceiving the king. He announces that the prince is lovesick, but that the object of his love is Erasistratus' own wife. The king begs him to give her up to save the boy, and Erasistratus asks whether the king would make the same sacrifice if Stratonice were at issue. The king claims he would, and Erasistratus tells him the truth. Seleucus in fact yields Stratonice to Antiochus and all ends happily. There is sometimes a parade of young ladies as in *AP*.

As with the story about Perdiccas, we cannot tell why or how this tale developed around the name of Antiochus. Mesk conjectured that the kernel of the story was simply the elevation of Antiochus to joint rule with Seleucus, embellished and transmogrified by the romantic imagination of various writers.[24] But it would be a curious metaphor for such a simple political step. Since there is nothing inherently incredible about the central situation of a young man mooning over a new queen (or a concubine), we should not rule out the possibility of a core of historical fact.

At any rate, the story in its full form exercised wide influence. Already for Galen, Erasistratus' fortunate diagnosis from the pulse was a model as he recounts his similar adventure (*de praecognitione* 6.1–16);[25] and Aristaenetus I.13 is a retelling of the entire tale, but now involving Polycles, his son Charicles, and the wise Dr. Panacius. Here, oddly, the (unnamed) lady is once again the mistress of the father, as in Soranus.

Thus there are two lines of tradition chiefly responsible for the story of *AP*. Of the first, the Perdiccas-Perdix combination, each extant version is distinctive in some significant feature not always reflected in *AP*. It is the second, the Antiochus tradition, which has exerted the stronger influence on our poem.[26]

Other Influences

Beyond these traditions dealing with the story itself, there are other materials which have influenced the poet. The forbidden relationships depicted for Antiochus and Perdica—love of stepmother and love of mother—make it inevitable that the myths of Hippolytus and Phaedra, and of

Oedipus and Iocasta, come into play. Mesk regarded the
Antiochus tale as strongly influenced by Euripides' *Hippolytus*, always recognizing that the direction of the passion is
reversed.[27] It is unnecessary to review the points of contact
between the two Greek sources, but we may note some
comparisons between the Hippolytus myth and *AP*. Hippolytus makes much of his rejection of Aphrodite and his service to Artemis. He goes to Athens to celebrate the Orphic
mysteries, and is ensnared there in the tragic relationship
with Phaedra. Perdica similarly offends Venus by failing to
pay her homage while he is in Athens and is thereby em-
broiled in a tragic passion.

Depending on the poet's sources, there may be more to
note. I think it unlikely that our unknown poet knew Euripides' tragedy directly, but rather that he knew Seneca's
reworking of the myth. As the Senecan *Phaedra* opens,
Hippolytus and his companions are traveling from Athens
into the country: Perdica likewise leaves Athens at the
beginning of *AP* with companions who are not otherwise
mentioned and play no real role. They seem to have been
added for this scene, and may have been suggested by the
tragic model. Perdica's sojourn at the grove may even be an
indirect reflection of Hippolytus' fondness for the wild.
Moreover, Seneca stresses that Phaedra is the victim of
Venus' revenge: again like Perdica, and like nothing else in
the tradition. In Phaedra's case Venus is pursuing all the de-
scendents of the Sun because he had exposed her adulterous dallying with Mars (*Ph.* 124ff.). This is also the theme
of Reposianus' poem and a popular topic in the African
poets. And finally, Perdica's meditations (272–81) on ways
to end his misery and his life are not unlike Phaedra's deliberations on the same topic (*Ph.* 258ff.). Both contemplate
the sword and leaping from a cliff and settle on hanging.
Phaedra has been wasting away in her passion, although
she decides to reveal and pursue her love rather than take
the secret to her grave.[28]

As to Oedipus, the comparison is inescapable, and Perdica makes it himself:

Oedipodem thalamos matris vult fama subisse
incestosque toros: satis est quod nescius ista
commisit culpamque tulit licet ille nefandam
exegit, sese privat dum lumine, poenam. (126–29)

Perdica assumes that greater guilt attaches to him because
he is aware that Castalia is his mother, but he did not know
that when he had his dream. Like Oedipus, he has been
separated from his parents since childhood and returns unaware to his mother. One can hardly miss the symbolic if
not ironic burden of lines 83 and 84 taken together:[29]

ardet in incestum pueri stimulante figura. . . .
ingrediturque suae regalia limina matris.

Note the shift from 18 (before the dream) *redeunti ad tecta
parentum*. Again one wonders whether Seneca may lurk
behind the poem. His *Oedipus* wallowed in the rhetorical
possibilities of the theme, including a vivid account of the
symptoms of plague afflicting the people of Thebes (180–
201), which is reminiscent of the symptoms so lavishly described by our poet. And we should not overlook the fact
that there are three references to Castalia, toward which
Laius was traveling when Oedipus slew him.[30]

Whatever may be the truth of these conjectures, it is
clear that this poet drew on Ovid's account of Myrrha's incestuous desire for her father (*Met.* 10.298–502).[31] Ballaira's account of the influences is thorough and largely convincing.[32] Those influences are most noticeable in the role
of the central figures, Castalia/Cinyras and Perdica/Myrrha.
For example, as Castalia in her anxiety asks Perdica the
name of his beloved, so Cinyras inquires of Myrrha (*Ap*
178ff.; *Met.* 356ff.). Both parents present a slate of candi-
dates, Cinyras bringing a list and Castalia actually bringing
the ladies. But none can satisfy Perdica, who sighs:

sunt niveae, sunt hic procero corpore pulchrae,
virgineoque nitent grato de flore puellae.
nulla tamen matri similis! (242–44)

and in similar terms, Myrrha explains her requirements:

consultaque, qualem
optet habere virum, "similem tibi" dixit. (363–64)

Ovid's story is important also because of the role of the
nurse, brought over from Euripides' *Hippolytus*.[33] Ballaira
argues plausibly that the story of Perdica must have retained the figure of the nurse at least to the point of the
tradition reported by Claudian. Thus our poet is likely to
be responsible for the deletion of the nurse and the assignment of some of her dramatic functions to Castalia. We can
therefore see the poet both borrowing carefully from his
sources and also moving with some independence into
novel turns of plot.

How then has the poet of *AP* used all these sources in
shaping his story? Clearly the *Aegritudo* is a variant on the
developed Antiochus story rather than on the original Perdiccas anecdote. Apart from the names of the hero and
physician, there are no points of contact which specifically
align the poem with Soranus rather than the Antiochus
tradition. The two strands may have come into contact
because of a confusion of names: Stratonice's mother and
daughter (thus Antiochus' half sister) were named Phila,
and Perdiccas had a sister named Stratonice. It is then
hardly surprising that the two families should attract the
same basic story. Lucian indicates the uncertainty in his
own day as to the correct subjects of the story:

οἷόν τι ἀμέλει καὶ Ἴκκος καὶ Ἡρόδικος καὶ Θέων καὶ εἴ τις
ἄλλος γυμναστὴς ὑπόσχοιτο ἄν σοι οὐ τὸν Περδίκκαν παρα-
λαβόντες—εἰ δὴ οὗτός ἐστιν ὁ τῆς μητρυιᾶς ἐρασθεὶς καὶ
διὰ ταῦτα κατεσκληκώς, ἀλλὰ μὴ Ἀντίοχος ὁ τοῦ Σελεύκου
Στρατονίκης ἐκείνης—ἀποφαίνειν Ὀλυμπιονίκην. (*Hist. conscr.* 35)

I would surmise that the story about Perdiccas and Hippocrates, as originally told—with what basis in fact we cannot know—was transferred to Antiochus as he became the

more famous and interesting personage.[34] Lucian's remark
suggests that the shift was in progress at that time.

Another influence which cannot be ignored is the prose
romance. The tale of Antiochus as found in Plutarch, ps.-
Lucian, and Julian, and above all in Aristaenetus, has much
of the tone of the romances, and this tone has carried over,
along with characteristic details of plot, to the Latin poem.
It is remarkable how many of the crucial texts for the understanding of this Latin epyllion are Greek. There is no Latin
version of the story which provides any significant portion
of the details found in *AP*. It is altogether likely that the
author of this poem knew Greek and drew on some part of
the Greek tradition for this fullest of Latin accounts.

Among the details of plot reminiscent of the romance are
the separation of the hero from his parents since childhood,
his consequent failure to recognize his mother, and the fact
that Perdica is a student in Athens. His royal status, even
vaguely conveyed, is also in harmony with this tradition.
Morelli went so far as to describe *AP* as a *novella* in verse.[35]
We may note also that the romances enjoyed attaching historical names to fabulous episodes merely for the interest
associated with a famous personage. Thus for instance in
the romance of Apollonius of Tyre, the wicked king who
entertains an incestuous desire for his daughter is named
Antiochus, a detail probably linked indirectly to the tradition we have been considering.[36]

And finally, the practice of the rhetorical schools influenced the poet heavily. The extravagant premises on which
the students composed *controversiae* offer many cases
which are similar to our story. Seneca's *Controversiae* VI.7
may typify the group:

Qui habebat duos filios duxit uxorem. alter ex adulescentibus
cum aegrotaret et in ultimis esset, medici dixerunt animi vitium
esse. intravit ad filium stricto gladio pater; rogavit ut indicaret
sibi causam. ait amari a se novercam. cessit illi uxore sua pater. ab
altero accusatur dementiae.

Other specimens include the pseudo-Quintilianic *Declamatio* 291 (with a more spectacular twist) and Calpurnius' *Declamatio* 46. Naturally there is no mention of princes or wise physicians in these brief summaries. They represent the lowest common denominator of the tradition, which no doubt enjoyed flamboyant development in the hands of students.

It is certain that at least some of the writers who provide us with accounts of Antiochus had encountered training such as the declamations suggest. Perry was surely too strict and idealistic in denying the possibility of cross-influences between the *declamationes* and the romances, just as Bornecque was too strict in demanding that the romance simply grew out of the school exercises.[37]

Since Carthage had one of the principal schools of rhetoric in the later Empire, and the topics for *declamationes* remained in use over very long periods of time, we may easily imagine that students in the Carthaginian school might be asked to dilate upon these same themes. Viewed from the other side, the poem certainly shows that its author had been trained in such a school. The unrestrained rhetoric, including the speeches which the prince and his mother deliver, smack unmistakably of this training. The *Anthologia Latina* and the *Romulea* of Dracontius both offer specimens of *controversiae* in hexameters: this poet may even have composed a *controversia* on this theme in school, of which the poem before us is a derivative.

There are two distinctive features of *AP*, as compared with any other part of the tradition. First, Perdica loves his mother, thereby making a tragic outcome inevitable; second, the poet has transferred the entire story from the realm of quasi-historical anecdote or even romance into the world of mythology.

Of particular importance is the change which the poet of the *Aegritudo* has wrought by composing a mythological narrative. In earlier versions of the tale, both Soranus and the Antiochus tradition, and even in the *controversiae*, we

moved in the everyday world or in the real world of historical figures. The gods appear not at all, and the miraculous
element is absent simply because the story hinges on human responses and ingenuity. We are not told why Perdiccas falls in love with Phila, or Antiochus with Stratonice. It
happens, and our interest is fixed on the solution. In *AP*,
however, we are immediately in the realm of myth, as the
poet allusively lists Amor's previous triumphs:[38]

> Dic mihi, parve puer, numquam tua tela quiescant?
> non sat erant frondes, non undae, nec fera nec fons?
> non Satyrus, non taurus amans, non ales et imber,
> non tristes epulae, post quas petit aera Tereus? (1–4)

From this point on, the poem is dominated by Venus' vengeance. Perdica is admittedly at fault for failing to worship
her, and as with Hippolytus or any other tragic figure, the
overwhelming blow may be traced to a genuine lapse. Perdica's actions are constantly compared to figures of myth.
The grove in which he rests evokes memories of Daphne,
Adonis, and Attis, and the spring evokes Narcissus and Philomela. As the god examines his arrows, we hear of Danae,
Leda, and Antiope (all adumbrated in the opening lines).
And when Perdica lies abed, his mother brings the young
ladies:[39]

> matronae veniunt forma cultuque micantes:
> hic erat Andromeda, hic altera Laudamia,
> ditior haec Danae, fulgentior altera Glauce,
> candidior Progne venit ‹altera et› altera Dirce. (228–31)

No doubt we are to admire the beauty of the women, but
we should note that they are all compared to women who
were involved in tragic episodes and draw our eyes back to
the realm of legendary heroines.

The fact that Venus sets all in motion fundamentally al-
ters the nature of the action. The use of the gods is more
than a means of externalizing Perdica's emotions and more
than casual literary convention. It links his dilemma to the

great sufferings of myth, and in particular lessens the guilt
which may attach to him despite his anguish.

It is idle to speculate on the poet's motives in using the
version involving incest. The theme smacks of the Hellenistic taste for the bizarre and the forbidden, as represented
by Parthenius' sketches of Periander's mother (*Path. Erot.*
xvii) and Leucippus (v) or Ovid's several tales of incest. As a
result of this choice, the hero will pine and sigh but there
can be no happy ending. From this fact flow other results.
The physician cannot succeed in finding a cure. Hippocrates still identifies the problem, but this is a chance discovery as in the Antiochus tradition. The interview with the
king is replaced by a soliloquy in which Hippocrates recites
the symptoms and mutters about his inability to help (155–
65). Thus the story changes from a demonstration of the
doctor's skill to a tragic narrative centered upon the young
man. Likewise the king, who elsewhere provides the happy
ending by yielding, is an unnecessary, awkward figure now.
The field must be clear for the son as it is for Oedipus.
Tecta parentum (18) is the only trace the king has left.[40]

We should note that Perdica is not guilty of incest. He is
lured in a dream by a vision of Amor. But even apart from
the substitution of Amor for Castalia, Perdica only dreams
of the erotic connection. It is a dream which, as Barbasz
notes, would have delighted Freud.[41] Perdica has not seen
his mother since he was very young, and his reminiscence
of her floods back in his dream now that he is a vigorous
young man. He cannot recognize her as his mother but
subconsciously he is drawn irresistibly to her sexually. But
how much guilt is there in such a dream?[42]

I wonder whether the Christian beliefs of the poet may
have influenced the matter, specifically the principle enunciated in the Gospel (Matt. 5:28) that "everyone who looks
at a woman lustfully has already committed adultery with
her in his heart." From this biblical perspective, as contrasted with the pagan view, Perdica could count himself
guilty despite having done nothing. Perdica is even further
detached from actual incest since it is not even a genuine

dream of Castalia. Charges of incest and the depiction of such themes were of considerable concern to Christian and pagan authors alike in the later Empire: John Chrysostom refers to the problem, especially in the theater. We know that the theme appeared in the mime and was the topic of declamation.[43] Thus the poet of the *Aegritudo* might well wish to avoid the direct representation of incest, even if not deliberately committed. By this device he can implicate the prince in the guilt of incest (and perhaps thereby point up a moral lesson) without having to present him as actually engaging in so offensive a deed.

This contrasts with the earlier pagan traditions of incest. Whether the guilty party is aware of the relationship (e.g., Myrrha) or unaware, like Oedipus, the guilt arises from the actual commission of incest. The same is true of such tales as ps.-Plutarch *de fluviis*, wherein Ganges, Tanais, and others unwittingly commit incest with their mothers and then fling themselves into the river upon discovering what they have done.[44] But in the Christian era, the accounts of Perdica/Perdix sterilize the notion—in *AP* as described and in Fulgentius both because the relationship is one of longing rather than action, and because it is then allegorized into a healthy love of land. Dracontius sets the tale in a context of deliberately shocking notions, and Claudian was not fervently Christian, if at all,[45] and in any case is probably reporting on a painting.

Structure

The structure of the poem is far from elaborate. The poet presents his story chronologically, without leaps ahead by prophecy or omen, and without flashbacks. His method is simply to pause over individual scenes, which, as we would expect, consist largely of descriptions and speeches. The indignant beginning addressed to Amor is matched by Perdica's final speech to the god: the question of line 1 (*numquam tua tela quiescant?*) is answered in the last verse (*hic Perdica iacet secumque Cupido peremtus*).

The first major scene is set in the grove of Amor. Two

purposes are served here. First it satisfies the popular taste for descriptions of the *locus amoenus*, and second, the details of the place provide ominous hints of calamities in myths associated with Venus:

> illis dispersi flores mixtique colores
> ostendunt Veneris quid amor. (32–33)

The charm of the *locus amoenus* has been charged with alarming connotations. The flowers are warnings of disaster, and the bird amid the branches is Philomela. The grove is beautiful but dangerous, like the goddess. Barbasz astutely notes[46] that Venus retained her associations with vegetation throughout antiquity, chiefly in the Vinalia, so that a grove specifically associated with her powers is natural enough. So is the connection with death, the principal crop of this soil.

But while we see the grove in alarming terms, Perdica does not. When the youth comes to the spring, the poet speaks only of the shade and fresh water it provides (59–65). Perdica is as unaware of peril here as in Athens.

The second tableau presents Amor waiting in the grove and preparing a new arrow. He makes it an occasion for reviewing past triumphs as he examines his used arrows: perhaps we should not ask why he still has the arrows already shot, or why he has kept them if they are useless for future targets. At any rate, he clearly requires a special arrow for each occasion. Now we watch him select a reed, and in a detail for which I can find no parallel, he plucks a feather from his own wing to use on the dart:

> post volucri cupiens vibramine abire sagittam
> pinnam de propriis ardentibus abscidit alis. (55–56)

The total effect of the passage is very Alexandrian, with its interest in the visual aspect of the action and its fascination with quasi-technical details. One is tempted to think that the poet may have had a picture in mind as he composed the verses.

The doctors in their bewilderment provide the next scene (137ff.). Here the poet displays his erudition in the technical medical language, although when all is said and done, Hippocrates has merely checked the patient's pulse. But the great physician is speculative and philosophical (*secum docto sermone locutus*):

> quid, medicina, taces? rationem redde petenti.
> non isti calor est pulsus nec vena minatur.
> nam sacrae partes,[47] quibus omnis vita tenetur,
> discordare parant, tum mox elementa resolvent,
> quae faciunt hominem, dum quattuor ista ligantur. (155–59)

The entire scene is apparently controlled by the poet's desire to array the technical terms of diagnosis, and to give prominence to Hippocrates' observation of Perdica. Again one is reminded of Galen's *de praecognitione*, which discusses the role of the pulse and in the process tells the story of Antiochus and Erasistratus.

No love epyllion would be complete without a sleepless night by the protagonist. Perdica endures two such nights, the first immediately after learning the identity of the lady. It is marked by all the conventional signs of lovesickness. The second comes after Castalia has tried to console him and made him even worse. Pudor and Cupido stand by his bed and compete for his heart (189–219). The two scenes are similar in pattern: Perdica alone is awake, and finally he breaks forth in lament and accusation. His speech in the first scene centers on his passion and guilt; in the second passage he is filled with defiance born of despair and tells Cupid to do his worst. The speeches serve to move the theme of the poem from Perdica's love to his death.

His final speech (264–90) admits defeat and merely deliberates the mode of death:

> quid dicis, Paphie? retulisti nempe triumphum:
> ad tantam maciem deducimur (264–65)
>
> . . . .
>
> quod superest, moriamur, Amor. (272)

The speech hinges on a paradox, that the hero is so weak and close to death that he cannot kill himself and thus faces prolonged life. I cannot discover any parallel for the notion that Amor will be killed if Perdica dies by hanging himself (but somehow will not be harmed by other methods).

Thus the selection of scenes to be developed shows a preference for paradox, for rhetorical possibilities, and for the exercise of imagination. Twists of logic and sentimental touches, personification of emotions—all these features remind us of Alexandrian taste, suggesting how enduring such conventions were, once they became established in the tradition.

Characters

As I have noted, the poem hinges largely on the presentation of the major characters, Perdica, Castalia, and Hippocrates. They are different from the traditional versions of these figures.

Perdica has but one characteristic: he is miserable. The poet does not use any title such as hero or even prince, but merely *iuvenis*. By the same token, Castalia is not the queen, but merely his mother. In short, the poet has concentrated on the relationship between these two rather than on their social stations, apart from *regalia limina matris* (84). This is a clear difference from the rest of the tradition, where the story turns on the fact that the young lover is a prince and gains the kingdom along with the queen. The kingdom not being at issue here, this is not mentioned. Similarly, the only epithets applied to Perdica are *miser* and *infelix*. The effect is to accentuate his helplessness: he is not exalted or strengthened by rank or prowess, until at last in his extreme condition he stands up to Amor and outwits the god.

When we first meet Perdica, there is rather more definition to him: he is a student and a pious soul (he does after all attend the altars of all the other gods). There is, moreover, the touch of heroic conduct as he reaches the grove:

ingressus postquam est lucos Perdica rigentes,
talibus est verbis socios aut voce secutus:
"o socii . . . ." (66–68)[48]

But the heroic gesture of addressing his companions thus is
softened by the fact that he is proposing a siesta amid the
flowers. The softness is enhanced by the pathetic touch in
85–86

quam (sc. matrem) parvus adhuc dimiserat olim,
cum peteret divae doctissima templa Minervae.

The verses emphasize his separation from parents and his
special attachment to Minerva, leading to his neglect of love
in favor of study. He is, in short, a vulnerable young lad who
once smitten predictably suffers extreme symptoms. The
description of this reaction is more like traditional accounts
of young women falling in love than young men.

He does not forget his training at school, but delivers
three speeches. His first reaction is to wonder how to present the case to his mother, and verbal failure seems to ap-
pall him as much as anything:

credamus! quid? hoc poteris conponere verbis,
aut vox qualis erit? adgressus namque parentem
"mater, ave" dicturus ero. quid deinde? tacebo! (123–25)

This characterization of Perdica vividly reflects the am-
bience in which the poem was created.

Castalia is not subtly developed as a character, but she
plays a more prominent role than is usually assigned to
the woman of the story. Nowhere is it actually suggested,
for example, that Castalia is beautiful, but only that Amor
has compelled Perdica to see her as such. The emphasis,
naturally, is on her identity as a mother and on her innocence. Even her name may point in this direction. The
name of the lady varies in the tradition, from Phila to Policaste, but nowhere else is she Castalia. In each case there
is some significance to the choice of name: Phila is obvious

enough, and Policaste may be an evolution from Iocaste (or Epicaste) and a hint at the Oedipus story.[49] Fulgentius goes on to *Policarpen, quod nos Latine multifructam dicimus.* As to Castalia, we may regard it as merely a further decline or evolution from Policaste, but I think it reflects her *castitas* by contrast with the *amor incestus* of her son.[50]

We should recall, as I noted earlier, how Seneca's *Oedipus* refers to Castalia in significant ways. Of particular interest is *Oedipus* (276–77) where Creon is describing how Laius was slain:

> frondifera sanctae nemora Castaliae petens
> calcavit artis absitum dumis iter.

The hero's approach to the grove, and the use of a name not elsewhere attached to Perdica's mother, suggests that the poet may have been thinking of Seneca. The detail recurs in the chorus' account of Theban history: *Castalium nemus / umbram Sidonio praebuit hospiti* (712–13).[51]

When Castalia hears of her son's arrival, she comes to greet him *memor nati*[52] and gives him *oscula materni plena doloris.* Irony pervades this scene with the play on *dolor* (Castalia), *cura* (Perdica) and *amor*. Castalia is solicitous when her son falls ill and assumes the role elsewhere played by the king in summoning the doctors. It is also she who devises the plan (usually assigned to Erasistratus) of bringing the eligible ladies past the bed. Thus the poet has moved Castalia into a central role, increasing her contact with the prince and thereby exacerbating the condition she seeks to alleviate. The irony of the situation is most clearly expressed when Castalia wonders whether Perdica is in love with a widow:

> inclita si virgo est, Hymenaeos iungere possum,
> sive suo matrona movet viduata marito;
> ne dubites. haec cura mea est, hoc maesta verebar,
> inlicitos ne forte toros temtare mariti
> cogeret acer amor matrisque gravaret honorem. (180–84)

The irony is complete if we read *Amor*.

This increase in Castalia's role is not merely an evolution of the woman's part which eventually assigns her more activities, but a double process which increases contact in direct proportion to its tragic effect.

Hippocrates is reduced in importance as compared with the earlier parts of the tradition. He cannot be the center of the story because he cannot succeed. However, in the mythological atmosphere of the poem he is more like a seer than a doctor. He is referred to as *magnus virorum* (170) and ponders at length the illness he cannot cure. His very failure lends added horror to the affliction, and he concludes *iam cetera di dent*.[53] The readers of this poem in Vandal Africa would no longer regard it as the reworking of a historical incident: Hippocrates was a legendary name, the father of medicine. He can function here rather as Chiron might in another setting.

Thus the poet of the *Aegritudo Perdicae* has worked many changes upon a story with a long heritage, and we end up with a most curious love story which blends history and mythology, tradition and innovation, artistry and ineptitude in strange and unequal proportions. But the poem is not without its charm, and it is a more important document in the history of the epyllion than has been recognized by most scholars. It is extremely difficult to assign the poem to an exactly defined place in that history, because the work remains undated and anonymous. What is remarkable for our purposes, however, is that the *AP* represents a different set of artistic choices and moves along a different path for the epyllion from what we see in the poems of Dracontius. It remains to consider how these two poetic approaches appear when set side by side and to see what lessons for the history of the miniature epic may be derived from this juxtaposition.

Chapter 8

Conclusion

WE HAVE NOW examined the epyllia of Dracontius, and the unassigned *Aegritudo Perdicae*. If we want to see the full dimensions of the epyllion tradition in Vandal Carthage, we must reexamine the persistent but erroneous attribution of the *Aegritudo* to Dracontius by scholars over the past hundred years.[1] As is already clear, there are differences between the two styles of poetry which make the attribution untenable, but the contrast itself is instructive.

The Aegritudo Perdicae *and Dracontius*

We may begin by considering the alignment of the *AP* with the epyllion tradition as a whole. It actually has a number of features which were characteristic of the classical epyllia—far more, indeed, than is the case with Dracontius. It preserves the much-favored emphasis on erotic pursuits of a bizarre or forbidden nature (for example, in Cinna's *Zmyrna*, Calvus' *Io*, the *Ciris*), and a fondness for descriptions of various kinds. This latter practice had been a standard feature of all poetry since the Silver Age, and yet is curiously rare in Dracontius. Likewise, the *AP* retains the epic tradition of catalogues, of which there is little trace in Dracontius. In all these ways, the poet of the *AP* reveals links with the epyllion tradition from earlier centuries which distinguish his work from that of Dracontius. Other features of the tradition are shared with Dracontius, principally the use of dreams and the invocation of the Muses, both of which Dracontius uses to good effect.

The greater similarity of the *AP* to the classical form is

245

important, however, and may even encourage the idea that
the poem is a translation or a reworking of a lost Greek or
Latin original.[2] There are two objections to such a view.
First, the central characters are historical in origin, and no
extant epyllion of the classical era treats historical figures.
It may indeed have been the resurgence of the historical
epic in the later period which encouraged the use of real
personages in such compositions as this. But for the *AP*, I
believe we should rather think of the romance, whose authors always showed total disregard for historical proba-
bilities and knew that real names made good box office in
an exciting story. On the other hand, it is likely that to fifth-
century readers, Hippocrates and Perdica were merely legendary or even unknown. But we should look at the matter
from the classical end: the names were widely known in
the first century, and at that time Hippocrates and Perdiccas would have seemed unfit subjects for a mythological
epyllion.

The second consideration is our fragmentary evidence on
the growth of the story. It is clear from Soranus and from
Lucian that in the second century, the Perdiccas story was
still in the anecdotal stage, and that the fuller version was
still associated with Antiochus. We should therefore regard
the fundamental story of the *AP*—including gods and incest—as developing after the time of Soranus but before
the time of Claudian, or rather before the date of the picture he describes in *Carmina minora* 8.

At the same time, there are features which will lead us to
assign the poem to a fifth-century context, and indeed to
the same context as Dracontius. For Dracontius is one of
the very few poets to mention the story of Perdica, along
with the poem from the *Latin Anthology*.[3] The theme apparently enjoyed some popularity in this place and at this
time. Like the *Hylas*, this is in all probability an exercise
related to the training in the rhetorical schools, although
we are not required to suppose with Baehrens and Vollmer
that the author of the *AP* belonged specifically to the school
of Felicianus along with Dracontius.

Moreover, similarities of incident provide links to Dracontius' work.[4] Both *AP* and *Hylas* present Venus offended
and sending Amor to exact revenge. Amor does so in both
cases by going to a spring in the woods and changing into
the likeness of a woman.[5] We have seen in both poems how
the god boasts of his former victories and reviews his weapons. These fairly specific touches point to a similar context
for the origin of both poems.

But the differences of style are equally striking. In addition to the features mentioned above, we should particularly notice Dracontius' fondness for long asyndetic series
of nouns or verbs. Not a single specimen of this occurs in
the *AP*. Instead, consider line 106:

> nox ipsi maesta est: vigilat metuitque tepetque.

Moreover, Dracontius is very fond of oxymoron, along with
all other forms of paradox. The *AP* presents paradoxical
concepts, but this poet prefers to bring them out by irony
rather than oxymoron. There is, for example, nothing remotely comparable to the opening lines of the *Orestes*.

In the last analysis, beyond any specific details, there is a
clear difference in the level of literacy and talent. If the *AP*
were the work of Dracontius, it would presumably have
been composed while he was still under the spell of the
school. This would make it a product of the same phase
of his poetic career as the *Hylas*, a far superior piece of
writing.

Thus the *AP* and Dracontius, set side by side, show two
clearly differentiated traditions of the epyllion. The author
of the *AP* is truer to the conventions of the epyllion tradition. He preserves more of the characteristic effects, is
more closely tied to the kind of subject preferred by the
classical epyllion, and shows how even a specialized form
such as the epyllion can be transplanted to a very different
world.

Dracontius: concluding observations

Dracontius' poems show a complex pattern of influences at work. High literary touches and broad effects from contemporary culture lie cheek by jowl. This is the work of an artist who reveals much about his own time, more so than a poet such as Claudian who strives to be consistently classicizing. Some impression of the general level of literary accomplishment in Dracontius' day may be had from the pages of the *Latin Anthology*. It is hard to believe that the authors of most pieces in the *Anthology* are contemporary with our poet, whose breadth of reading and sense of artistry are on so different a plane. But it is precisely this combination of traditional and current that makes Dracontius so alive and interesting to read. His semibarbarisms of vocabulary and vulgarisms of syntax are inextricably interwoven with the sonorities of Vergilian and Statian verse. Both speak to the reader directly from the poet's imagination.

Dracontius is not afraid to create new directions for his stories and to draw new lessons from them. The presence of so many innovations and the combination of inherited literary expression with current vulgar language show how alive the poetic tradition was to the poet. His relation to that tradition was not one of museum keeper, but rather of a creative renovator of an old and beloved building, for which new uses are being devised along with a new façade to make it more attractive to modern visitors.

In pursuit of this goal Dracontius draws from whatever source or form will serve his purposes. One result of this eclecticism is that the poems are quite different from each other as well as from the traditional treatments of the individual themes. One poem is like a pantomime, the next like a tragedy, and the next like a romance.

If then we ask how Dracontius' epyllia compare with the classical phase, the answer must be that they diverge rather sharply from the prevailing norms of the Hellenistic-Roman period. This is hardly surprising. In the classical phase epic dominated whatever other traits the individual poems had.

But when we turn to Dracontius, the manner of treatment shows wide variations, including the stamp of several non-poetic forms and even nonliterary materials. The center of gravity of the tradition has been lost.

Yet some crucial features do persist. The interest in elaborate structure is a quality which Catullus would have recognized with approval. The recurring interest in erotic themes, including the more peculiar byways of the subject, is a heritage going back to the Alexandrian beginnings of the miniature epic. Moreover, the epyllion had always shown a preference for little-known myths and for obscure or invented versions of famous stories. Certainly Dracontius' poems accord with this tradition, although as we have seen, the reasons for his innovations are somewhat different from those of Callimachus or Ovid.

And so we return to the point of departure. This openness to experiment is itself the strongest legacy from the classical epyllion. The range within which poets moved was relatively restricted during the Hellenistic-Roman phase and is far wider in these fifth-century ventures. Dracontius' experiments are not basically different from those which his predecessors had conducted, but inevitably the equipment available to him had changed during the intervening five centuries. The dominance of prose forms in the Empire meant that Dracontius was inescapably influenced by those forms. The same is true of rhetorical training in light of his personal education and professional interests. Dracontius simply saw a different profile to the history of literature.

Dracontius is at the heart of a major transition. His world was dominated by forces which had little awareness of the highest periods of the Roman literary tradition. He is at the juncture between the ancient and medieval worlds in several respects. The reader of these poems meets medieval literary tastes as well as ancient: the chronicle effect of the stories as Dracontius tells them, the interest in magic and miracles, and above all the persistent presence of Christian attitudes, even if sometimes disguised, all bespeak an outlook which will become more familiar in the centuries ahead. The language of the poems likewise contains numerous features which would seem more natural to Jordanes than to any writer before Claudian.

Dracontius mediates between the classical and medieval, between pagan and Christian; and in some fashion he also provides a bridge between the Roman world which produced the forms and subjects of his poetry, and the Germanic people who ruled the world he lived in. Although he is in many ways so Roman that one could almost forget that he came from a context dominated by barbarians, yet his praise for Felicianus for bridging the gap between the two peoples shows his interest in bringing the two cultures together. The Vandals are a silent people in the realm of letters, and ironically their best voice is the Roman who shared their life and perhaps their lineage, and whose ear was keen enough to hear a variety of voices and harmonize them.

Notes

CHAPTER 1

1. K. Gutzwiller, *Studies in the Hellenistic Epyllion* (*Beiträge zur klassische Philologie* 114: Meisenheim 1981).
2. M. M. Crump, *The Epyllion from Theocritus to Ovid* (Oxford 1931).
3. W. Allen, "The Epyllion: a Chapter in the History of Literary Criticism" *TAPA* 71 (1940) 1–26.
4. On the notion of an elegiac epyllion, cf. C. N. Jackson, "The Latin Epyllion" *HSCP* 24 (1913) 37–50; D. F. Bright, "The Art and Structure of Tibullus I.7" *Grazer Beiträge* 3 (1975) 42ff.
5. Crump went so far as to assert that the epyllion—along with all other departments of Latin poetry—saw no development after Ovid (p. 48).
6. By·classical I mean the poems of the Hellenistic-Roman phase normally associated with the term *epyllion:* such works as Theocritus *Id.* 13, 24, 25; Callimachus' *Hymn* 6 and *Hecale;* Catullus *c.* 64; the *Ciris* and *Culex;* the Aristaeus episode of the *Georgics* (4.315–566); and—if we accept Crump's premise—each of the 186 stories of Ovid's *Metamorphoses.*
7. This poem of some 124 verses was first published by R. Roca-Puig, *Alcestis. hexàmetres Llatins* (Barcelona 1982); cf. also W. Lebek, "Das neue Alcestis-Gedicht der Papyri Barcinonenses" *ZPE* 52 (1983) 1–29; P. J. Parsons, R. G. M. Nisbet & G. O. Hutchinson, "Alcestis in Barcelona" ibid. 31–36; J. Schwartz, "Le papyrus latin d'Alceste et l'oeuvre de Claudien" ibid. 37–39; M. Marcovich, "Alcestis Barcinonensis" *Illinois Classical Studies* 9 (1984) 111–34. The papyrus itself belongs to the 4th century, early in the century according to Lowe (*Codices Latini antiquiores* Suppl. 1782), C4² in Roca-Puig.
8. Latin: in addition to the five poems studied in this volume, the list includes the *Alcestis* mentioned in the previous note; Claudian's *De bello Getico, De bello Gildonico,* and *Gigantomachia;* Reposianus' *De concubitu Martis et Veneris;* and—depending on how broad the definition is—perhaps Prudentius' *Psychomachia,* Avitus' *De transitu maris rubri,* the Vergilian centos in the *Anth. Lat.* and even

some of Prudentius' *Peristephanon* (e.g., carm. 9). Greek: Triphiodorus, *Iliou halosis*, the *Orphic Argonautica;* Colluthus' *De raptu Helenae;* and Musaeus' *Hero et Leander.*

9. On the large question of later Latin poetry's relation to the genre distinctions, implicit religious content, and mixture of effects in the earlier tradition, cf. Jacques Fontaine, *Études sur la poésie latine tardive d'Ausone à Prudence* (Paris 1980), esp. 1–23 ("Le mélange des genres dans la poésie de Prudence") and 25–83 ("Unité et diversité du mélange et des tons chez quelques écrivains latins de la fin du IVe siècle: Ausone, Ambroise, Ammien").

10. A. M. Quartiroli, "Gli epilli di Draconzio" *Athenaeum* NS 24 (1946) 160–87; 25 (1947) 17–34.

11. J. M. Diaz de Bustamante, *Draconcio y sus carmina profana* (Santiago de Compostela 1978).

12. Cf. text below, Chapter 8.

13. On the origins of *vandal/vandalism* in their modern sense cf. Christian Courtois *Les Vandales et l'Afrique* (Paris 1955) 59. The usage begins in earnest only during the 18th century (Voltaire 1732, and in particular Grégoire, Abbé of Blois, who coined *vandalisme* in 1794) but is an extension of the Renaissance Italian view of the early Germans as embodying all that is uncivilized and destructive: hence Gothic. Cf. also *OED* for early uses of *vandal* and its derivatives in English (late 17th century and later).

14. Among the more flamboyant ancient accounts of the Vandals are Procopius, *De Bello Vandalico;* Victor of Vita, *Historia persecutionis Africanae provinciae;* Victor of Tunnuna, *chron.;* Prosper of Aquitaine, *De ingratis, De providentia Dei;* Paulinus (of Béziers?), *epigramma* (cf. *CSEL* XVI p. 503 for text); Isidore, *Historia de regibus Vandalorum;* Salvian, *De gubernatione Dei*, offers a flattering picture of the Vandals, but principally to prove his point that the sins of the Romans were to be contrasted with these savages who behaved less wickedly than the champions of civilization. As Courtois remarks, "On déchirera volontiers l'image romantique du Barbare sanglant, professionnellement dressé sur des ruines fumantes, mais pas pour lui substituer l'image, tout aussi romantique, du 'bon Barbare', descendant transrhénan du 'bon Sauvage'" (p. 61). For a comprehensive presentation of contemporary views, cf. P. Courcelle, *Histoire littéraire des grandes invasions germaniques*, 3d ed. (Paris 1964), esp. 79–90, 183–215.

15. From the vast bibliography on the early Germans, and specifically on the Vandals, one item rises above the rest for our purposes: Courtois' *Vandales*, a work of astonishing richness and unfailing interest. See also L. Schmidt, *Geschichte der Wandalen.* 2d ed. (Munich 1942); J. Randers-Pehrson, *Barbarians and Romans* (Norman 1983) 132–88. Cf. also n.20 below.

16. Victor of Vita *Historia* (I.2) is explicit that this figure included women and children and slaves, not just the army (as Procopius believed: *B.V.* I.v.18). As Courtois notes, the only reason Gaiseric would have conducted a census at Gibraltar was in order to plan the logistics of transporting his people across the straits to Africa, and for that he had to have a head count not just of his troops but of all who needed passage (cf. pp. 215–17).

17. J. B. Bury, *History of the Later Roman Empire* (London 1923) I.247. We have a vivid sketch of Gaiseric in Jordanes, *Getica* 168: erat Gyzericus iam Romanorum clade in urbe notissimus, statura mediocris et equi casu claudicans, animo profundus, sermone rarus, luxuriae contemptor, ira turbidus, habendi cupidus, ad sollicitandas gentes providentissimus, semina contentionum iacere, odia miscere paratus. He was—as Hobbes would say—nasty, brutish, and short.

18. The Vandal "era" counted from the capitulation of Carthage in 439, and so Gaiseric's regnal years are calculated in the same manner even though he had ruled since 428. The series of kings were: Gaiseric 439–77; Huneric 477–84; Gunthamund 484–96; Thrasamund 496–523; Hilderic 523–30; Gelimer 530–34. See Courtois 260–71 (La galérie des rois) for sketches and sources; 390–409 for a more extensive genealogy of the Asdingi, sources and chronologies.

19. On the Donatists under the Vandal regime, cf. Courtois 285, esp. n.5. Our knowledge of the role played by Donatists at this time is very shaky, but scattered references lead us to believe that they fared somewhat better under the Vandal oppressors than under their traditional Catholic enemies (although this may simply be grumbling in the Catholic sources).

20. Chr. Courtois et al., *Tablettes Albertini. Actes privées de l'époque vandale* (Paris 1952).

21. For a very thorough examination of the problems and of the scholarship, see Díaz 33–96.

22. Cf. the *subscriptio* of *Rom. V:* exp. controversia statuae viri fortis quam dixit in Gargilianis Thermis Blossius Emilius Dracontius vir clarissimus et togatus fori proconsulis almae Karthaginis apud proconsulem Pacideium.

23. H. Malfait, *De Dracontii poetae lingua* (Paris 1902) xix, adopted Baehrens' alteration of *Rom.* V.117 from *Carthago invita volensque* to *invicta valensque* (strangely trying to avoid the most characteristic feature of Dracontius' style, the oxymoron). If then the *controversia* were delivered before 439, the poet's birth would have to be pushed back to or beyond 420. But a boast such as *invicta valensque* is likely only in hindsight, after the city had in fact been conquered, and the change is quite unconvincing. It would also entail a very implausible age for the poet during the reigns of Gunthamund and Thrasamund at the end of the century.

24. D. Romano, *Studi draconziani* (Palermo 1959) 13: between 450 and 460.
25. D. Kuijper, *Varia Dracontiana* (Diss. Amsterdam: The Hague 1958) 7ff.
26. Diaz 38ff.
27. Cf. text pp. 66–68 below.
28. E.g., Pierre Courcelle, *Late Latin Writers and their Greek Sources,* 2d ed. (Cambridge Mass. 1969) 217–21.
29. Originally by Fr. von Duhn *Dracontii carmina minora* (Leipzig 1873). The conjecture was picked up and its implications pursued by F. Corsaro, "Problemi storico-letterari del cristianesimo africano nel V⁰ secolo. Studi su Draconzio" *Miscellanea di studi di letteratura cristiana antica* 11 (1961) 8ff. Diaz (61) approves and embellishes.
30. H. Papencordt apparently advanced the suggestion first in his *Geschichte der vandalischen Herrschaft in Africa* (Berlin 1837), but it quickly became an article of faith, stated as an established fact in every discussion of Dracontius, the Vandals, or Zeno. A fleeting voice of doubt comes in Vollmer's *RE* entry, but he shows no doubt in his *MGH* edition. Finally P. Chatillon spelled out the difficulties, "Dracontiana" *Revue du Moyen âge latin* 8 (1952), esp. 195ff., and since then no specialized study of Dracontius has argued for Zeno.
31. Kuijper 13ff.
32. See the criticisms in Romano 16f., and Diaz 57ff.
33. Corsaro 12–16.
34. Dracontius seems to imply such a motivation in his remarks on the informer (*Rom.* VII.127–31):

> non male peccavi nec rex iratus inique est,
> sed mala mens hominis, quae detulit ore maligno,
> et male suggessit tunc et mea facta gravavit.
> poscere quem veniam decuit, male suscitat iras
> et dominum regemque pium saevire coegit.

35. Schmidt 135; Romano 75f.
36. Cf. E. Baehrens, "Neue Verse des Dracontius" *RhM* 33 (1878) 313–16.
37. Romano (74) suggests both; Diaz (94) agrees.
38. Cf. *Hel.* 350–62 (simile of lion) and *Sat.* 137–46. If indeed the *Sat.* simile is the model, then the epyllion belongs in or after the prison years. The *Med.* and *Or.* may both be later than *Hel.*, to judge from other adaptations by the poet, which would place all but *Hylas* in the middle or late stages of his production.
39. Vollmer recognized this (*MGH praef.* Vff.) and developed an elaborate theory about lost poems, the original multibook arrangement, etc. Extensive analysis in Provana 36ff., Diaz 102–109. The lack of

meaningful order (*pace* Vollmer) and the separation of *Or.* from the
rest of the nontheological poems make it virtually certain that we
have only a remnant in the present *Romulea.* The title is presumably meant to classify the poems on traditional Roman themes as
distinct from expressly Christian topics.

40. All the poems are hexameters except I (troch. tetr. catal.).
41. The titulus gives the premise: Vir fortis optet praemium quod volet.
    pauper et dives inimici. bellum incidit civitati. dives fortiter fecit;
    reversus praemii nomine statuam petiit et meruit. secundo fortiter
    egit: reversus petiit praemii nomine asylum fieri statuam suam et
    meruit. tertio fortiter fecit: reversus petiit praemii nomine caput
    pauperis inimici. pauper ad statuam divitis confugit. contradicit.
42. On the tangled question of the relative chronology of Dracontius'
    poetry, cf. C. Lohmeyer, "De Dracontii carminum ordine" *Schedae
    philologicae Hermanno Vsener . . . oblatae* (Bonn 1891) 60–75;
    Provana 33–38; Diaz 109–19.

CHAPTER 2

1. The comprehensive presentation of ancient materials by Gustav
   Türk is still invaluable: *De Hyla* (*Breslauer, philologische Abhandlungen* 7.4: Breslau 1895); cf. also the lengthy review of Türk by G.
   Knaack in *Göttingische Gelehrte Anzeigen* 158 (1896) 867–88.
2. On the extant poems cf. A. S. F. Gow's *Theocritus;* H. H. Koch, *Die
   Hylasgeschichte bei Apollonios Rhodios, Theokrit, Properz und Valerius Flaccus* (Diss. Kiel 1955); G. Serrao, "Problemi di poesia ales-
   sandrina II: Ila in Apollonio e in Teocrito" *Helikon* 5 (1965) 541–65;
   H. Fuchs, *Die Hylasgeschichte bei Apollonios Rhodios und Theokrit*
   (Diss. Würzburg 1969); K. J. Gutzwiller, *Studies in the Hellenistic
   Epyllion* (Meisenheim 1981) 19ff.
3. Türk 1–9.
4. Hesychius, s.v. Ὕλας· κρήνας Κιανοί· καλοῦνται δὲ καὶ βαρβά-
   ρων γένος οὕτως.
5. The brief treatment of the story in the *Orphic Argonautica* (639–
   57) is studded with peculiar inventions: cf. Türk 44–45.
6. R. M. Agudo Cubas, "Dos epílios de Draconcio" *Cuadernos de filología clásica* 14 (1978) 323.
7. Türk 40–41; schol. Theoc. XIII.7; schol. Ap.Rh. I.1207.
8. For an interesting but incautious review of possible sources and
   points of original invention, see G. Procacci, "Intorno alla composizione e alle fonti di un carme di Draconzio (*Hylas. Rom. II*)"
   SIFC 20 (1913) 438–49.
9. Cf., for example, Diod. Sic. IV.12.1–2: τρίτον δὲ πρόσταγμα
   ἔλαβεν ἐνεγκεῖν τὸν Ἐρυμάνθιον κάπρον ζῶντα . . . κατὰ τὴν
   μάχην ταμιευσάμενος ἀκριβῶς τὴν συμμετρίαν ἀπήνεγκε τὸν
   κάπρον ζῶντα πρὸς Εὐρυσθέα.

10. Of course Vergil has no hint of Hylas in his Aristaeus tale, but he is familiar to all (*G.* 3.6), and Silenus sings his story in *Ecl* 6.43–44.
11. Cf. Türk 13–15; Fr. Dübner, ed. *Scholia graeca in Aristophanem* (Paris 1883) *ad loc. & adnot.* pp. 607–608.
12. Also Ὕλαν κραυγάζειν; cf. Türk 45–48 for relevant texts.
13. Procacci 448; Provana 57.
14. Procacci 446.
15. Cf. ibid. 442.
16. The *Latin Anthology* (264R.) contains Propertius' famous couplet on the *Aeneid* (II.34.65–66), but the lines were presumably excerpted long before that time and preserved because of their bearing on Vergil.
17. There is surely no reason to accept Türk's argument (p. 63 n.2) that derives the name from Apollonius' Dryope rather than from Vergil's Deiopea.
18. It is impossible to tell whether Dracontius is also reflecting Ovid (*Met.* 5.364ff.) or whether they sound alike because both poets are imitating Vergil.
19. *Hyl.* 104/VF I.549; 123/III.531; and according to Procacci (p. 442) 66–67/I.218–20, but if so the echo is fainter than any Hylas ever made.
20. Provana 59.
21. Cf. Agudo Cubas 306–18; Diaz 137–49 also assumes a four-part structure.
22. Procacci 440; cf. also Provana 57.
23. Quartiroli 165, 173–74.
24. Diaz 137.
25. C. Morelli, "L'epitalamio nella tarda poesia latina" *SIFC* 18 (1910) 319–432, esp. 405ff.; cf. also Procacci 440 n.2; Quartiroli 174.
26. See text pp. 35–37 below.
27. Clymene alludes to two myths not known in any other poet: *Lycastum zelat Amazon* (119) and *Furias amat ipse Cupido* (120). Dracontius mentions the second myth again in *Med.* 460. Procacci (444) suggests the idea may have arisen from Val. Fl. IV.13, *i, Furias Veneremque move*, but this cannot possibly be correct. There might be some remote association with *Anth. lat.* 240R., *Cupido amans*, where Cupid cries *in furias ignesque trahor* (8), but this is clearly not the same as a specific myth. Agudo Cubas (321) prefers the assumption of a lost source. The fact that Dracontius alludes to the myth twice without any attempt at explanation suggests that it was current in his day, and in view of the many innovations in mythology which distinguish the period, I think it likely that the novel version had developed only in that general place and period.
28. By contrast, Venus' first word to Amor in *Aen.* 1.664 is *nate;* and in Ovid, the two ideas are intertwined: "*arma manusque meae, mea, nate, potentia*" *dixit* (*Met.* 5.365).

29. Agudo Cubas 310.
30. Procacci 440 n.2.
31. Cf. Agudo Cubas 312.
32. On the pantomime see L. Friedländer, *Roman Life and Manners under the Early Empire*, 7th ed. (repr. London 1965) vol. II, pp. 100–11; E. Wüst, s.v. "Pantomimus" *RE* XVIII. 833–69; H. Bier, *De saltatione pantomimorum* (Diss. Brühl 1920); V. Rotolo, *Il pantomimo* (Palermo 1957); M. Bieber, *The History of the Greek and Roman Theater*. 2d ed. (Princeton, N.J. 1961) 235 ff. Among ancient sources, the most extensive is Lucian's *de saltationibus*.
33. E.g., Lucian *de salt.* 63; Suet. *Calig.* 54.
34. See M. Bieber, s.v. "Maske" *RE* XIV 2070–2105.
35. See the detailed account of this particular pantomime in Apuleius *Met.* X.29–34.
36. A point noted but not pursued by H. Bier (n.32 above) 113.
37. G. Traversari, *Gli spettacoli in acqua nel tardo-antico* (Rome 1960).
38. G. d'Ippolito, "Draconzio, Nonno e gli 'idromimi'" *A&R* 7 (1962) 1–14.
39. *Cantabat* has seemed so inappropriate that some have resorted to "emendation": *transibat* (Bücheler), *cursabat* (Baehrens).
40. Valerius saw the similarity to Ascanius, and imitated the famous Vergilian line, *sequiturque patrem non passibus aequis* (*Aen.* 2.724): *haeret Hylas lateri passusque moratur iniquos* (3.486).
41. Diaz 387.
42. Provana 58.
43. G. K. Galinsky, *The Herakles Theme* (Oxford 1972) 81.
44. See the discussion of Theocritus' humorous treatment in these epyllia by Gutzwiller (n. 2 above) 10–38.
45. Cf. M. Simon, *Hercule et le christianisme* (Paris 1955); F. Gaeta, "L'avventura di Ercole" *Rinascimento* 3 (1954) 227ff.; Galinsky 188f.
46. "Veramente in ogni epillio, tranne che nell' Ila, si leggono invettive contro gli dei, implorazione di mitezza, e di amore, che possono nascere dal nuovo concetto di Dio padre, misericordioso: ma questo è espresso solo negativamente" (pp. 168–69).

CHAPTER 3

1. Provana's first sentence on the poem is surely wrongheaded on almost every count: "Nessuna novità importante troviamo nell' ultimo epillio . . . ; il poeta non ha qui altro intento, che quello di narrare le geste di Medea" (p. 70).
2. Quartiroli (17–25) and Provana unrelentingly insist on lost sources where no extant model can be identified. Those who believe Dracontius invented his peculiarities of plot are especially harsh. For example, J. H. Goedhart ends his summary of post-Euripidean treatments of the myth with Hosidius and then Dracontius: "Ul-

timus nobis restat Hosidio etiam indignus versificator nomine Dracontius. . . . Parodiam legere nobis videmur." (De Medeae mytho apud antiquos scriptores et artifices [Diss. Leyden 1911] 39–40).

3. Quartiroli 17.

4. Cf. H. Bardon, La littérature latine inconnue, vol. 2 (Paris 1956) 214–16.

5. J. J. Mooney, Hosidius Geta's Tragedy "Medea" (Birmingham, Ala. 1919) 8; N. Dane, "The Medea of Hosidius Geta" CJ 46 (1950) 77; F. Desbordes, Argonautica (Brussels 1979) 84; G. Salanitro, Osidio Geta, Medea (Rome 1981) 74.

6. Her. 12; Met. 7.1–424; Tr. 3.9. He seems to be avoiding in these works the events which would normally fall in the tragedy, as if to prevent duplication. But the general tenor of his treatment is clear from these extant works.

7. There is nothing to encourage Diaz' view (p. 224) that the unspeakable nature of Medea's crimes accounts for the invocation of muta Polyhymnia.

8. W. H. Friedrich (Vorbild und Neugestaltung [Göttingen 1967] 70) comments on this problem in broad terms. Nowhere is the gulf as obvious as in Dracontius, precisely because the other poets tried to focus on one aspect or the other. Even Apollonius is uncomfortable blending the lover and the murderess.

9. Lines 36–39 are most reminiscent of Claud., Rapt. Pros. 1.1ff. Quartiroli's comparison with Accius fr. 1R. is strained and unconvincing.

10. Iuno cum ad flumen Euhenum in anum se convertisset et staret ad hominum mentes tentendas, ut se flumen Euhenum transferrent, et id nemo vellet, Iason Aesonis et Alcimedes filius eam transtulit: ea autem irata Peliae quod sibi sacrum intermiserat facere, effecit ut Iason unam crepidam in limo linqueret.

11. So Diaz 226.

12. Hymenaeus is not used elsewhere as a messenger of this sort. No doubt his presence here is due to the influence of the epithalamium on the entire scene. Cf. Morelli, "L'epitalamio nella tarda poesia latina" SIFC 18 (1910) 319ff.

13. "Draconzio, Nonno e gli 'idromimi'" A&R 7 (1962) 5.

14. If the text is sound, Dracontius introduces both comparatum and comparandum with sic (102, 110). This may be an indirect Graecism, i.e., rendering both ὡς and οὕτως by sic: in that case, it would suggest a Greek model for the simile.

15. For the most comprehensive treatment of the theme, see R. van den Broek, The Myth of the Phoenix in Classical and Early Christian Traditions (Leiden 1972). Earlier, J. Hubaux & M. Leroy, Le mythe du Phénix dans les littératures grecque et latine (Paris 1939). Dracontius almost certainly knew the poem of his compatriot Lactantius de ave Phoenice (cf. esp. M. C. Fitzpatrick, Lactanti de ave Phoenice [Philadelphia, Pa. 1933], and M. Walla, Der Vogel Phoenix in

der antiken Literatur und der Dichtung des Laktanz [Diss. Vienna 1969]). He shares with Lactantius, for example, the use of the feminine in referring to the bird, which was either bisexual or asexual (see van den Broek 359ff. on the sex).

16. Note that Dracontius uses the phoenix thus in *DLD* 1.653ff.; without such overtones in *Rom.* V.115–16.

17. Cf. the similar scenes in *AP* and *Hyl.*

18. Cf. Z. Pavlovskis, "Statius and the Late Latin Epithalamia" *CP* 55 (1960) 160–77, and Morelli, (n.12 above) 406f., who sees specifically the influence of Claud., *Nupt. Hon.* 77ff. He is probably right (contra: Quartiroli 20).

19. This comparison may be intended to remind us of the task which the hero usually faces in Colchis, the yoking of the fire-breathing bulls.

20. Cf. e.g., Herod. IV.102 on the Scythians (a wonderfully general ethnographic designation in later ages, especially in the writers of the Empire).

21. On the subject of human sacrifice, see esp. F. Schwenn, *Die Menschenopfer bei den Griechen und Römern (Religionsgeschichtliche Versuche und Vorarbeiten* 15.3. Giessen 1915, repr. Berlin 1966); W. Burkert, *Homo necans. Interpretationen altgriechischer Opferriten und Mythen* (ibid. 32. Berlin 1972; Engl. ed. Berkeley, Calif. 1983); and A. Henrichs, "Human sacrifice in Greek religion: three case studies" in *Le sacrifice dans l'antiquité (Entretiens Hardt* 27. Geneva 1980) 195–242.

22. W. H. Friedrich (n.8 above) 69.

23. See Lawrence E. Stager, "The rite of child sacrifice at Carthage" in *New Light on Ancient Carthage,* ed. J. Pedley (Ann Arbor, Mich. 1980) 1–11.

24. Note how Dracontius has used visual effects to shift the focus of action: first the dizzying view from on high as Cupid looks down, and now, as the action returns to the human realm, we see through Jason's eyes as he lies on the altar looking up.

25. Diodorus apparently derived the story from Dionysius Skytobrachion, whom he followed for much in this book.

26. See Seeliger's art. "Medeia" in Roscher II.2.2484; and L. Séchan, "La légende de Médée" *REG* 40 (1927) 235.

27. Contra: C. Lohmeyer, "De Dracontii carminum ordine" in *Schedae Philologae Hermanno Vsener a sodalibus seminarii regii Bonnensis oblatae* (Bonn 1891) 71–72, who regards *Or.* as the latest of the three major epyllia (*Hel., Med., Or.*), all of which he dates after the poet's release from captivity.

28. Note that both Cupid and Medea begin by calling Jason *pirata;* interestingly, it is Cupid who adds *decore* (210), whereas Medea, even while proposing, calls him *nefande.* The use of *pirata* is probably a vestige of the usual version in which Jason is known to be after the fleece.

260 NOTES

29. Sch. Ap. Rh. 4.1217: Τιμῶναξ ἐν α' τῶν Σκυθικῶν ἐν Κόλχοις φησὶν Ἰάσονα Μήδειαν γῆμαι Αἰήτου αὐτῷ ἐγγυησάντος. The scholia (ad 4.1153) also report Antimachus' version: Ἀντίμαχος ἐν Λύδῃ [φησὶν] ἐν Κόλχοις πλησίον τοῦ ποταμοῦ μιγῆναι; but μιγῆναι is to be distinguished from γῆμαι, especially in Antimachus' erotic work and in view of the telltale detail of the riverbank.
30. Contrast the wedding of Jason and Glauce, to which the Furies come as participants and witnesses (Medea 479–83).
31. There is some confusion in the ceremony as Dracontius describes it. Medea calls Jason her husband immediately after releasing him from the altar (257) and dresses him in regal robes (cf. Dido's treatment of Aeneas after the cave), and the messenger reports natam ignoto nupsisse marito (312–13). But the events described in 257–70 are the sponsalia, the betrothal celebration with its attendant feasting and other ceremonies. The wedding proper appears in 336–39, after Aeetes has formally given his blessing and Medea dons the bridal wreath for the ceremony.
32. On this parallel, cf. W. Schetter, "Medea in Theben" Würzburger Jahrbücher (1980) 211.
33. Contrast Argia, who is fida coniunx.
34. See also in text pp. 65ff. below on the possible influence of the fairy tale on the morphology of this story.
35. Vollmer noted that the ultimate source of this scene in literary terms was Vergil (Aen. 4.296ff.). The ghost of Vergil seems to hang over these lines in such details as the rhythm of this verse: compare ad thalamos, regina, tuos with Aeneas' inadequate excuse to the shade of Dido: invitus, regina, tuo de litore cessi (6.460).
36. So Ap.Rh. 4.162ff.; Val. Fl. 8.68ff.; Diod. Sic. 4.48; and others.
37. This is the view of Schetter (n.32 above) 211.
38. For the separate elements, see S. Thompson's Motif-Index of Folk-Literature (Bloomington, Ind. 1957): note esp. F.374, the hero in fairyland longing to visit his home, and Q.247, the lapse of time in fairyland. The motif is of course familiar in classical literature, from Odysseus on Ogygia to Psyche and Cupid.
39. On the theme generally, see E. S. Hartland, "The Supernatural Lapse of Time in Fairyland" in The Science of Fairy Tales (repr. Detroit, Mich. 1968) 161–254.
40. Friedrich 68–76; cf. Schetter 210, n.7.
41. Friedrich 71.
42. Kuijper 7–9.
43. Ibid. 8
44. Hosidius does not indicate where the play is set and has a chorus of Colchian women instead of the Corinthians found elsewhere. But cf. Mooney (note 5 above) on the relationship between Hosidius and Ovid.

45. Quartiroli 21 n.3 (referring both to this initial setting and to the epilogue).
46. Hyginus (*Fab.* 25.2) speaks of *Creon Menoeci filius rex Corinthius*, but the son of Menoeceus was the Theban Creon.
47. See Schetter (212–13) for other proposed, but false, explanations.
48. Ibid. 212–21.
49. Cf. text pp. 79–80 below on the epilogue.
50. Especially developed in Seneca (e.g., *Med.* 920ff.) and Euripides (e.g., *Med.* 1260) as taunts by Medea to Jason.
51. A comparison with Dracontius' other murderous protagonist is striking: Clytemestra settles on the murder of Agamemnon because she does not wish to forfeit the benefits of her adultery with Egistus (*Or.* 179).
52. Cf. Schetter 215ff.
53. The scholarship on magic and sorcery in classical literature, and especially on affiliations with the nether powers, is enormous. Of particular relevance here are A. M. Tupet, *La magie dans la poésie latine* (Paris 1976); S. Eitrem, "La magie comme motif littéraire chez les Grecs et les Romains" *Symbolae Osloenses* 21 (1941) 39–83; R. Cagnat, *La sorcellerie et les sorciers chez les Romains* (Paris 1903).
54. Catull. 64: wedding scene 31–49/265ff; the intervening lines describe the wedding coverlet and include the intervention of Bacchus—another theme in this poem.
55. S. Blomgren is undoubtedly correct in reading 479–81 as follows:

> "conventum pactumque" sonat signatque tabellas
> horrida Tartareo veniens de gurgite virgo
> Tisiphone.

See "In Dracontii carmina adnotationes criticae" *Eranos* 64 (1966) 63.
56. For a lengthy catalogue of such passages, cf. V. P. Loers, *Ovidi Nasonis Heroides* (Cologne 1829–30) *ad Her.* 2.115. See also H. Jacobson, *Ovid's Heroides* (Princeton, N.J. 1974) 392–93. There are two branches to the tradition: the wedding which ends in the bride's death on her wedding night, and the marriage which will eventually prove to have been ill starred from the wedding day.
57. Provana 71–72. Quartiroli 19 more cautiously asserts an indirect derivation and adds the necessary modification that Dracontius in any case coincides with Hyginus only in this second half of the story.
58. These two symbols are similarly important in *Orestes*.
59. The name of the princess wavers throughout the tradition between Glauce and Creusa: e.g., Apollodorus has Glauce (I.ix.28), Seneca has Creusa. Hosidius also calls her Creusa, but of course in his Vergilian cento he naturally would use the name which by a happy

chance he found already present in Vergil's text (*Med.* 243 from *Aen.* 2.778). Hyginus shows a fine eclecticism in calling her Glauce in 25.2 but Creusa four lines later (25.3).

60. D. Page, *Euripides, Medea* (Oxford 1939) xxvi.

61. E.g., schol. Eur. *Med.* 117; Apollod. I.ix.28; Hyg. *Fab.* 25, 239; Paus. 2.3.6; Tzetzes *ad* Lyc. 175, 1315. Many of the variants are laid out in Roscher II.2.2490ff.

62. *Fab.* 25.3 *natos suos ex Iasone Mermerum et Pheretum interfecit.* The MS in both transcriptions reads *ferentes;* Baehrens restored the name. Forcellini reports it as Feretus.

63. Anouilh plays on this same emotional irony to excellent effect in his *Médée.*

64. Medea was linked to Hera in a variety of ways: cf., e.g., Apollod. I.ix.28 on Hera Akraia. She is even reported (*Suda,* s.v. αἴξ) as the founder of the cult of Hera in Corinth. The death of the children was also variously reported as due to accident, to Medea's deliberate crime, and to the revenge of the Corinthians. The last then, in turn, was related to the cult of Hera, as the Corinthians expiated the murder (schol. Eur. *Med.* 264; Paus. II.3.7).

65. Ap.Rh. 4.1176ff; Apollod. I.ix.23.

66. Note also that Cadmus was the son of Agenor and brother of Europa, to whom Dracontius compares Aeetes and Medea (314ff.).

67. Kuijper's emendation of 590 may be viewed as certain:

> tibi mater, Iacche,
> Thebana de stirpe *et, arator,* tibi Diones
> Harmoniam nupsisse ferunt.

cf: *Varia Dracontiana* 78.

68. Schetter 220.

69. So also Quartiroli 25. Provana calls the epilogue "una protesta contro tutte le irrazionalità e le barbarie del mito" (p. 70), but that is not necessarily the same as Christian polemic.

70. The overall distinction between these scenes is clear enough, but the poet slides from one to the other without even a sentence break in 257. He employs a similar manner in skipping from Colchis to heaven (49); so also at 382 and 556. By this device Dracontius creates an impression of unity among otherwise sharply separate components—and incidentally by contrast emphasizes the abruptness of such breaks as 365/366 and 469/470.

71. For example, there is a lacuna at 543/544 which would alter the line count.

72. S. Gamber, *Le livre de la "Genèse" dans la poésie latine au Vᵉ siècle* (Paris 1899, repr. Geneva 1977), esp. pp. 19–24 on Dracontius.

CHAPTER 4

1. Provana 67.
2. Cf. text pp. 210–11 below.
3. *Fata* are invoked or blamed in this poem at 15, 57, 68, 131, 156, 162, 191, 198, 201, 465, 535, 539, 629.
4. Cf. Quartiroli 179.
5. For a similar approach, see Agudo Cubas 269.
6. See ibid. (291ff.) on the question of whether Colluthus influenced Dracontius. I think Agudo Cubas is wrong in dismissing the possibility of influence on the ground that Dracontius knew no Greek, but she is certainly correct that the two poems are "tremendamente dispares."
7. So also Eur. (*Hel.* 27ff.; *Troad.* 930); Ovid (*Her.* 16.85); Hyg., *Fab.* 92. Cf. Morelli 95.
8. Cf. Apul. *Met.* 10.32: Venus polliceri videbatur, si fuisset deabus ceteris antelata, daturam se nuptam Paridi forma praecipuam suique consimilem.
9. Agudo Cubas (292) notes that this tradition is not found before Propertius (2.2.13), but is frequent thereafter. We should beware of thinking that a theme which is common in both Greek and Latin versions began with Propertius simply because he is the earliest witness we now have. I suspect he had Alexandrian models.
10. But Vat. Myth. (II.197) speaks of a nurse in whom Hecuba confides.
11. Servius *ad Aen.* 5.370: sane hic Paris secundum Troica Neronis fortissimus fuit; adeo ut in Troia agonali certamine superaret omnes; ipsum etiam Hectorem, qui cum iratus in eum stringere gladium, dixit se esse germanum, quod allatis crepundiis probavit, qui habitu rustico adhuc latebat.
12. Cf. also Eur., *Alexandros*, and Ennius' imitation; Hyg. *Fab.* 90; Serv. *ad Aen.* 5.370; Vat. Myth. II.197. See esp. F. Jouan, *Euripide et les légendes des chants cypriens* (Paris 1966) 113–42.
13. The device of a festival as the setting for tragic action is old and much used, and for this specific passage one need not try to pin down a model. Ovid also introduces the idea of festivity, but from a different approach, in *Her.* 16.89–92 by claiming that Paris' return is in itself what makes this a red-letter day.
14. The symmetry is characteristic of the poet: at Paris' first return, joy is changed to sorrow in the prophecies of Helenus and Cassandra, and his second return (with Helen) changes sorrow into joy. Cf. also Agudo Cubas 273.
15. See R. Scodel, *The Trojan Trilogy of Euripides* (Göttingen 1980), for a thorough discussion of Euripides' *Alexandros* and its relation to Ennius' play.
16. F. Buecheler, "Coniectanea XVI" *RhM* 27 (1872) 477.
17. Morelli 101–103.

18. See the judicious remarks by T. C. W. Stinton, *Euripides and the Judgement of Paris. JHS* Suppl. XI. (1966) 54ff., on the separateness of these events and the impossibility of constructing a secure relationship.
19. The *Cypria* already had both. See Quartiroli 181 n. 1, who properly attributes the "similarities" to the underlying idea rather than to specific imitation.
20. This vision of Trojan heroes perishing should be set against Telamon's catalogue (319–26) of the Greek heroes who will win fame from the war.
21. So Helenus says *me fortuna potens exspectat Pyrrhus et ingens* (133—if Ianelli's repair of the line is correct).
22. Morelli comments on the dramatic qualities of the whole poem from a different perspective (114): Atqui in tam panso orationum corpore actio minime languet; immo saepe tam sunt motae, tantis impletae furoribus, ut interdum non epicum opus sed tragicum legere videamur.
23. It is admittedly unreasonable for Apollo to contradict his own spokesmen, as Quartiroli (182) objects, and it makes for an awkward scene. But there could be no stronger way to underscore Cassandra's inability to gain credence than to have her own source of inspiration repudiate her.
24. Cf. Morelli 104 on *Aen.* 3.90ff. as a model.
25. It is difficult to agree with Diaz, who presents a lengthy argument (pp. 120–34) that *Rom.* VIII and IX (Achilles deliberating whether to restore Hector to Priam) are the first pieces of a grand project to tell the early history of Rome. Apollo intervenes, says Diaz, so that Troy may fall but, more importantly, so that Rome may rise. The Vergilian phrase *imperium sine fine dabit* is not merely an echo to be recognized but the key to the whole poem: this use of the Helen story as the first step in Rome's history is what Dracontius means by his claim to proceed *meliore via.* But Diaz shows no clear or necessary link between this poem's version and Rome, beyond what was inherent in the tradition (Aeneas' role in the embassy is hardly sufficient for the purpose).
26. *Ecl.* 1.82: et iam summa procul villarum culmina fumant.
27. Apollod. *Bibl.* 2.136; Soph. *Ajax* 1299ff.; Hyg. *Fab.* 89.
28. The MS gives *dat . . . faciet,* which is surely amiss. Priam is expressing the hope that Paris will meet a suitable young lady on his travels. Baehrens saw the difficulty, and conjectured *det,* but left *faciet.* It is preferable to have parallel subjunctives (which may have a kind of future force, as often in this period): *det . . . faciat.*
29. On the idea that Dares was a source for Dracontius here, cf. also C. Wagener, "Beitrag zu Dares Phrygius" *Phil* 38 (1879) 120; Provana (65ff.) is dubious, preferring a common source for the two accounts.
30. On the shift from Sparta to Cyprus, cf. text on pp. 121–23 below.
31. See Agudo Cubas 276.

32. Quartiroli 183.
33. The separation of Paris from the other *proceres* (who were likewise *regis pignora,* after all) is surprising at first glance. But the poet's purpose may be not so much to enhance Paris as to distinguish him from the legates who are going to be speaking. It is another bit of evidence that in Dracontius' mind—and probably in his source— Paris had no role to play.
34. Viz., 261, 262, 263 (*regia*), 268, 272, 275, 276, 284. Note also sur-*rexisse* in 272.
35. Viz., 267, 268, 280 (*regnante*).
36. In addition, however, Dracontius' readers might recognize that *iacet ingens* is Vergilian, referring to the sprawling corpse of Priam murdered by Neoptolemus (*Aen.* 2.557): *regnatorem Asiae. iacet ingens litore truncus.*
37. Dracontius is not quite alone in presenting Telamonian Ajax as the son of Hesione (despite Agudo Cubas 277). Italicus (*Il. Lat.* 624) has the genealogy, and that poem is echoed several times by Dracontius; but it is perhaps of more interest that Dares likewise mentions it (19). This is another link between these two authors. Dracontius makes more of it than either of the other two, as he has Telamon's anger and prediction of the war stem in part from paternal pride in the young hero. Cf. also vv. 314–15 for further use of the relationship.
38. This time an Ovidian touch: cf. *Met.* 13.505 *iacet Ilion ingens.*
39. The hint of Paris is enhanced by *festivas extingue faces* (308), which brings to mind the image of Paris as the firebrand in Hecuba's vision and Helenus' prophecy (122).
40. Note also *Aen.* 1.249, where Aeneas—speaking of Antenor—says *nunc placida compostus pace quiescit.*
41. Servius (*ad Aen.* 10.91) also tells of two missions by the Trojans, but in his version Priam himself leads the first, and Paris the second. Servius is copied, almost verbatim, by Lactantius Placidus (*ad* Stat. *Ach.* 21 and 397) and Vat. Myth. II.199.
42. Apollodorus likewise reports (*Epit.* iii.4) that Paris was driven from Greece to Sidon and Cyprus, and it is not impossible that Apollodorus got his information from the *Cypria.*
43. The passage was imitated in detail by Venantius Fortunatus (*Vita S. Martini, praef.* 11ff.), who may also have had in mind *DLD* 2.175f.
44. Agudo Cubas (279ff.) amplifies on the Vergilian sources: note esp. *G.* 3.400–401/*Hel.* 414–17; *Ecl.* 1.74–76/*Hel.* 406–409; *G.* 3.212–23/*Hel.* 418–19.
45. I accept Baehrens' emendation; N's *et* interrupts the asyndetic series in a most unlikely manner.
46. See Apollod. *Epit.* III.4, with Frazer's note *ad loc.* (vol. 2, p. 175 n.2) for other relevant passages and discussion.
47. The piety of the Spartan queen in coming all the way to the sacred

birthplace of Venus is somehow reminiscent of the practice of pilgrimages to the sacred sites of the Holy Land by Christian ladies (one thinks first, naturally, of Aetheria's *Peregrinatio ad loca sancta*).

48. Note the play on words—very characteristic of our poet—in *cretum* 443: just two lines earlier we hear that Helen's husband was detained in Crete (*retinet dum* Creta *maritum*), and now in some subliminal way Paris is taking his place by this repetition of the same pattern of sounds announcing his arrival as those which announced Menelaus' absence.

49. The symbolism connected with birds in classical literature is complex and pervasive. Among the more general or comprehensive works, see esp. E. W. Martin, *The Birds of the Latin Poets* (Stanford, Calif. 1914); D'Arcy Thompson, *A Glossary of Greek Birds*, 2d ed. (Oxford 1936); André Sauvage, *Étude de thèmes animaliers dans la poésie latine. Le cheval, les oiseaux* (*Collection Latomus* 143: Brussels 1975); John Pollard, *Birds in Greek Life and Myth* (London 1977). For the naturalist dimension (and references to sources), O. Keller's *Die antike Tierwelt*. 2 vols. (Leipzig 1909–13) is still indispensable; for the linguistic dimension see J. André, *Les noms d'oiseaux en latin* (Paris 1967).

50. The hawk in pursuit of the doves is perhaps drawn in part from Silius Italicus 4.105ff. (so Quartiroli 184), where the omen occurs just before the battle of the Ticinus. But the pursuit of the dove by the hawk is a standard symbol as old as the contrast between Mars and Venus: note for example Ovid *Ars Amatoria* 2.363, speaking indeed of Menelaus' folly in leaving Helen accessible to Paris: *accipitri timidas credis, furiose, columbas*.

51. Statius identifies a seer as Theodomas, son of Melampus (*Theb.* 3.454ff.; 8.278ff.), and Dracontius may have that in mind, although he speaks of his augur merely as *de gente Melampi*.

52. The idea that Ganymede invented augury is as silly as it is novel. Perhaps the poet merely wanted to bring in Ganymede because he was Trojan and, like Paris, played a role in starting a Trojan war. That he was loved by Zeus and was taken to heaven may have suggested a greater knowledge of what the gods did. But Polles occurs (apart from this line) only in the *Suda*, s.vv. Πόλλης, Μελάμπους, where this role is also assigned to him. Dracontius may also have come upon this role for both Polles and Ganymede in some mythographic source.

53. The epithet carries some bite here as well: we may recall Horace's reference to this very meeting (*Carm.* 1.15.1–2) which juxtaposes these very terms: *Pastor cum traheret per freta navibus/Idaeis Helenen perfidus hospitam*.

54. Morelli 109.

55. I might add that Morelli's comment *similia leguntur apud Daretem* is simply wrong, as is his reference to Dictys I.5.

56. But cf. below at 573 which suggests a pretext at least: Menelaus has come to Cyprus *sacra dicare* (as had Helen), but there is no basis for any such action in the entire tradition. Dracontius simply has a need to account, however unsatisfactorily, for Menelaus' timely arrival.

57. The match is underscored by the descriptions of their lamentation: *ingemit et flavos extorquet vertice crines* (Menelaus: 576); *plangit et albentes immundat pulvere crines* (Priam: 589).

58. The cenotaph for Paris is a detail found also in Hyginus (*Fab.* 90): *fecit in Ilio Priamus cenotaphium Paridi.* But there it refers to the early stage of Paris' life, after the king has ordered him killed at birth (*quem natum iusserat interfici*).

59. The troika of Hector, Troilus, and Polites appeared also in the first Trojan scene (84), but is almost unknown elsewhere. Morelli (98) notes that the François Vase bears a scene showing Achilles pursuing Troilus, who is being rescued by Polites and Hector. C. Robert (*Bild und Lied* 17) believed the scene was derived from the *Cypria*. Morelli speculated that the *amicitia* of these three warriors likewise derived from the Cyclic poem. Certainly it is odd to find such a detail in a vase of the 6th century B.C. and the work of a poet (who could not have seen the vase) in the 5th century after Christ; and this may add to the probability that Dracontius at least knew the Greek source, even though he seems not to have followed it for the major elements of his plot.

60. It is possible that this scene is influenced by pantomimic sources. We have seen that Dracontius drew on pantomime in both *Hylas* and *Medea,* and Luxorius confirms that the abduction of Helen was indeed a subject of pantomime in this very period: cf. *Anth. Lat.* 310R.

61. Cf., in this poem, vv. 31–32, 61–65; and elsewhere, e.g., *Med.* 177ff. (triple *iam*), 341 (2 pluperfects leading into the present). In the present passage, Dracontius overdoes it: *iam* six times in 4 lines.

62. The Vergilian echo also sends us back to Helenus' vision of the *mille carinas* (126) coming to Troy.

63. The total for Cyprus allows for the lacuna after 461.

64. Cf. Agudo Cubas for the proportions of speeches to narratives in each segment. The total for Troy₁ through Cyprus (61–585) is 278/526.

CHAPTER 5

1. Among the indispensable items on the *Orestes* must be listed the following: B. Barwinski, *Quaestiones ad Dracontium et Orestis tragoediam pertinentes. Quaestio II: de rerum mythicarum tractatione* (Programm Deutsch-Krone 1888); K. Rossberg, *In Dracontii carmina minora et Orestis quae vocatur tragoediam observationes crit-*

icae (Stade 1878); id. *Materialen zu einem Commentar über die Orestis tragoedia des Dracontius* (Hildesheim 1888); E. Rapisarda, *La tragedia di Oreste*, 2d ed. (Catania 1964); Quartiroli 25–34; and G. Aricò, "Mito e tecnica narrativa nell' *Orestis Tragoedia*" *Atti Acc. Palermo* 37 (1977–78) 405–95. W. H. Friedrich also has brief but valuable observations in *Vorbild und Neugestaltung* (Göttingen 1967) 176–81.

2. On the implications of the title, cf. W. Cloetta, *Beiträge zur Litteraturgeschichte des Mittelalters und der Renaissance*, vol. 1 (Halle 1890) 4–7.

3. Both in his edition/translation (above n.1) and also in "Il poeta della misericordia divina I. L'unità del mondo religioso di Draconzio" *Orpheus* 2 (1955) 1ff.; "Fato, divinità e libero arbitrio nella 'Tragedia di Oreste' di Draconzio" *Historisches Jarbuch* 72 (1958) 444ff. Rapisarda specifically argued that Dracontius was Christianizing the Orestes myth as found in Aeschylus by reinterpreting its symbolic value throughout.

4. Also involved is the question of whether Dracontius knew Aeschylus directly or via intermediate sources: cf. Quartiroli 27; Aricò (408–10) not only is skeptical about direct imitation of Aeschylus, but is perhaps too ready to assume that Dracontius did not use Greek sources at all.

5. Barwinski (n.1 above) p. 11; Quartiroli (29 n.2) is inclined to see the *Orestes* as a more mature work and thus to date it after the other epyllia. Aricò's view that the poem antedates Dracontius' acceptance of Christianity would become very problematic if the *Orestes* is assigned even to the poet's middle period. On the general question of the chronology of the poems, cf. Romano, *Studi draconziani;* Diaz 33ff.; C. Lohmeyer, "De Dracontii carminum ordine" *Schedae H. Vsener oblatae* (Bonn 1891) 60–74. Cf. also text pp. 57–58 and n.27 above.

6. Cf. text pp. 149ff. below. Provana 51 and Barwinski 11 take the opposite view.

7. Lines 427–52 were moved to their present place after 540 by Vollmer. Cf. text pp. 178ff. below for a new solution.

8. See Aricò 422–23; note also G. Polara, "Ricerche sul proemio nella poesia latina" *Rendiconti dell' Accademia di Napoli* 49 (1974) 135–53, not directly on Dracontius but presenting an extensive theoretical study of the poetic *proemium.*

9. *Pius* occurs 11 times, *pietas* 16 more. Note that Dracontius uses *pietas = pater* (cf. 38), a common Christian usage which may argue that he was a Christian at the time of the *Orestes.*

10. I follow Rapisarda in accepting Maehly's supplement for 16. Rapisarda notes the defense is needed against the admitted deeds of Orestes, which would seem to offer a clear convicting case. I would add that one of the distinctive features of Dracontius' story is

the absence of the Furies in their usual role. Haase's *damna‹vere sorores›* is in fact not true to the story (it is accepted by Vollmer and Aricò).

11. *Rex ille regum, ductor Agamemnon ducum, / cuius secutae mille vexillum rates / Iliaca velis maria texerunt suis.*

12. Cf. also *gemina lustra/duo lustra* (Sen.): Dracontius apparently had the Senecan lines in mind throughout this section.

13. Rapisarda *ad loc.* notes that *veneranter adorat* (48) is a phrase used only by Christian authors.

14. The role of Ulysses in bringing Iphigenia to Aulis is far from original with Dracontius: it figured prominently in Eur. *IT*, and in minor versions such as, e.g., Apollod. *Epit.* iii.22, but the assignment of blame to his treachery rather than to the orders of Agamemnon reflects the strong and constant distrust of the wily Ulysses in Latin letters.

15. It would hardly seem necessary for Iphigenia to explain any of this to the commander of the Greek fleet. I suspect that beyond the immediate purpose of exculpating Agamemnon before his murder, Dracontius is also indulging his usual desire to include the full story of his characters. As with Medea and Paris, he wants a comprehensive myth, and this flashback is the simplest way to include the events at Aulis (the alternative place would have been the end of the prologue—cf. *Hel.* 31–60 for the Judgment of Paris—but that spot was used for the moralizing on Agamemnon's character). Iphigenia's sanitized version of the story can then in the process show how nearly blameless her father was.

16. Cf. Rapisarda 103 (*ad loc.*).

17. So also Antenor, in appealing to Telamon for the release of Hesione, had juxtaposed frequent references to Priam as *rex* and Hesione as *soror* (*Hel.* 261ff.: cf. esp. 272–73 *nisi iam, rex magne, sororem / reddideris regi*).

18. As we saw especially at the conclusion of the episodes in Colchis (*Med.* 340ff.) and Cyprus (*Hel.* 585ff.).

19. Barwinski 11: summo iure mirandum est quid sit quod non tum cum Agamemnone sed postea demum cum Oreste fratre Iphigenia aufugiat et quod Agamemnon domum reversus rem illam iucundissimam non statim cum suis communicavit. It is only fair to recall that Agamemnon has his head split open immediately upon his arrival at Mycenae, and hardly has time even for such electrifying news.

20. Dracontius uses *interea* and *dum* to mark the beginning of several scenes in this poem: *interea* 41, 108, 682; *dum* 108, 232, 453, 820, 862; cf. also *illa nocte* 515. The other principal indicators of a new scene are a change of locale (453, 515, 682, 862) and the lapse of time (453, 803, 887). In 41 especially, as we move from the prologue to the main narrative, it is clear that *interea* is a mere narrative marker, since there is no change of person or of place. The duplicate

interea in 108 creates the impression that 41–107 may have been inserted into an original design which followed the traditional sequence of prologue—Mycenae—return of Agamemnon.

21. Cf. Aricò (427–30) on these lines.
22. Line 194.
23. That Mycenae is not a seaport was presumably beyond the ken of Dracontius. Homer likewise sets the murder in Mycenae; Aeschylus speaks more loosely of Argos, by which he meant the region rather than the city alone. Seneca, like the rest of the Roman poets, speaks of Mycenae (cf. Tarrant on Sen. *Ag.*, pp. 160–61, for a review of the tradition). But Seneca and Aeschylus also have Agamemnon reach the palace after a ride in a chariot, not by stepping directly off the ship. Dracontius follows another tradition in combining Mycenae and the shore—a tradition alluded to by Servius *ad Aen.* XI.267: in ipso limine imperii, id est in litore, qua Clytaemnestra Agamemnoni occurrit ad litus at illic eum susceptum cum adultero imteremit. The account referred to by Servius is admittedly not quite the same (cf. text p. 154 below) but shows that the confusion need not have originated with our poet. In any case, the detail will surely not have disturbed his readers, who have endured much worse geography in both *Helen* and *Hylas.*
24. See the useful remarks by Quartiroli (30–34) on the psychological development of Clytemestra as compared with the cloddish Egistus and the monotonous Agamemnon. But the queen herself ends by being a character-type, as will appear.
25. It is part of Dracontius' use of Seneca that Cassandra arrives first, and delivers her prophecy before Agamemnon arrives on the scene. Cf. Aricò 429. K. Stackmann, "Senecas Agamemnon" *Classica et Mediaevalia* 11 (1950) 194ff., conjectures a possible common source for Seneca and Dracontius in this respect; but the use to which Dracontius puts this feature is original with him, and the conjecture of a lost Greek play is risky if the only evidence for it is the totally different use of a single feature in Seneca and Dracontius. See also Tarrant's edition of Sen. *Ag.* (Cambridge 1976) p. 15 n.1.
26. Barwinski (p. 11) comments on the episodic quality of Dracontius' poems, in which individual scenes have no articulated relationship to the poem as a whole. The neglect of Cassandra is an obvious illustration of this tendency, although Barwinski is far too sweeping in his judgment.
27. The sobriquet occurs 16 times, to which add *pastoralis = Egisti* (270) and the elaborate calumny by the poet in 275–76. It is worth noting that Seneca's Cassandra hints at the term as well (*Ag.* 732) where she refers to Paris as *pastor,* and then warms that *agrestis ille alumnus* (i.e., Egistus) will destroy the House of Mycenae. But the developed use of the term as a reproach is Dracontius' own. It is a

blend of social deficiency and moral failure set against the unimpeachable credentials of Agamemnon in both regards. On the social aspect cf. W. Trillitzsch, "Der Agamemnonstoff bei Aischylos, Seneca und in der 'Orestis tragoedia' des Dracontius," in *Aischylos und Pindar* hsg. E. G. Schmidt (Berlin 1981) 273.

28. One could also look in an entirely different direction: the golden lamb by which Thyestes had claimed the kingdom of Pelops. Thyestes seduced Atreus' wife Aerope, who then delivered to her lover the golden lamb, possession of which carried with it the throne of Pelops (cf. Apollod. *Epit.* ii.10–13 and Frazer's note there for further references. The lamb is frequently mentioned, one of the most interesting passages being Sen. *Th.* 222–35). This treachery is then repeated in the next generation with Clytemestra and Egistus. In calling Egistus a "good shepherd" Cassandra may refer sarcastically to this treacherous act of shepherding by Egistus' father. In objection to this line of analysis one may note that it would presumably not account for the insistent use of *pastor* throughout the poem.

29. Note also 200–202, where Clytemestra points to Helen as one who has successfully slain many kings by causing the war and now lives in peace.

30. Cf. text p. 139 above.

31. She has a similar moment of "feminine" weakness in 219, when she concludes her account of their bloodthirsty plan by bursting into tears.

32. Line 203 contains a problem of long standing: nec metuam Danaos: heredem *sterno* Thyestis. So the MSS. But should it be *servo* (L. Mueller, Baehrens, Rapisarda)? Who is *heres Thyestis?* The obvious answer is Egistus. As Rapisarda notes, Dracontius elsewhere in this poem refers to both Agamemnon and Menelaus as Atrides. But it would also be accurate, albeit unexpected, to call Agamemnon the heir of Thyestes. If we begin with the thought implied by the entire line, it must be admitted that the general populace is more likely to approve the removal of one who represents the inheritance of the criminal Thyestes, than that it should condone regicide because it protected Egistus—whom we have seen as a mewling nonentity rising only by his illicit association with the king's wife. Even Clytemestra (who in fact seems to have little respect for Egistus) would not regard him as a personage to sway public opinion in this way. And we should note that Clytemestra uses the same phrase in referring to the slaying of Agamemnon just a dozen lines before: *victorem sternere ferro* (190). Thus the queen is saying that she can get away with murder because the victim is the heir of the felonious Thyestes: keep *sterno* and understand her to intend Agamemnon. But there is irony as well; for by launching this plot, Clytemestra is sealing the doom of the man most naturally termed *heres Thyestis:* Egistus.

33. It is apparently unique with Dracontius that the king comes after so long a journey, including his imposing first appearance in the prologue and his visit to Iphigenia, still dressed in battle garb; and it stretches verisimilitude even further that the queen should anticipate his arriving in such a condition. Dracontius is of course working with the symbolic value of the gory clothing. The king displays on his person the violence and death which his return brings. It is typical of Dracontius' tidy imagination that the queen should incorporate this feature into her plan, so that when he arrives in this condition, the accuracy of her plot becomes the more apparent.

34. Cf. Aricò (431) on the elimination of the nurse.

35. Rossberg's conjecture that Dracontius may have derived this otherwise unattested picture from Claudian's lost *Gigantomachia Latina*. is plausible enough: it is not the sort of picture which the poet himself is likely to have invented, certainly not for the purposes of this poem, and it is certain that Dracontius made extensive use of Claudian's poems.

36. Rapisarda (253–58) provides a lucid survey of all incidents and characters found in this poem, compared to the other ancient sources in which they appear: for this detail, cf. 253–54, and see also Frazer's note on Apollod. *Epit.* vi.23.

37. For a more detailed consideration of the Servian accounts, see Aricò 434–36.

38. I do not understand why both Aricò and Rapisarda include Dracontius among those who have only Egistus kill Agamemnon. To be sure, he alone swings the axe, but Clytemestra is pinning the victim in the shirt and signaling Egistus when it is his moment to act. This is a shared deed as surely as if both wielded axes.

39. For the full range of relevant texts, see Höfer, s.v. "Orestes" in Roscher III.955–1014. Among the most important are Hom. *Od.* 3.304ff.; Pind. *Pyth.* 11.34ff.; Aesch. *Cho.* 677ff.; Soph. *El.* 11ff.; Hyg. *Fab.* 117; Sen. *Ag.* 918ff.; Apollod. *Epit.* 6.24–25; Serv. *ad Aen.* 2.16.

40. This discrepancy with the subsequent tradition disturbed Zenodotus, who amended ἀπ᾽ Ἀθηνάων (307) to ἀπὸ Φωκήων. Eustathius comments *ad* 3.307: Τὸ δὲ ἂψ ἀπ᾽ Ἀθηνάων, τινὲς γράφουσιν ἂψ ἀπὸ Φωκήων, ὡς ἐκεῖ ὄντος παρὰ τῷ θείῳ Στροφίῳ τοῦ Ὀρέστου. οεραπεύουσι μέντοι καὶ τὸ ἀπ᾽ Ἀθηνῶν οἱ παλαιοί, λέγοντες ὡς ἀπὸ Φωκίδος εἰς Ἀθήνας κατὰ ζήτησιν σταλεὶς Ὀρέστης μαθήσεώς τε καὶ παιδεύσεως, ἐκεῖθεν κατελθὼν οἴκοι, ἐποίησεν ἅπερ ἐποίησεν. ἵνα εἶεν δύο καταγώγια τῷ Ὀρέστῃ Φωκὶς μὲν ἐπὶ ἀναστροφῇ, Ἀθῆναι δὲ ἐπὶ παιδείᾳ. It may be from some such tradition developed in later antiquity that Dracontius felt free to develop this picture of Orestes' school days; or it could be the other way around, and the later scholiastic tradition

derived, from accounts such as Dracontius, the "evidence" for
Orestes being a student during his exile.
41. So Hyg. *Fab.* 117: Electra Agamemnonis filia Orestem fratrem *in-
fantem* sustulit, quam demandavit in Phocide Strophio. Dracontius
suggests this tradition—perhaps only through casual use of language—in 685 *viderat Atrides muros quos liquerat infans.*
42. See C. Morelli, "Sulle tracce del romanzo e della novella" *SIFC* NS
1 (1920) 81; Quartiroli 33.
43. The passage contains a curious allusion:

> atque utinam iuvenem per bella feriret Amazon
> Penthesilea fremens, quam vix evasit Atrides. (344–45)

The incident is elsewhere reported only in Dares (ch. 36: Penthe-
silea . . . exercitum contra Agamemnona educit. fit proelium ingens, per aliquot dies pugnatur. Argivi fugantur in castra, oppri-
muntur. cui vix Diomedes obsistit, alioquin naves incendisset et Ar-
givorum universum exercitum devastasset.), although it is worth the
caution of observing that it was Diomedes who was resisting, not
Agamemnon. We may suppose that Dracontius and Dares shared a
source, although this conjecture troubled Rapisarda, who predictably wanted Dracontius to have drawn even this directly from Aeschylus: *Eum.* 625 refers to the Amazons, but there is no hint of the
incident Dracontius mentions, and we are a long way from this passage in both content and location. Seneca likewise mentions the
Amazons as a potential source of death for Agamemnon (*Ag.* 217–
18), and if we did not have the far closer correspondence with Dares
we might be tempted to settle for a Senecan source.
44. Ovid. *Met.* 5.130, 12.80; Stat. *Theb.* 2.571; 3.13.
45. See Rapisarda *ad* 353.
46. See text p. 36 above.
47. Haec plangens funestam currit ad urbem / et querula sic voce boat
(366–67).
48. A case in point is *remige planta* (375), which seems to have a tragic
ancestry. Eur. *IA* 138 (Agamemnon to Presb.) ἴθ᾽ ἐρέσσων σὸν
πόδα is remarkably close, from a play on a related theme, and is an
odd expression. It is a pity that we cannot assess more accurately
Dracontius' knowledge of earlier Roman drama, especially Ennius.
By a coincidence we have what may be Ennius' rendering of this
phrase (*Iph.* fr. XCVIII Joc.: representing either *IA* 139–40 or *IA*
1–2), and it shows no sign of the image found in both Euripides and
Dracontius. Note also Nonnos VII.185 Χεῖρας ἐρετμώωσα δι᾽
ὕδατος ἔτρεχε κούρη. Vergil's *remigium alarum* (*Aen.* 1.301, 6.18)
turns the image in the other direction, but is likewise borrowed
from tragedy (cf. Aesch. *Ag.* 52).

49. Rapisarda 150.
50. The phrasing is apparently influenced by Vergil *G.* 1.508, from which Jerome derived his language in rendering the text of Is. 2.4; but Vergil speaks of the opposite process (*et curvae rigidum falces conflantur in ensem*).
51. There is a faulty correction of 401 and 403 originating with Vollmer. He reads:

> deliciis epulisque bonis refovete *senectam*,
> pignora natorum dulces nutrite nepotes.
> unica mors restat morbis finire *salutem*.

But A has *senectam* in 403. Vollmer assumed it to be an intrusion from 401, but the parallel from Lucan is surely decisive: *liceat morbis finire senectam* (V.282). In fact he has corrected in the wrong direction: 401 should read *salutem*. Clytemestra is alluding to the state of deprivation and suffering she alleged in 387: *visceribus vacuis*. And 403 should read *senectam* following Lucan.

52. Rapisarda (*ad* 415) provides an ingenious explanation of *ipse sibi genium facit* as pointing to Egistus' self-deification.
53. Lines 427–52 are certainly not in their correct place in the manuscripts. Vollmer thought that they formed a part of Agamemnon's speech to Orestes and moved them to follow 540. Other solutions such as incorporating them in the poet's meditations on fate (following 271: L. Mueller) or keeping them in place but positing a lacuna after 426 (Giarrantano, Peiper) are untenable. I have moved the lines to follow 749. See text pp. 169f., 177–80 below for discussion.
54. See Hyg. *Fab.* 117; Apollod. *Epit.* vi.24.
55. And of course the pseudo-Senecan *Octavia* likewise employs the ghost of Agrippina (*Oct.* 593–645) in a speech which may have had some influence on Dracontius here. See Tarrant's edition of Sen. *Ag.* pp. 157–59 on the ghost-prologues tradition which Seneca inherited and greatly enhanced, and which was to be very prominent in Renaissance drama.
56. Eur. *Hec.*, esp. 37ff., 521–82; Sen. *Troad.* 938ff., 1118–1164; Ovid, *Met.* 13.439–80; Hyg. *Fab.* 110; Triph. *Iliu halosis* 686ff.; Dictys 5.13; Quint Smyrn. 14.210–38.
57. Cf. below on Clytemestra's modesty at the moment of her death (787–91), derived from Polyxena's similar gesture (*Met.* 13.478–79); and Iphigenia's account of being summoned to the altar of sacrifice (79ff.) likewise has echoes of Ovid's narrative.
58. The prayer format is closely similar; line 483 echoes *Theb.* I.57 and 85; Tisiphone finds the path to Thebes familiar (*notum iter ad Thebas* 101): cf. *notum iter invenient* (sc. *Furiae*), *Or.* 487. Aricò (445) gives other parallels.

59. Apparently *altus Orestes* (516) means *iam adultus*, as contrasted with *brevis et parvus* (193).
60. There is surely little point in interpreting *flatibus alternis* as "alternating between inhaling and exhaling" (Rossberg)—as if there were some other way to do it! Cf. also Rapisarda *ad loc.*
61. Note especially the ghost of Laius (Stat., *Theb.* 2.1ff.) and Hector (Sen. *Troad.* 443ff.), both of whom find echoes in this passage.
62. Observe that Agamemnon shifts from addressing both men to the singular *necabis* in 540. This is both because the moral dilemma of matricide rests only on Orestes, and also because in fact it is Orestes alone who kills Clytemestra, while Pylades dispatches Egistus.
63. Cf. text p. 177 below for their significance after 749.
64. In 546, Vollmer reads *noster amor Danais, sunt odia saeva duorum.* But the MSS read *deorum.* Rossberg's *reorum* is a far preferable correction, as this is how the poet elsewhere refers to Clytemestra and Egistus.
65. Rapisarda raises pointless objections to interpreting *tempore sidereo* (556) as "during the night," and tries to make it mean "in celestial, i.e., divine, manner." Dracontius, however, is not being mystical, only pedantic in mentioning (again) that it is nighttime!
66. Again in 579, A seems to have preserved a true reading which has been spurned by editors: *muliercula tristis / aspiciat moechum, quae* gaudens *vidit Atriden* (*garrula* B). Giarratano defended *garrula* by adducing 319 where the word is indeed used of Clytemestra but not with reference to the murder scene. Far more persuasive is the contrast between *tristis* and *gaudens.*
67. This reminder of the events at Agamemnon's tomb has another purpose as well. With the next scene, the arival of Orestes at Mycenae, we will finally rejoin the sequence of events in *Choephori.* That sequence began with the servants' lament. Dracontius, as we have seen, used precisely that event to open his "Orestes" and now he brings us back to it as he prepares to resume the traditional story.
68. Note another link with the *Helen: Or.* 671 is nearly identical with *Hel.* 110, although it is difficult to say in which direction the poet's self-borrowing moved. Cf. however 727 *ossibus effractis minuunt per mille secures:* an odd expression, but one which may be a spin-off from the more natural *mille carinae* of *Hel.* 126, 646 (a Vergilian borrowing, in any case).
69. The poet's chronology is wavering again: cf. 572. Either this is a casual use of *infans = puer* or it is a vestige of the mythographic tradition (cf. Hyg. and n.41 above).
70. There is, as noted earlier, a broad similarity between the return of Orestes and the return of Odysseus. It is interesting to see that at this moment, the parallel is rather with the son of Odysseus and the son of Agamemnon: the servants recognize Orestes by his father's

features, as Telemachus was recognized because he had the eyes, feet, hands, and other features of his father. Compare *Or.* 696 and, e.g., *Od.* 4.149–50.

71. Aricò is surely wrong to mark a new segment of the poem in 700: so closely are these lines bound together that 700–705 report the reactions to the sound heard in 699.

72. See Rapisarda *ad loc.* It is clearly better to assign the lines (with Rapisarda) to Clytemestra than (with Vollmer and others) to Egistus. The lapidary notation *terretur Egistus* is most effective alone.

73. *Durissima* is not (*pace* Rapisarda) a comment on the sturdiness of limb produced by the shepherd's life. It is a moral comment, not physiological.

74. The text is uncertain. The MSS read *possedit regnum*, which would seem to be beside the point being made. The essential fact about Tamyris was her revenge on the Great King: *regem* (Maehly) is almost certain. And either Vollmer's *praecidit* or Maehly's *occidit* will serve well. Given the exact nature of Tamyris' vengeance (cutting off Cyrus' head and plunging it into a skin filled with human blood), *praecidit* is apparently more precise.

75. Once again note the difference between this statement and the poet's own presentation elsewhere. Here Medea did not kill Jason (*incolumi viro*), which agrees with the dominant tradition, but Dracontius himself has Jason killed in the conflagration along with the entire royal house: *Med.* 519.

76. Usually the lines are punctuated so as to treat 434 as a single unit, which combines the adversative *sed* with the conjunctive *-que* even though the two ideas are incompatible; and links *in crimine tanto* only to the Scythian women.

77. This interpretation of the lines allows us to keep *fuit* rather than essaying *subit* ("ma sta dinanzi il ricordo di Alcesti") with Rapisarda.

78. The two Greek examples are found together elsewhere: cf. Ovid *Tr.* 5.14.37–38 (which also alludes to Andromache); Mart. 4.75.5–6. Hyg. *Fab.* 243 (*Quae se ipsae interfecerunt*) includes both in a list of 25 suicidal heroines.

79. For the idea cf. Sen. *Th.* 1077ff.

80. Cf. note 57 above.

81. Rapisarda p. 201.

82. Quartiroli 32.

83. Reading *pacta* (Baehrens) in 807, not *rapta(m)*.

84. See chiefly Eur. *Andr.* 967–81, Hyg. *Fab.* 123, and of course Ovid *Her.* 8 (which Dracontius echoes: 815/*Her.* 8.9). There is a wealth of confusing snippets and conflicting images scattered through the scholiastic literature (e.g., schol. Eur. *Andromache* 32, Serv. *ad Aen.* 3.332). For a valuable survey of our information and how it

does not fit together cf. H. Jacobson, *Ovid's Heroides* (Princeton, N.J. 1974) 43ff.; and Frazer's notes on Apollod. *Epit.* vi.14 (vol. ii pp. 252–57).

85. Married: Ovid, Vergil; pregnant: Philocles (reported in schol. Eur. *Andr.* 32).

86. Quartiroli 28 n.2.

87. *Ast illum ereptae magno flammatus amore / coniugis et scelerum furiis agitatus Orestes / excipit incautum patriasque obtruncat ad aras* (*Aen.* 3.330–32). But note that in Vergil as elsewhere, Orestes is already mad and is driven by the Furies—both differences from the Dracontian account.

88. Note that Vergil mentions the stage in describing this Orestes: was Vergil drawing on a dramatic source? Servius *ad loc.* says that Pacuvius thus depicted Orestes (in his *Orestes?*), but it is very unlikely that Dracontius saw or used the early tragedy.

89. Quartiroli 33.

90. I read *igne* (A) with Rapisarda: *angue* B.

91. The two passages are further linked by *mortale minatus* 617/*mortale minatur* 823.

92. The poet presents us with three kinds of madness: Lycurgus, king of the Edoni, who attempted to rape his mother and then killed his wife and son (cf. schol. *Il.* 6.130; Hyg. *Fab.* 133; Apollod. *Bibl.* 3.5.1); Hercules, who was driven mad by Megaera and unwittingly slew his wife Megara and his sons (Eur. *Herc.*, Sen. *HF:* these two are found in the same order in Lucan I.574–78, which may have suggested them to Dracontius); and Ajax, who presumably represents self-destruction.

93. See Rapisarda (210–11) for a more detailed evaluation of Orestes' symptoms.

94. Tyndareus: Hyg. *Fab.* 119, Hellanicus frag. 169; cf. Tzetz. *ad* Lyc. 1374. Erigone: Marm. Par. 40; Dictys VI.4. Both: *Etymologicum magnum*, s.v. Αἰώρα.

95. "Depend on it, Sir," said Dr. Johnson, "when a man knows he is to be hanged in a fortnight, it concentrates his mind wonderfully."

96. The line is virtually the same as *Med.* 246 and raises the question of priority. I am inclined to regard this poem as the original setting for the line, and the *Medea* as the reapplication. As will appear immediately, there are other similarities between the two poems, none inconsistent with the priority of the *Orestes.*

97. Barwinski p. 11; cf. n.19 above.

98. Hyginus (*Fab.* 119) puts the trial in Mycenae, the logical place if one has detached the purpose of the trial from the Areopagus. We cannot now tell whether this simplification appeared elsewhere in the mythographic tradition, but in any case, Dracontius has chosen

278 NOTES

to stay with the dominant literary tradition. This strengthens the impression that the novelties in the poem come not from lost mythographers but from the poet himself.

99. So Rapisarda; Aricò, hesitantly.

100. But Molossus himself proposes exactly the same kind of vengeance in his suggested punishment.

101. The hyperbole that one sack will not suffice is borrowed from Juvenal's assault on Nero (VIII.213–14). The specifics of this punishment are found in the *Digest* (XLVIII.9.9): poena parricidii more maiorum haec instituta est, ut parricida virgis sanguineis verberatus deinde culleo insuatur cum cane gallo gallinaceo vipera et simia, deinde in mare profundum culleus iactetur. hoc ita, si mare proximum sit; alioquin bestiis obiciatur, secundum Divi Hadriani constitutionem.

102. This line of argument accepts the relocation of 925–26 after 933. The lines have always been recognized as intrusive where they occur in the MSS, and already Rossberg had moved them to follow 933; Maehly after 920 (an impossible notion); Giarratano after 930 (tentatively: an attractive idea if only because it would reduce the harshness of *obiciat facinus* 930/*forsitan obiciat* 931, but it still leaves three changes of subject in five lines). Rapisarda, like Vollmer, keeps the lines in place, but his explanation is that sudden shifts of topic are in keeping with Orestes' excited state. This is not true: Orestes is a passionate orator, but he moves adroitly through his argument. The last failing one should accuse him of is meandering.

103. For a most valuable summary of the scholarship on this question, see D. A. Hester, "The Casting Vote" *AJP* 102 (1981) 265–74. Hester supports the view that the jurors are deadlocked and Athena produced a majority to acquit. For the view that her vote yielded a tie, see e.g., M. Gagarin, "The Vote of Athena" *AJP* 96 (1975) 121–27.

104. Apollod. *Epit.* vi.24; *Marm. Par.* 25.

105. Especially when the Olympians are the jury: cf. Eur. *Or.* 1650; Aristides *Panath.* 348; Dem. 23.66. Lucian (*Pisc.* 21; *Harmonides* 3) has a human jury but Athena produces a tie and thus acquittal.

106. Schol. *ad* Eur. *Or.* 1650; Aristid. *Or.* 2.24. That a tie-breaking vote was called the vote of Athena (Aristid. *loc. cit.*; cf. Julian *Or.* 3.114) points to this tradition also.

107. Rapisarda quotes Sen. *Epist.* LXXXI.26: Quemadmodum reus sententiis paribus absolvitur et semper quicquid dubium est humanitatis inclinat in lenius. It is clear that Dracontius would have hesitated to accept the second part of this sententia as readily as the first.

108. A technical usage. On *potestas* in its multiple forms see Gaius *Inst.* I.

109. Cf. *Med.* 572–73 *linquite mortales miseroque ignoscite mundo, / parcite iam Thebis;* also 588ff.
110. Aricò (469), who also stresses how they are separated by "enorme distanza, oltre che chronologica, sopratutto culturale." But that accounts for the differences, not the similarities.
111. A useful list of apparent echoes of Seneca's *Ag.* in *Or.*: Aricò 470 n.157.
112. The one exception is minimal: the servant girl who announces *venit Orestes* (708).
113. Valuable comments in Aricò 488–91; cf. also Quartiroli 30.
114. Note that Aricò (489) gives 51 lines for the longest speech, but this assumes 427–52 are to be assigned to Agamemnon's speech to Orestes. As noted, I dispute this placement. The longest speech is now Clytemestra's (163–203).
115. Divergences from Seneca are collected in Aricò 470 n.158.

CHAPTER 6

1. Quartiroli 167.
2. Cf. E. Rohde, *Der griechische Roman* (Leipzig 1914) 124ff.
3. This is in the strongest possible contrast to Quartiroli (164): "Gli svolgimenti e i particolari nuovi . . . non sono invenzioni dell'autore, pel quale il mito e casa morta che presenta un interesso solo erudito, bensi derivano per lo più da fonti a noi ignote."
4. *Hel.* 540ff.; 369ff.
5. H.-P. L'Orange, *Art Forms and Civic Life in the Late Roman Empire* (Princeton, N.J. 1965), esp. 9ff., 70ff.
6. Ibid. 21.
7. On the transformation of portrait sculpture, see ibid. 105ff. and earlier his *Studien zur Geschichte des spätantiken Porträts* (Oslo 1933). The evolution of the aesthetic inherent in this change is analyzed in Gervase Mathew, *Byzantine Aesthetics* (London 1963).
8. For a broad analysis of the relationship between function or office and gesture or act, see R. Brilliant, *Gesture and Rank in Roman Art* (New Haven, Conn. 1963).
9. Sabine G. MacCormack, *Art and Ceremony in Late Antiquity* (Berkeley, Calif. 1981) for a rich and stimulating study of *Adventus*, *Consecratio*, and *Accessio*.
10. Cf. also the valuable material, over a long perspective, in A. Grabar, *L'empereur dans l'art byzantin* (London 1971).
11. Cf. MacCormack 259f.; M. Lawrence, "The Iconography of the Mosaics of S. Vitale" *Atti del VI Congresso Internazionale di Archeologia Cristiana. Ravenna 1962* (Vatican City 1965) 123–40.
12. MacCormack 19.
13. *Or.* 27, *Martia* bellipotens referebat *classica* princeps/Tib. I.1.4

Martia cui somnos *classica* pulsa fugent. *Sulphure puro* (*Med.* 391/Tib. I.5.11) is even less remarkable.

14. *Rom.* VII.73/Prop. II.25.5.
15. B. Barwinski, "De Dracontio Catulli imitatore" *RhM* 43 (1888) 310–11.
16. H. D. Jocelyn, *The Tragedies of Ennius* (Cambridge 1967) 56f.
17. *Anth. Lat.* 21 (Riese I.1 p. 85), 193 (Riese p. 162).
18. W. Cloetta, *Beiträge zur Literaturgeschichte des Mittelalters und der Renaissance* I (Halle 1890) 5–6.
19. Aricò 417–18.

CHAPTER 7

1. First published by E. Baehrens, *Unedirte lateinische Gedichte* (Leipzig 1877) 5–26, with supplementary notes by E. Rohde, p. 46–48; and again with a significantly revised text in *Poetae Latini Minores* V (Leipzig 1914) 112–25. A new edition was prepared by S. Mariotti and apparently available for limited circulation in 1966, but it was not actually published. There is also an *Index verborum Aegritudinis Perdicae* by S. Rizzo (Rome 1968).
2. Mariotti's restoration of 98 is very satisfactory—*est sed caeca ‹meas infestaque flamma medullas›: RFIC* 97 (1969) 390. Rohde (above n. 1) thought there was also a lacuna after 179, but the conjecture is needless.
3. A small industry of conjecture and emendation was prompted by the condition of the text. Among the more useful discussions: Baehrens' notes in his edition; R. Ellis, *JPh* 5 (1874) 252–62; K. Rossberg, *Fleckeisen Jahrbücher* (1878) 428ff., (1881) 357ff.; Barbasz, *Eos* 27 (1924) 29–39; Morelli, *SIFC* (1920) 75 n.1; Mariotti, *RFIC* 97 (1969) 385–92.
4. See text pp. 245ff. below.
5. There is a contradiction between this excuse for Perdica's ignorance, *quam* (sc. *matrem*) *parvus adhuc dimiserat olim* (86–87), and the poet's earlier statement, *nuper Athenas venerat* (19–20). The discrepancy may reflect clumsy integration of differing sources or mere inadvertence.
6. Soranus, *Vit. Hipp.* 2: cf. Westermann Βιογράφοι (Brunswick 1845) 450.
7. Dumb. Oaks 37.31. Published by A. de Longpérier, *Revue archéologique* 1 (1844–45) 458–61. See the discussion by G. M. A. Richter, *Catalog of the Greek and Roman Antiquities in the Dumbarton Oaks Collection* (Cambridge, Mass. 1956) 32ff., and the brilliant article by F. Chamoux, "Perdiccas" *Hommages à A. Grenier* I (*Collection Latomus* 58 [1962]) 386–96.
8. M. Robertson, *A History of Greek Art* (Cambridge 1975) 558.
9. *Three Critical Periods in Greek Sculpture* (Cambridge, Mass. 1951)

32, where the link is reported as the unpublished proposal of B. Segall and A. M. Friend.

10. Ὁ μὲν Πέρδιξ σαφῶς ὄνομα κύριον. Ἄλλως· κάπηλος ἀντὶ τοῦ μάγειρος. ἔσκαζε δὲ οὗτος. εἴρηται δὲ ἐν τοῖς πρόσθεν, ὅτι χωλὸς οὗτος ὁ Πέρδιξ, ἀφ᾽ οὗ φασι τὴν παροιμίαν, Πέρδικος σκέλος, ἐπὶ τῶν λεπτοπόδων. Ἄλλως· ὁ Πέρδιξ ὄνομα καπήλου. χωλὸς δὲ ἦν οὗτος . . . τούτου δὲ πολλοὶ μέμνηνται. ἀπὸ τούτου δέ φασι τὴν παροιμίαν, Πέρδικος σκέλος, ἧς καὶ Ἀριστοφάνης ἐν ταῖς ἀμέτρος παροιμίαις μνημονεύει.

11. Published by J. Carcopino, *Revue archéologique* (1922) 211–30.

12. Robertson (n.8 above) says, "Something is lost, which was held on the knee under the left hand," but this is only because of the odd position of the hand, sufficiently explained by Chamoux' article of which Robertson was apparently unaware.

13. Baehrens *ULG* 8.

14. Provana 53 n.1.

15. G. Ballaira, "Perdica e Mirra" *RCCM* 10 (1968) 219–40.

16. The age of the youngster is variously estimated, but certainly a nursing child is a very different person from a student prince.

17. On Perdix, see Höfer in Roscher III.2 cols. 1946–55.

18. Sister: Apollod. *Bibl.* III.15.8; *Suda, s.v.* Πέρδικος ἱερόν; Tzetz. *Chiliades* I.493; inferred from Diod. Sic. IV.75.4–7; Paus. I.21.4; schol. Eur. *Or.* 1648. Nephew: Soph. *Camici* fr. 323R, *apud Suda, s.v.* cit.; Serv *ad G.* I.143, *ad Aen.* VI.14; Isid. *Orig.* XIX. 19.9; Ovid *Met.* 8.236–59. Höfer lists these as: (1) Perdix the mother of (2) Perdix the son (alias Talos, a.k.a. Kalos).

19. Cf. also Hyginus *Fab.* 39, 274; Fulgentius *Myth.* III.2.

20. Vat. Myth. I.232, II.130, III.7.3.

21. Provana 52 argues that Fulgentius represents a stage beyond Soranus and Lucian (concubine, stepmother, mother), and that *AP* must be dated after Fulgentius, or Fulgentius would have followed the story as presented in the poem. Thus he places the *AP* in the late sixth century. But obviously the argument can run the other way (if Fulgentius had been available, why would *AP* not follow him more closely) and should be cast aside. Cf. text pp. 246–47 below for features supporting a date contemporary with Dracontius.

22. For a careful and illuminating study of this tale, see J. Mesk, "Antiochus und Stratonike" *RhM* NS 68 (1913) 366–94. Rohde was the first to recognize the link between the Antiochus and Perdica stories (*Der griechische Roman* 58), but he assumed Perdica was a variant on Antiochus, whereas I believe it was originally the other way around. Cf. also Baehrens *ULG* 1–12.

23. Versions in Val. Max. V.7 *ext.* 1; Plut. *Demetr.* 38; App. *Syr.* 59–61; ps.-Lucian *de dea Syra* 17–18; Julian *Mis.* 347 Hert.; *Suda, s.v.* Ἐρασίστρατος.

24. Mesk (n.22 above) 368f.

25. Galen *de praecognitione*, ed. V. Nutton, *Corpus Medicorum Graecorum* V.8,1 (Berlin 1979) pp. 100–105 and notes pp. 194–97.
26. Mesk also provided a valuable assessment of the relationship between *AP* and the Antiochus tradition: "Aegritudo Perdicae" *Wiener Studien* 57 (1939) 166–72.
27. Mesk (n.22 above) 391ff.
28. That is, Seneca has followed the *Hippolytus Kalyptomenos* of Euripides rather than the extant *Hipp.* For a discussion of the influences of these two versions on subsequent poets, including Ovid and Seneca, cf. A. Kalkmann, *De Hippolytis Euripideis quaestiones novae* (Bonn 1882) 66–90. The Phaedra who takes the initiative is more reminiscent of Dracontius' Helen and Medea.
29. Baehrens transposed 84 to follow 87, and this arrangement has not been challenged. The intervening 3 verses describe why Perdica did not recognize his mother, and are clearly parenthetical whatever the position of 84. I wonder whether 84 should not be returned to follow 83 as in the MS, and allow its full impact to be felt.
30. Cf. text p. 243 below.
31. See the very full comments by Fr. Bömer, P. Ovidius Naso, *Metamorphosen* Bd. 5 (Heidelberg 1980) pp. 110–65; and W. S. Anderson, *Ovid's Metamorphoses VI–X* (Norman 1972) pp. 501–17.
32. Ballaira (n.15 above) 221–24. Earlier brief remarks in Morelli, "Sulle tracce del romanzo e della novella" *SIFC* NS 1 (1920) 87; G. Barbasz, "De Aegritudinis Perdicae fontibus, arte, compositionis tempore" *Eos* 30 (1927) 158.
33. Ovid presumably also drew heavily on such classic treatments of the Myrrha story as Cinna's epyllion *Zmyrna*. Cf. Bömer 111–12, 115–16.
34. Morelli (85) saw the importance of Antiochus' fame as a stimulus to embellishing the tale, but never doubted that it began with Antiochus rather than Perdiccas.
35. Morelli 76.
36. *Historia Apollonii regis Tyri*, ed. A. Riese (Leipzig 1893). See the analysis by B. E. Perry, *The Ancient Romances* (Berkeley, Calif. 1967) 294ff.
37. Perry 331–33 n.7; H. Bornecque, *Les déclamations et les déclamateurs d'après Sénèque le Père* (Lille 1902).
38. Some of these are unclear. I take the list as referring to Daphne, Asterie (or Helle), Callisto, Hylas (or Narcissus), Antiope, Europa, Leda, Danae and Procne (Philomela).
39. Again the names reflect the myths evoked in lines 1–4. The supplement in 230 is from Baehrens: *alii alia*.
40. Soranus' story does not hinge on the fact that Alexander is dead: it happens to be the case (Morelli misstates the dynamics of the story by implying it is like the Oedipus myth, where the father *must* be dead).

41. Barbasz 157 n.2.
42. Dreams of intercourse with relatives were subjected to very elaborate interpretation and fine distinctions (is the mother alive or dead, is one's son more or less than five years of age if he is the partner, is the father rich or poor, etc. etc.). According to Artemidorus, not all dreams of an incestuous encounter with one's mother are to be viewed as boding ill: indeed, such a dream betokens good for artisans and laborers (especially farmers: cf. Fulgentius' treatment of this myth), demagogues and politicians. Cf. *Oneirocriticon* I.78ff. (79 on mothers). For other literature on dreams and their interpretations in antiquity, see N. Lewis, *The Interpretation of Dreams and Portents* (Toronto 1976); J. G. Wetzel, *Quomodo poetae epici et Graeci et Romani somnia descripserint* (Diss. Berlin 1931); A. Grillone, *Il sogno nell' epica latina* (Palermo 1968); R. G. A. van Lieshout, *Greeks on Dreams* (Utrecht 1980) with extensive additional bibliography.
43. Note Jerome *Epist.* CXVII.7: *legimus in scholis puerum aliquem ossibus vix haerentem inlicitis arsisse amoribus et ante vita caruisse quam peste*—a description which sounds remarkably like *AP.* On the general theme: O. Rank, *Das Inzest-Motiv in Dichtung und Sage* (Leipzig 1912). Note also the further link between our poems and the pantomime.
44. For these interesting parallels, see Morelli 83.
45. On the question of whether Claudian was at least nominally Christian see A. Cameron, *Claudian* (Oxford 1970) 214ff.
46. Barbasz 154–55.
47. This apparently technical term seems not to be paralleled elsewhere. *Sacer*, like ἱερός, occurs in several specific terms (e.g., *sacer morbus*/ἱερὴ νοῦσος of epilepsy, ἱερὸν ὀστέον/*sacrum os; ignis sacer*), but here the word simply means "vital." I would conjecture that it was a quasi-technical usage from popular medical terminology.
48. Thus e.g., Verg. *Aen.* 1.198–99, *O socii . . . o passi graviora;* 2.387, and frequently.
49. So Morelli 81.
50. *Casta:* so also Ballaira 220 n.8.
51. Cf. also *Oed.* 229, *sancta fontis lympha Castalii.*
52. The reading is Baehrens' conjecture: it is supported by the contrast with Perdica's lack of memory in 85–86.
53. H has *ceteri dicant.* Baehrens emended to *cetera di dant,* but Hippocrates surely ends on a note of prayer or prophecy rather than statement. The subjunctive is needed, even if it is felt to have a future force, as frequently in this period (cf. line 1 *numquam tua tela quiescant?*).

284 NOTES

CHAPTER 8

1. Vollmer, s.v. Dracontius, *RE* V.1644 attributed the poem to Dracontius; and despite cogent objections by Provana (50–53: but see above for his equally improbable dating), Weymann (*Literarisches Zentralblatt* 1915, p. 297) and Morelli (75, n.11), the idea found adherents as recently as Chamoux (1962). By contrast, Ballaira presents the odd notion that the poem is an imitation of Dracontius from early seventh-century Spain.
2. So, for example, Mesk, *Wiener Studien* 57 (1939) 166.
3. Cf. above p. 225.
4. Cf. G. Ballaira, "Perdica e Mirra" *RCCM* 10 (1968) 224ff.; earlier Baehrens *ULG* 8ff.
5. The similarity of the scenes prompts me to wonder about the text of *AP* 64, for which editors print *inriguas respexit aquas lymphasque recentes*, where H reads *nymphasque regentes*. The pleonasm *aquas lymphasque* is not in the style of this poet, whereas the presence of the presiding nymphs at the spring both enhances the supernatural atmosphere as Amor arrives and provides yet another point of similarity with the *Hylas*. Most important, *nymphasque regentes* is the reading of the MS, which need not be rejected.

Select Bibliography

(Abbreviations in brackets)

Agudo Cubas, R. M., "Dos epílios de Draconcio. *De raptu Helenae y Hylas*" *Cuadernos de filología clásica* 14 (1978) 263–328.

Aricò, G., "Mito e tecnica narrativa nell' *Orestis tragoedia*" *Atti dell 'Accademia di Palermo* 37 (1977–78) 405–95. [= Aricò]

Baehrens, E., "Zu Orestis tragoedia" *RhM* 26 (1871) 493–94.

———, *Unedirte lateinische Gedichte* (Leipzig 1877). [= *ULG*]

———, "Neue Verse des Dracontius" *RhM* 33 (1878) 313–14.

———, *Poetae Latini minores* t. V (Leipzig 1914).

Ballaira, G., "Perdica e Mirra" *RCCM* 10 (1968) 219–40.

Barbasz, G., "In *Aegritudinem Perdicae* (*Anth. Lat.* 808R) animadversiones" *Eos* 27 (1924) 29–39.

———, "De *Aegritudinis Perdicae* fontibus, arte, compositionis tempore" *Eos* 30 (1927) 151–69.

Barwinski, B., *Quaestiones ad Dracontium et Orestis tragoediam pertinentes. Quaestio I. de genere dicendi* (Diss. Göttingen 1887). *Quaestio II. de rerum mythicarum tractatione* (Programm Deutsch-Krone, 1888).

———, "De Dracontio Catulli imitatore" *RhM* 43 (1888) 310–11.

Blomgren, S., "In Dracontii carmina adnotationes criticae" *Eranos* 64 (1966) 46–66.

Boissier, G., *L'Afrique romaine* (Paris 1901).

Bornecque, H., *Les déclamations et les déclamateurs d'après Sénèque le Père* (Lille 1902).

Broek, R. van den, *The Myth of the Phoenix in Classical and Early Christian Traditions* (Leiden 1972).
Brown, Peter, "Christianity and Local Culture in Late Roman Africa" *JRS* 58 (1968) 85–95.
Cameron, A., *Claudian. Poetry and Propaganda at the Court of Honorius* (Oxford 1970).
Chamoux, F., "Perdiccas" *Hommages à A. Grenier*. t.1 (*Collection Latomus* 58. Brussels 1962) 386–96.
Chatillon, F., "Dracontiana" *Revue du moyen âge latin* 8 (1952) 177–212.
Clerici, E., "Due poeti. Emilio Blossio Draconzio e Venanzio Fortunato" *Rendiconti del istituto dei Lincei* 107 (1973) 108–50.
Cloetta, W., *Beiträge zur Literaturgeschichte des Mittelalters und der Renaissance*. Vol. 1 (Halle 1890).
Corsaro, F., "Problemi storico-letterari del cristianesimo africano nel V° secolo. Studi su Draconzio" *Misc. di studi di lett. crist. antica* 11 (1961) 5–32.
Courcelle, P., *Histoire littéraire des grandes invasions germaniques*. 3ᵈ ed. (Paris 1964).
———, *Late Latin Writers and Their Greek Sources* (Cambridge, Mass. 1969).
Courtois, Christian, *Les Vandales et l'Afrique* (Paris 1955). [= Courtois]
———, C. Leschi, Ch. Perrat, C. Saumagne, *Tablettes Albertini. Actes privés de l'époque vandale (fin du Vᵉ siècle)* (Paris 1952).
Diaz de Bustamante, J. M., *Draconcio y sus carmina profana* (Santiago de Compostela 1978). [= Diaz]
Duhn, Fr. von, *Dracontii carmina minora* (Leipzig 1873).
Ellis, R., "On the Newly Edited Poems of Dracontius" *JPh* 5 (1874) 252–62.
Frazer, J. G., ed., *Apollodorus. The Library*. 2 vols. Loeb Classical Library (Cambridge, Mass. 1921).
Friedländer, L., *Roman Life and Manners under the Early Empire*. 7th ed. (repr. London 1965).
Friedrich, W. H., *Vorbild und Neugestaltung* (Göttingen 1967).

Fuchs, H., *Die Hylasgeschichte bei Apollonios Rhodios und Theokrit* (Diss. Würzburg 1969).

Gamber, S., *Le livre de la "Genèse" dans la poésie latine au Vᵐᵉ siècle* (Paris 1899; repr. Geneva 1977).

Giarratano, C., *Blossii Aemilii Dracontii Orestes* (Naples 1906).

———, *Commentationes Dracontianae* (Naples 1906).

Grillone, A., *Il sogno nell' epica latina* (Palermo 1968).

Gutzwiller, K. J., *Studies in the Hellenistic Epyllion (Beiträge sur klassische Philologie* 114: Meisenheim 1981).

Hubaux, J., and M. Leroy, *Le mythe du Phénix dans les littératures grecque et latine* (Liège 1939).

Hudson-Williams, A., "Notes on Dracontius and on the 'Aegritudo Perdicae'. I. Dracontius" *CQ* 33 (1939) 157–62.

d'Ippolito, G., "Draconzio, Nonno e gli 'idromimi'" *A&R* 7 (1962) 1–14.

Jacobson, H., *Ovid's Heroides* (Princeton, N.J. 1974).

Jocelyn, H. D., *The Tragedies of Ennius* (Cambridge 1967).

Jouan, F., *Euripide et les légendes des chants cypriens* (Paris 1966).

Kuijper, D., *Varia Dracontiana* (Diss. Amsterdam. The Hague 1958). [= Kuijper]

Labriolle, P., *Histoire de la littérature latine chrétienne.* 3ᵈ ed. 2 vols. (Paris 1947).

Langlois, P., "Dracontius" *Reallexikon der antiken Christentums* IV. cols. 250–69.

Lohmeyer, C., "De Dracontii carminum ordine" *Schedae philologicae Hermanno Vsener a sodalibus seminarii regii Bonnensis oblatae* (Bonn 1891) 60–75.

Maehly, J., *Anonymi Orestis tragoedia* (Leipzig 1866).

Malfait, M., *De Dracontii poetae lingua* (Diss. Poitiers. Paris 1902).

Mariotti, S., "Imitazione e critica del testo. Qualche esempio dall' *Aegritudo Perdicae*" *RFIC* 97 (1969) 385–92.

Mesk, J., "Antiochus und Stratonike" *RhM* NS 68 (1913) 366–94.

————, "*Aegritudo Perdicae*" *Wiener Studien* 57 (1939) 166–72.

Monceaux, P., *Les africains* (Paris 1894).

Morelli, C., "L'epitalamio nella tarda poesia latina" *SIFC* 18 (1910) 319–432.

————, "Studia in seros Latinos poetas" *SIFC* 19 (1911) 82–120.

————, "Sulle trace del romanzo e della novella" *SIFC* NS 1 (1920) 25–100.

Pavlovskis, Z., "Statius and the Late Latin Epithalamia" *CP* 60 (1965) 164–77.

Pedley, J. S., *New Light on Ancient Carthage* (Ann Arbor, Mich. 1980).

Procacci, G., "Intorno alla composizione e alle fonti di un carme di Draconzio (*Hylas. Rom.* II)" *SIFC* 20 (1913) 438–49.

Provana, E., "Blossio Emilio Draconzio. Studio biografico e letterario" *Mem. reale Acc. sc. Torino* 62 (1912) 23–100. [= Provana]

Quartiroli, A. M., "Gli epilli di Draconzio" *Athenaeum* 24 (1946) 160–87; 25 (1947) 17–34. [= Quartiroli]

Randers-Pehrson, J., *Barbarians and Romans. The Birth Struggle of Europe* A.D. 400–700 (Norman 1983).

Rank, O., *Das Inzest-Motiv in Dichtung und Saga* (Leipzig 1912).

Rapisarda, E., "Il poeta della misericordia divina. Vol. 1, L'unità del mondo religioso di Draconzio" *Orpheus* 2 (1955) 1–9.

————, "Fato, divinità e libero arbitrio nella "Tragedia di Oreste" di Draconzio" *Historisches Jahrbuch* 77 (1958) 444–50.

————, *La Tragedia di Oreste.* 2ᵈ ed. (Catania 1964). [= Rapisarda]

Riese, A., ed., *Anthologia Latina* (Leipzig 1894).

Romano, D., *Studi draconziani* (Palermo 1959). [= Romano]

Rossberg, K., *In Dracontii carmina minora et Orestis quae vocatur tragoediam observationes criticae* (Stade 1878).

————, "Zur Orestis Tragoediam" *Jahrbuch für klassische Philologie* 29 (1883) 569–75.

————, "Neue Studien zu Dracontius und der Orestis tragoedia" 33 (1887) 833–60.

————, *Materialen zu einem Commentar über die Orestis tragoedia des Dracontius.* Vol. 1 (Programm 293: Hildesheim 1888); Vol. 2 (Programm 295: Hildesheim 1889).

Rotolo, V., *Il pantomimo* (Palermo 1957).

St. Margaret, Sr. M., *Dracontii Satisfactio. Text, Translation and Commentary* (Diss. U. Penn.: Philadelphia 1936).

Salanitro, G., *Osidio Geta. Medea* (Rome 1981).

Scaffai, M., *Baebii Italici Ilias Latina* (Bologna 1982).

Schetter, W., "Medea in Theben" *Würzburger Jahrbücher* NF 6 (1980) 209–21.

Schmidt, L., *Geschichte der Wandalen.* 2ᵈ ed. (Munich 1942).

Scodel, R., *The Trojan Trilogy of Euripides* (*Hypomnemata* 60. Göttingen 1980).

Shackleton Bailey, D. R., "Echoes of Propertius" *Mnemosyne* 5 (1952) 307–33.

————, *Towards a Text of "Anthologia Latina"* (*Camb. Philol. Soc. Suppl. Vol.* 5. 1979).

Speranza, F., "Noterelle critiche alla 'Medea' di Draconzio" *A&R* 6 (1961) 168–73.

————, ed., *Blossi Aemili Draconti Satisfactio una cum Eugeni recensione* (Rome 1978).

Stackmann, K., "Senecas Agamemnon. Untersuchungen zur Geschichte des Agamemnonstoffes nach Aischylos" *C&M* 11 (1950) 180–211.

Stinton, T. C. W., *Euripides and the Judgement of Paris* (*JHS Suppl.* XI. 1966).

Tarrant, R. J., ed., *Seneca. Agamemnon* (Cambridge 1976).

Thieling, W., *Der Hellenismus in Kleinafrika* (Leipzig 1911).

Traversari, G., *Gli spettacoli in acqua nel tardo-antico* (Rome 1960).

Trillitzsch, W., "Der Agamemnonstoff bei Aischylos, Seneca und in der 'Orestis tragoedia' des Dracontius" in

Aischylos und Pindar hsg. E. G. Schmidt (*Schriften zur Geschichte und Kultur der Antike* 19. Berlin 1981) 268–274.

Tupet, A. M., *La magie dans la poésie latine* (Paris 1976).

Türk, G., *De Hyla* (*Breslauer philologische Abhandlungen* 7.4: Breslau 1895). [= Türk]

Vollmer, F., s.v. "Dracontius" *RE* V. cols. 1635–44.

————, *Fl. Merobaudis reliquiae, Blossii Aemilii Dracontii carmina, Eugeni Toletani episcopi carmina et epistulae* (*MGH. Auct. ant.* XIV. Berlin 1905). [= Vollmer]

Wagener, C., "Beitrag zu Dares Phrygius" *Phil.* 38 (1879) 91–125.

Index

Achilles: 99, 111, 172, 181
Admetus: 101
Adonis: 39, 236
Adventus: 214–15
Aeacus: 112
Aeetes: 55, 58–59, 61–62, 64, 71
Aegritudo Perdicae: viii–ix, 8, 34,
    40, 51, 86, 156, 220, 222–44
    passim; attributed to Dracon-
    tius, 8, 245–47; structure,
    238–41; characters in, 241–44
Aelius Aristides: 197
Aeneas: 104, 115, 118–19, 168
Aeolus: 51
Aeschylus: 20, 138–39, 146, 152–
    53, 155, 201; see also *Agamem-
    non; Choephoroi; Eumenides*
Agamemnon: 141 ff., 214–15; in
    land of Taurians, 143–46; mur-
    der of, 151 ff.; ghost of, 167–71,
    188
Agamemnon (Aeschylus): 144,
    158, 161, 162
"Agamemnon" (*Orestis trag.* 41–
    426): 139, 143–63
Agamemnon (Seneca): 138, 142,
    152, 165, 178, 204
Ajax: 111, 117, 175, 265 n.37
Alani: 9–10
Alcestis: 179
Alcestis (poem): 5, 251 n.7
Alexander (Ennius): 94
Alexandros (Euripides): 94
Allecto: 75
Amor: 32, 34, 223, 235, 237–39,
    241; see also Cupido

Andromache: 178, 188
Antenor: 104, 106–109, 110 ff.
Anthology, Latin: 12, 218, 225,
    235, 246, 248
Antiochus I: 229–30, 233, 235–
    36, 240; see also Stratonice
Antiope: 236
Aphrodite: 52, 88, 125, 231; see
    also Venus
Apollo: 34, 38, 94, 99, 101, 190,
    194
Apollodorus: 201
Apollonius of Rhodes: 21–24, 33,
    42, 52, 217; scholia on, 24, 58
Apollonius of Tyre: 234
Apsyrtus: 73, 211, 214
Aquatic mimes: 36, 52, 160; see
    also mimes; pantomime
Architecture, late antique: 212–13
Areopagus, Court of: 192–93
Argonauts: 21–22, 23, 42, 49; sup-
    pressed in *Hylas*, 23; Greek tra-
    dition of, 23; in *Medea*, 47 ff., 79
Ariadne: 209
Arianism: 11
Aristaenetus: 230, 234
Aristaeus (in Vergil's *Georgics*):
    23–25
Aristophanes: 24, 225
Artemis: 231
Asdingi: *see* Vandals
Astyanax: 97
Athamas: 79
Athena: 196; see also Minerva
Athens: 154, 156, 164, 172, 191,
    222, 231, 239

291

The Miniature Epic in Vandal Africa

was set in various sizes of Caledonia and Goudy by G&S Typesetters and printed on 60-pound Glatfelter B-31 by Cushing-Malloy, with case binding by John H. Dekker & Sons.